LESBIAN

LESBIAN Bedtime Stories

Gathered and Edited by Terry Woodrow

Tough Dove Books

Cover design by Koelle and Gillette, Willits, CA
Illustrations by Rainbow,
except for those on pages 135 and 224 by Jesse Cougar
Cover photo by Rachel Epstein
Cover model: Jan Cox

Most of these stories were previously unpublished.
Another version of *A Sleeping Cherub* by Marjorie Morgan first
appeared in *New Gay Life*, April, 1977.
Another version of *Dracula Retold* (under the name Marilynn
Woodsea) first appeared in *Feminary*, Spring, 1981.
Telling Mom by Karen Dale Wolman first appeared in *Dimensions*,
October, 1988.

ISBN 0-9615129-1-1
Library of Congress Catalog Card Number: 89-90036

This book was printed in the U.S.A. on recycled paper (70%).
Save the Trees! Don't just recycle, buy only recycled products.

Your comments are welcome, but we are not now soliciting books
or stories.

Tough Dove Books
P.O. Box 1152
Laytonville, CA 95454

To Our Loves and Our Lives

About The Editor

Terry Woodrow is an author and editor who collected so many good stories for this book she had no room to print any of her own creative writings. Clean air, clean water and natural beauty are more important to her than mechanical comforts; she lives along a creekbed in a tiny cabin without hot water, electricity or phone. One of the submissions for this book was left at the top of her long dusty driveway, under a rock.

Terry Woodrow has called herself Bluejay for the past thirteen years, and she published her first novel, *It's Time,* under that name. Bluejays are common, loud, and clever, and so are working class Lesbians who also deserve great respect for their acute insights and powerful tenacity. Every twilight Bluejay prays for a world full of peace, freedom and justice, for all beings.

If we live it, then it is.

Introduction and Acknowledgments

I have some good news! All of the wonderful stories in this book have happy endings; they also truly reflect the nature of our lives. In these pages you'll find sexy dykes, working dykes, political dykes and bar dykes, happy dykes and smart dykes and lots of dykes in love. You can read this book start to finish, or you can use the description found on the title page of each story (Humor, Erotica, Fantasy, Relationships, etc.) to find a story to suit your mood. I hope you enjoy all of them!

It's been my very deep pleasure to actualize this book. Many Lesbians have helped and I thank them heartily. My lover, Jesse, by proximity and good nature became my co-editor. Lots of local Mendocino County Lesbians (Andrea, Barbara, Sally, Morgan and Willow) read the submissions and gave initial feedback, which was essential. Ann brought me into the computer age, and Robin kindly coached me and loaned me her computer for typesetting. Jan posed for the cover; Rachel took the picture; Jean designed the cover and contributed valuable professional consultation; Carol, Jesse, Hannah and Andrea did the proofreading. Thanks goes to Donna for the seed idea. I thank Rainbow, our illustrator, not only for her wonderful drawings but also for her flexibility. Hannah and Carol are very kind to be storing these books in their shed. Moonyean provided great advice. Zoe's a great coach.

To all the women who have submitted their stories for this project, both to those published and to those (this time) who weren't, thank you so much for your cooperation throughout the mammoth and sometimes tedious process of consensual editing. More power to feminist process. It can be done!

I hope this book brings our community countless hours of enjoyment, and the relaxation and self-validation we deserve at the end of our busy days. Sweet dreams to you!

Terry Woodrow

Illustrations

by Rainbow

Rainbow: This is the magic name of Sue Parker Williams, fifty-five, who lives by the ocean with her cat, Generic, and loves music (especially dulcimer), art, architecture, and St. Augustine. Also, this is a curved arc of colors made of light and water. Blessed be!

She loves doing illustration and hopes doing these will lead to more! 2854 Coastal Highway, St. Augustine, Florida 32084.

Table of Contents

Intrigue

The Woman in the Off-Black Pantyhose

by Patricia Flinn

Patricia Flinn extends her love and highest thoughts to all who read these pages.

The Woman in the Off-Black Pantyhose

A most extraordinary thing happened to Angela Atwood one day at the Tunesboro Foodtown Supermarket.

It was one of those late afternoons in early spring just before twilight, when time seems to crystalize and the whole world sparkles with an unearthly luminosity, when Angela, feeling a rather odd emptiness in the center of her heart, stepped from her car and walked slowly across the parking lot. At the front of the store she took hold of one of the shopping carts that were lined up neatly against the wall.

Almost instantly her eyes caught sight of a small piece of paper lying at the bottom of the wagon.

She sighed as she bent to pick it up. If there was one thing she couldn't stand, it was other people's litter. Gum wrappers, old candy boxes, torn sheets of paper, crumpled coupons or debris of any kind at the bottom of her cart never failed to irritate her. When she went shopping she liked her wagons nice and clean. It was a matter of principle.

If only people would learn to pick up after themselves, she thought, glancing down at the paper which was bright pink and finely grained, an expensive sheet, no doubt, from someone's personal stationary.

It was covered with large black letters that curled and looped across the entire page.

How odd, Angela wondered. Who would use expensive stationary to write a grocery list, and in *calligraphy* , no less?

Her eyes ran across each item—a pair of off-black panties and pantyhose, a bottle of ketchup, a jar of kosher dill pickles, a package of Thomas' English Muffins, mascara, Kleenex, lipstick.

She turned the paper over.

2

> *Against a pale and raging moon*
> *When all the world lies hushed*
> *I lie alone upon my bed*
> *And dream again of you.*
> *The silence of your secret eyes,*
> *The arms I knew so well,*
> *The tender lips and burning thighs,*
> *That speak the soul of you.*
> *Darleen, sweetheart, meet me at 9 sharp.*
> *You know where.*
> *I'll be waiting. Wear your blue bra.*

For a moment Angela was stunned. It was almost as if a stranger had come out of the darkness and embraced her. She glanced around nervously. There was no one in sight except a young retarded boy in a large cowboy hat and boots whom she knew worked for the store and was in charge of rounding up the stray wagons.

Angela read the poem again, trying her best to imagine where it had come from and what kind of person could have written it.

She brought the paper up to her nose. It smelled faintly of perfume. Obviously it belonged to the woman who had come to the store in search of panties and pantyhose and pickles and—

And *what* ?

Angela took another quick look around before her eyes fell onto the paper again.

> *I lie alone upon my bed*
> *And dream again of you.*
> *The silence of your secret eyes*
> *The arms I knew so well—*

Was it some type of joke or what? Darleen was a woman's name and yet the poem had apparently been written by a woman, a woman who was calling another woman *sweetheart* and asking her to wear a blue bra. What on earth did the whole thing mean?

Angela glanced to her right, then to her left. A tall attractive

3

woman in a bright yellow dress was strolling across the parking lot toward her. Angela watched as the woman approached. Had the poem been intended for her?

The woman passed by without a glance, disappearing into the doorway of a nearby bookshop.

Angela took a deep breath and tried to think. She didn't know whether to stick the note back into another cart or simply drop it into the nearest bin.

But suppose someone sees me, she thought. *They might think the note was for me!*

She closed her eyes, trying to imagine why anyone—male or female—would write such a thing on the back of a grocery list and then leave it behind in a public shopping cart for anyone to find. Was it possible that it was all perfectly innocent, the absent-minded scribbling, say, of some bored but highly imaginative person trying to pass the time on a long check-out line? Or had she actually stumbled upon the real makings of some secret and passionate assignations involving two women?

The question left her somewhat lightheaded, especially since nothing like this had ever happened to her before.

She stood there, fingering the note, wondering what she should do. After a few moments, however, she found herself thinking about the women. She tried to imagine what they were like. Where they lived. How they had met. Whether they were young or old, married or single, attractive or not.

Despite herself, strange and unsettling scenarios began flashing through her brain: A young, very beautiful woman in a lacy blue bra was walking along a rain-splashed street; a tall, slender woman with thick auburn hair was slipping her lovely hips into a pair of tight black panties; two women, fair as moonlight, were embracing in the shadows of a thick lush garden.

Angela shuddered. Years before she had had such dreams of women. Dreams that had left her vaguely uncomfortable and somehow unsettled, but that had been a long time ago when she was much younger. A *girl* really. Certainly long before she had married and begun raising a family.

Nervously, she glanced at her watch. It was almost five-thirty. What in the name of God was she doing? She still had dinner to make and a lot of work to do. Larry and the children would be waiting. She couldn't afford to waste any more time wondering about some silly old poem.

She grabbed hold of her cart and pushed it through the automatic swinging door, moving swiftly past the fruit and vegetable aisle.

She shot up the cookie lane and turned right into the dairy department where she grabbed a quart of Tuscan Low-Fat Milk and a package of Diet-Delight, sodium-free yellow cheese. In the bread aisle she picked up a box of Thomas' English muffins.

On her way to the check-out counter she passed several shapely young women in high heels and business suits. One of them was standing in front of the condiment section eyeing a large jar of kosher dill pickles. Angela couldn't see her face, only the back of her head. She was slender with long flowing blonde hair that curled gently across her delicate shoulders.

For one brief moment—possibly two—a pair of marble-smooth burning white thighs flashed through Angela's brain. Startled, she jerked her cart forward, running smack up the heels of a fat hairy man in purple pants and a Mickey Mouse T-shirt.

"Hey, what the hell do you think you're doin'?" he shouted. "Why don't you watch where you're goin', lady?"

"I'm—I'm terribly sorry," Angela stuttered. "I—I didn't see you there."

"Didn't see me?" he shouted, lifting his foot and giving his heel a vigorous rub. "What are you, blind? Am I supposed to wear taillights or somethin'? I was standing right in front of you. What do you mean you didn't see me?"

"I—I really am sorry," Angela said, her face reddening, as she caught a glimpse of the woman with the long blonde hair gliding past her. "My mind must have been somewhere else."

"That's for sure," the man said. "Somewhere like Mars, maybe."

"Right on!" shouted a glassy-eyed teenager with pimples and a mohawk hair-cut who zigzagged between them.

Angela's eyes were on the blonde woman as she came to a stop at the rear of the express lane a few feet away. A medium-sized bottle of pickles sat demurely at the bottom of her shopping basket.

Angela watched as the woman settled patiently into the long line,

5

slipping her right foot out of her shoe and rubbing it lazily behind the back of her leg. She was wearing off-black pantyhose.

"Next time watch where you're goin', OK?" the man said, limping painfully away. "You women nowadays are a menace."

Over by the canned vegetables two middle-aged men in blue workmen's clothes were pointing and laughing.

Angela steered her cart toward the check-out counter where the blonde woman was now absent-mindedly thumbing through a copy of *Mademoiselle*.

Angela inched up behind her, hoping to catch a whiff of her perfume, but all she could smell were oranges.

Leaning over the woman's shoulder, Angela peered into her shopping basket. Sure enough, there were four oranges there, scattered among the jar of pickles, three bottles of Perrier, a wedge of Blue cheese, and a box of Tampax.

But there were no panties, no pantyhose, no lipstick, no mascara—

Angela paused.

What on earth was she doing, snooping in some strange woman's shopping basket? Whatever had possessed her? Was she losing her mind?

Her hands and underarms began to perspire. Quickly, she folded the poem and stuck it into her purse. She was acting like a child. An utter fool. She had to get hold of herself.

She took another deep breath to steady herself.

It was all so absurd. What had ever led her to believe that *this* woman was the one who had written the poem? Was it only because she'd seen her pick up that bottle of pickles? Was it the off-black pantyhose?

And why should she have cared whether the woman had written the poem or not? What was it to her? Certainly it was none of her business if some person she had never seen before had chosen the Tunesboro Foodtown as the site for some illicit affair.

Angela was so embarrassed she could have kicked herself. In fact, she would have left the store right then and there if another customer hadn't come behind her, blocking her exit.

Slowly the line moved forward.

She watched as the blonde woman bent over her cart, grabbing hold of each item. She wished she could at least see her face, but the woman's soft golden hair hung thickly in the way. She saw her fingers, though. They were long and thin, her nails sharp and blood red. There was no ring, however. Not even an engagement ring.

If she *was* the woman, Angela thought, and she *did* have a female lover, she was certainly *free* enough to meet her some place other than the parking lot of a public supermarket. Why all the secrecy then? Why all the mystery?

The answer shot like a bolt through Angela's body. More than likely the poem that now rested in her purse had been intended for some woman like herself, *who was married.* A someone with some sweet, unsuspecting soul of a husband and a couple of nice, ordinary, wholesome kids.

Angela could almost picture this woman: an older, fairly handsome lady with soft eyes and a gentle smile. The kind of person a younger, more attractive, but infinitely less experienced woman would feel comfortable with.

Curious, Angela turned and panned the store. The woman behind her was short and rather stubby. She was wearing a long gray dress and holding a thick loaf of Italian bread and a package of Boorshead Salami. She seemed nice, but smelled heavily of garlic. Behind her was the mohawk with the pimples.

Angela looked away. The only woman in the place who even *faintly* resembled a kindly, *dignified* person was the female butcher who was grinding chop meat. But if the poem had been intended for her, why had it been left sitting outside in a shopping cart?

Frustrated, Angela turned back to the woman in front of her. Her slender hand was reaching out for the box of Tampax at the bottom of her cart.

Angela's heart began to race madly, her thoughts flying and spinning like wild birds through an immense blue sky. She longed to lean over and talk to the woman, to find out who she was and what she was like. But she was afraid, fearful of what might happen. Of what the woman might think.

Perhaps she wasn't the person who had written the poem. Perhaps she had no lover, no one she lay awake for, longed for atop her bed while the pale moon raged and the world lay hushed.

Perhaps the only thing that had ever come between *her* burning

7

thighs was an innocent Tampax.

Angela grew dizzy. She didn't know what to do, what to think. And there was no way for her to find out, either. In fact, she really didn't know *anything* about this woman. Nothing at all. Not even the shape of her face or the color of her eyes.

She watched as the blonde woman's cool, white hands slipped into her purse. Perhaps she would write out a check. Sign her name. Give her phone number and address. Instead, she handed the clerk two twenty dollar bills, took the change, and disappeared out the door with her bag of groceries without once turning her head.

By the time Angela reached the parking lot, the woman was gone. She wandered up and down, in and out between the cars for some time, but there was no trace of her anywhere.

Was the woman gone forever?

That night, while Angela sat beside Larry in their living room, she thought about the woman. Every so often, when Larry wasn't looking, she took out the poem and read it. All through the night she dreamed of the blonde woman, who was lying atop a narrow, white bed holding out her arms and softly calling Angela's name; outside her window a pale moon raged, and stars exploded in great, white bursts.

Early the following evening Angela found herself again at the supermarket, her eyes scanning all the shopping carts and the checkout lines, but there was no sign of any note, no trace of any secret rendezvous.

For weeks she returned every twilight. She diligently searched every scrap of paper, every crumpled note that she would find at the bottom of some cart. Once or twice she thought she saw the blonde woman disappear into a car and drive away, but she was always just a little too late to know for sure.

It was frustrating, and terribly depressing at times, especially when Larry began to complain that she didn't seem to be her old self anymore. But despite it all, Angela refused to give up.

Night after night she returned to the supermarket, hoping to find another poem, another trace of the blonde woman.

She knew she was out there. *Somewhere.*

She could sense it.

She just had to be patient...

Zarathustra's Secret

or How I Found the Meaning of Life

by Jessie Lynda Lasnover

I, Jessie Lynda Lasnover, live in Southern California with the woman I love. We share our home with several pigeons, rabbits, Cavalier King Charles spaniels, a collie and a calico cat. I have four children and my lover has three children and five grandchildren. Although none of them live with us, they visit often, adding the happy noise of childhood to the more usual peaceful harmony of our home. I am a freelance writer of both journalistic non-fiction articles and mostly fantasy-type fiction. I'm writing a novel now which I hope to finish soon. I earn my living working as a psychiatric technician in a hospital program for chemical dependency, and I am in training to work as assistant editor for the Los Angeles based Lesbian News. *Recently I've been investigating feminist religion, studying paganism and Goddess worship. I am proud to call myself a witch. I believe strongly in the philosophy implied by my story and I think we create our own realities. I am withdrawing my energy from the patriarchy and one of the ways I plan to do this is that my lover and I are hoping to move to the Oregon wilderness as soon as I complete my Master's in English.*

Zarathustra's Secret

or How I Found the Meaning of Life

Priscilla and I went off to the mountains to find out about life. I wasn't so sure about going—I mean, what if I didn't like what I found out? But Priscilla is a calico cat, and so much more definite about things than I am.

For example, Priscilla never loses anything, but recently I spent half an hour looking for my slippers because I couldn't remember where I put them. I finally had to be content with some turquoise booties my grandmother crocheted for me years ago before she died. I found those under a pile of laundry in the clothes room.

I've been meaning to get a dresser but it seems I don't think of it when I have the money and then when I remember I've already spent all my money on tropical fish or houseplants. Oh well. So I just throw all my clothes on top of the bed in the extra room which is now called the clothes room. Nellie's no better, either. She used to throw her clothes in *all* the bedrooms before I came, and sleep in the living room. Now Nellie and I share one room, my computer and Priscilla share another, and the third room is the "clothes room."

Once in a while, for old time's sake, we all still sleep in the living room with the fish and the bird, but it's just not comfortable; we're both too old now for that and so we wake up all sore with cramps in our necks. Do young people get cramps in their necks? I forget, now, how it felt then.

Well, I've been wanting to go to the mountains for years and years. Sometimes I go for short little spaces and smell the trees, and hear the bugs and birds, and smile at the wind, but I don't stay long enough to find much out. I never guessed Priscilla wanted to go and discover things, too. She seemed to be content until one night I just happened to mention to her that I'd been wanting to go. She immediately told me that she'd been wanting to go also and why didn't we leave this weekend?

Well, of course I told her all sorts of reasons why not—such as I'd miss Nellie, and who would sing to my bird and take care of the fish? Nellie would miss me too. But Priscilla told me I was just making excuses. The bird could sing to himself for awhile and the fish could care less whether I was there or not; Nellie would feed them. As for Nellie, well, what was I anyway, a big baby? Couldn't I be away from my sweetheart for a few weeks while I discovered the meaning of life? Nellie would miss me, but I'd be back, and in the meantime she could have a friend or her grandkids over to keep her company. We'd both survive the separation.

Priscilla can look awfully sarcastic when she wants to, and now her tail curled up in a highly critical manner. She didn't have to mention that she considered me to be much too wishy-washy, her tail said it for her.

What can I say? My cat talked me into it and Nellie didn't object as much as I'd expected (hoped?) so off we went. I had to stop every couple of hours to send a postcard to Nellie. I pretended I was stopping for coffee or gas. After the first couple of stops I had to limit sending my love-notes to the times when Priscilla made her nature calls because of the way she looked at me, it was too embarrassing; I know she though I was a big baby.

We eventually made it up to the Desolation Wilderness in Northern California. There're some backpacking trails up there and it's still pretty cold during that time of year, with snow up in the higher elevations. I figured we wouldn't see too many people. I had a nice little tent, a subzero sleeping bag (just in case), and various other supplies to keep us for a while. I was hoping to live off the land once we got settled so I only brought lightweight food—mostly beef jerky and raisins. Priscilla assured me she knew how to catch her own food, and I figured I could live off my fat in an emergency; I'd fasted before.

I found a parking area off the road that looked like a good starting place for one of the trails, left my car parked and locked, with a note on the dash to the rangers about my approximate destination and dates I'd be in the wilderness. Then I shouldered my pack and we started off.

I didn't see anybody else on the trail. I wore a flannel shirt over a T-shirt: jeans, thick socks, tennis shoes and my big wool hat from Peru. A canteen hung from my pack, a Sierra cup from my belt on one side, a Buck knife from the other.

Right away Priscilla took off. She'd be gone for twenty minutes or so and then she'd check in with me, telling me the sights she'd seen off the trail on either side of me. Sometimes she scouted ahead and told me when we were approaching a stream, a spring, or some particularly beautiful scenery. She especially loved a spot of color, and would make sure I knew where to look for a striking purple bloom, or a group of red and yellow blossoms. It was Spring, and in the low elevations there were many lovely flowers along the trail.

She got impatient with me because I needed to rest more often than she did but I pointed out to her that I was past my prime and out of shape. She looked me over and agreed. Really, sometimes she's a little too honest; it even borders on rudeness. We hiked up and down the trail—mostly up—for a couple days. It was getting colder now at night. After the sun went down, as well as for the first hour or two in early morning, I had to wear my gloves. I was getting really tired of the beef jerky so I dug out my little book on edible plants and sampled a few leaves and flowers. I hadn't got hungry enough to try a bug yet, though I'd heard they were very nutritious. They just looked so unappetizing; I'd grown up with the fear of bugs most American girls seem to be cursed with. Priscilla brought me a mouse once but I told her I'd rather not eat it. She got rather huffy about people who don't appreciate gifts, and said she'd keep her future catches to herself. There was no way to send a postcard to Nellie. The next best thing was to start a journal and address it to her. Whenever I felt a real pang, missing her, I'd stop and write her a note. Priscilla would watch me. Her posture managed to convey a mixture of disapproval, sarcasm, and pity but she never commented other than to start calling me Baby; to this day she still calls me that. I stopped objecting long ago.

Finally, just when I thought my old muscles were not going to be able to take any more aches, we reached what I felt was the perfect spot for us to stop at. Priscilla agreed it was just right. I'd been setting my tent up along the trail on the way but now I thought I'd build a shelter. There was a stream which fed into a small lake that had a sort of beach, surrounded by large granite boulders, small trees and bushes. Above the rocks and vegetation was another clear area which had the mountain rising on one side and pine woods all around. We could see some snow far up on the mountain but there was none close by. Priscilla told me there was a hollow in the mountainside near the woods. We could build our shelter there. I checked it out and the hollow was nearly a cave; I could stand up in it and it extended inside for about five feet. The opening was three or four feet across. I set up my tent inside the hollow—it fit perfectly. Then I searched around and, with my knife, I cut some branches which I tied into poles and dug into the ground in front of my cave, crossing and tying some across the top to make a framework. I gathered up a lot of smaller branches and wove them through the poles, so I had an extension of my cave. Next I took my solar blanket (a plastic sheet) and tied it over the shelter so it could either fall down in front or be thrown back over the top. I put small rocks all around the front and built it up some. I hoped the sheet and rocks would keep out most of the weather and the tent would keep out the rest.

I piled some stones up against the rocky mountainside to shelter my fire, just enough so the wind wouldn't blow it out every time I tried to kindle one. It wasn't too windy; the mountainside and the woods were effective windbreakers. Priscilla found us a good toilet area in a small clearing on up the trail a bit—not too close to the water or our home, and not up against the woods either. I am paranoid enough to feel uncomfortable squatting right next to trees and bushes where somebody might be hiding. It was sheltered from the trail by a pile of boulders which hid the spot from any possible passersby. That probably wasn't too important since we hadn't seen anybody up here but it made me feel more comfortable. I get constipated if I think somebody can see me. Priscilla thinks this is one of my more stupid traits, but even she can't intimidate me into squatting right out there in the open.

By the time I got everything set up that first day, it was almost dusk...a good time to fish. I dug my fishing pole out of my pack and put the segments together. Priscilla brought me a bug and I stuck it on the hook. I walked down to the beach and scouted around the rocks looking for a deep part of the lake. I found one near a big rock, cast out my line, and sat down to wait. Priscilla sat with me and, in pure contentment, we watched the sun set. Just as the orange glow was fading from the sky I got a bite. It didn't take long to reel in the fish. It wasn't very big but it was enough for our dinner. I skinned, boned, and gutted it. Priscilla ate the inside parts raw. I built up my fire and stuck the fish on a pointed stick and roasted it. It only took a few minutes to cook the fish; I ate most of it and Priscilla ate the rest.

We sat for a while watching the stars. Priscilla agreed with me that this was the perfect place to find out about life; all we had to do was wait here, letting the mystical peace and beauty of the place soak into us until we were ready to receive it, and the meaning would come to us. It was a magical spot. There are magical places here and there, but it seems most people are just too busy to find them. Alot of people don't even believe in them, but cats do. If people would take the time to talk to their cats they would find out about the magical places and about a lot of other things as well, maybe even how to live. I've noticed that it's rare to find a person who really knows how to live; a happy person. Nellie knows how to live. She watches everybody and learns from their mistakes. She can laugh at life, she can laugh at people. She knows how to live and that's why I love Nellie; she's a kind-hearted person; a happy person.

While I was getting all sentimental thinking about Nellie, Priscilla started to get disgusted. She told me I was becoming a gushy romantic and she stalked off into the night with as much dignity as she could express in her stiff tail. Oh well, I thought, and went to bed.

In the middle of the night I had a dream. I saw a glowing light surrounding a shining figure, floating up above the ground. I was standing below, looking up at the light, feeling the loving warmth it sent to me, content with just that, when it added to my joy by speaking to me in a beautifully deep, melodious voice. I felt happy, at peace. It was God and She told me everything was just fine. I trusted Her completely and accepted what She told me totally, without question. I *knew* everything was fine. I felt so good, suffused with happiness throughout my body. The feeling just got too big to contain and it woke me up. There was Priscilla, sleeping on my stomach and purring. I stroked her and thought about how much I loved her, even if she did tend to be a little sarcastic. That thought apparently woke her up because she opened her eyes and told me I was stupid, but she loved me anyway and now, go back to sleep. I didn't dream any more that night.

The next week passed peacefully and happily. We fished, we hiked, I ate flowers and leaves, and we watched the days go by in harmony. I felt safe and content. Gradually, though, I became aware of another presence there in the woods with us. It wasn't anything really overt, just that at times it felt like somebody was watching us. I'd hear the sound of rustling leaves and smell the scent of some other person floating in the air, but when I'd turn to look I'd see nobody, nothing. The bushes and trees would look the same, or so I thought.

Maybe a squirrel would scamper by and I'd think, oh, that was what I heard (or felt or smelled or saw out of the corner of my eyes). I'd see Priscilla's ears perk up at sounds I couldn't hear and she'd get that super-alert look that cats get, but she never said a word to me about it. Gradually, but without fear, I came to believe there was somebody there in the forest with us. I was curious and getting a little impatient. Together, Priscilla and I waited for our visitor.

At the end of the week a woman came to see us. She was slender and short, about five feet tall, with long silver hair and a mole on her left cheek. She had a few gray hairs on her chin and a very fine white moustache. Her skin was dark honey brown and her eyes were bright blue. She wore a plaid flannel shirt, blue jeans and leather cowboy boots, dusty and worn with age. She carried a stout, gnarled tree branch as a staff.

Priscilla and I have been waiting for you, I told her. The woman told me she had been watching us for several days. She told me her name was Zarathustra and that she hadn't ever had much luck speaking to people—she usually talked with eagles, snakes, and nature faeries. She said she'd decided to take a chance on me because it had been about a hundred years since she'd talked to any humans, and no women had spoken to her since Sumerian times; sometimes she'd thought the men had killed them all. She told me she was very glad to see they still existed. In fact, it was because I was a woman that she'd decided she should try, once again, to speak with a human. She hoped I wasn't the sort who threw rocks at prophets?

I assured her I wasn't and Priscilla told her she'd never seen me throw a rock at anybody. She relaxed, then. After all, Priscilla was a cat and could be trusted. There was one thing I wanted to know. I wondered why Nietzsche described her as a man? Zarathustra looked at me. Then she told me that was the way things were, ever since men forgot the Goddess. Nietzsche could not see her for what she was; his prejudice got in the way. He saw and heard only what he wanted because he did not want to learn from a woman.

I invited her to eat with us. She was a vegetarian, so we gathered up several flowers and plants and Zarathustra showed me where to find roots, tubers, and a few berries as well. We mixed them all up into a salad with some of the raisins I had left and I brewed a tea from leaves Zarathustra gave me. She'd brought her own cup, a Sierra cup like mine but older. She said she'd found it years ago along the trail. She'd got her clothes a little less honestly, she admitted. A party of men had camped up here a couple years ago and while they slept, she took some of their clothes and the boots because her own were worn out. She'd left a pile of uncut gemstones to pay for the items, but she still felt a little bad about it because she hadn't given them the opportunity to barter.

The three of us gathered around the fire and had a very nice little party. We ate together and drank together, we watched the stars together and then we sang and danced together. Zarathustra taught us some of the dances of the nature faeries and a song snakes and eagles sing. Priscilla taught her some splendid cat songs and I showed her the dance I dance for Nellie. I told her about my dream and she told me what she meant by the "Superman." She said she never meant for anyone to use the idea of the Superman to oppress other people; anyone could be a Superman, it wasn't limited by race, sex, age or species. The Superman is a quality of being heroic and gentle, strong yet open, it is the ability to see our own beauty and the beauty of the world around us. Everyone has the seed of the Goddess inside; it is in our souls and we just need to reach in and connect with Her. Once we connect with our Goddess, we are the Superman; we grow beyond the pettiness inherent in patriarchal society and we are free. The Nazis so distorted the Superman that they used it to justify the worst form of elitist, sexist racism. Her absolute disappointment with the Nazi perversion of the Superman had almost decided her to give up men altogether. They can't seem to understand truth, she told us, snakes are much more honest.

Yes, I felt inside me the truth of what she'd said. Then I wondered, what is the meaning of life? That is what Priscilla and I came to find.

Zarathustra looked at us a moment in silence. Then she told us that we were on the way to finding the answer. She wanted to know why should she spoil our quest by making it easy?

We watched her and felt confused. Zarathustra saw this. She looked in our eyes and promised us, one day we would know the answer. It may be we wouldn't realize it until we died; but we would know it.

We easily accepted this because it seemed reasonable and besides, it was the only choice we had. We drank the rest of the tea and danced the night away while Priscilla sang for us. Close to dawn a group of very small, maybe three feet tall, beings joined us in our dance. They were pleasingly fat and looked sort of like people except that their skins were a soft bluish color and their eyes a shining tawny yellow. They were dressed in braided leaves and flowers which had been made into skirts hanging below their waists down to a few inches above their knees. Their plump little bodies twisted, twirled, and leaped into the air with an amazing grace and agility. We all danced in honor of the rising sun.

Priscilla and I curled up on the ground together and watched as Zarathustra left with the nature faeries. We stayed in the mountains another two days enjoying the sky and the scenery and watching the lives of the bugs and animals unfold around us. Then it was time to go.

The snow had never reached us; it stayed higher up in the mountains. And although it hadn't rained except for a light mist in the mornings, it started to drizzle on our last day hiking back to my car. Priscilla looked extremely dissatisfied as she marched along the trail in front of me. I told her we'd been very lucky up to now; one last day's rain wasn't worth getting upset about. Priscilla declined to answer.

When we reached the car she curled up on the seat and immediately went to sleep. I had a hard time changing in the car but finally managed to get some dry things on.

On the drive home I listened to the radio, getting used to the world again and thinking about Zarathustra. I knew it would be fun to teach Nellie the faerie dances. I looked at Priscilla there next to me, purring in her sleep. I felt happy going home to my bird, the fish, the clothes room, and especially Nellie. And then, suddenly, I had it; I knew the meaning of life. I smiled.

Pretty

by Martha Miller

Martha Miller is a mid-western writer who looks for diversity in women's fiction. She's tired of plots about slim, pale, young women with flat stomachs. She says story-worthy things happen to other women too.

Her latest work reflects experiments in syntax and style—what she calls the "neo-lesbian erotic voice." She thinks that lesbians shouldn't have to use traditional heterosexual words to describe their love making. Some day she'd like to see Tee Corinne's Dreams of the Woman Who Loved Sex *taught in college Lit. classes alongside of Woolf, Joyce, Faulkner and other great literary pioneers.*

Pretty

My mistake was demanding an answer. I knew she was angry and had had too much to drink. But *I* was angry, too, and I pushed it.

"Why?" I asked.

Every time I brush my teeth, comb my hair, or simply pass by a mirror, I hear her answer. It comes to me at the damndest times. I drive down the street and from nowhere the impact knocks the wind out of me. Twice I've had to pull the car over. I divide my life into two phases, before and after her answer.

"I just wanted to be with someone pretty," she said.

Later she'd tried to atone, sent flowers and a card, "I really screwed up. I won't see her again."

I leave a note under the wiper blade of her jeep, "I'll miss you."

As I walk away I think, I'll miss the lavender dildo more (probably not true, but I'm still angry). We'd bestowed a female persona on it and named her Lilith (feared and fearless lady of the night, tamer of wild beasts, and Adam's first wife who refused to submit to oppression and invasion). She was shaped more like a slender woman than a penis. Strapped to Danille's pubis by a black leather holder, she'd brought me to orgasm when all else failed. We'd picked her out together, but it was clear from the first who would wear her, who she belonged to. Danille will be dipping Lilith into someone else now—someone "Pretty."

Danille is tall and slim. Her hair is cut short and spiked on top. Brown. When we went to the bar she'd moussed it up—so handsome. Her figure is slim and boyish, except for her hips and convex stomach where she carries what little weight she carries. I knew from the beginning she could have had any woman. But until her parting shot, I never wondered, *'Why me?'*

Now I'm obsessed with it.

I try to masturbate. By the end of the first month it's all I can think about. She was always better with my body than me. Slow. Gentle. I get in a hurry, press too hard—hurt.

•

I brush my hair each morning. I wet it down, but it won't lie right. I see freckles across my nose, pock marks (remnants of adolescent acne) on my cheeks, blonde fuzz on my upper lip.

I step before a full length mirror. If there were a children's book of pictures, 'this is a man,' 'this is a woman'; my picture would be under, 'this is a lesbian.' My breasts are too large, my waist too thick, my legs too short.

'I will lose some weight,' I think over a breakfast of Count Chocula and bananas.

•

I start Monday morning. After a poached egg on dry, whole wheat toast, grapefruit juice, and black coffee with sweet 'n low, I drive to the park.

It is quiet this early. I set out at a brisk pace. I walk for awhile; my legs cramp, my stomach rumbles and sweat runs out of my hair—into my eyes. The shady quiet feels oppressive. The squirrels and birds get on my nerves. An old woman carrying a walking stick passes me, calls, "Good morning," then disappears up a hill and around the corner.

Two plump women in pink and white shorts, with fuzzy pompoms on their tennis shoes, accost me.

"Have you been doing this long?" one asks.

"Yeah," I say, "about ten minutes."

They giggle. "We mean do you come here often?"

"No," I puff. "Just started."

They slow and fall into stride beside me.

"Jennifer here used to be a cocaine addict," the tall one says. "I drank a lot. Then we found God."

"Cocaine is a great weight-loss drug," I say. A bead of sweat burns my eye. I am momentarily blinded and bump into Jennifer.

"Oh my," she says not breaking stride.

"We've been walking for five months. I've lost 40 pounds," says the one who used to drink. "Jennifer has lost 27."

"Jesus saves." Jennifer raises her voice.

22

"I'm a pagan, myself," I say and cut off to the right.

Later, I see them coming again.

"The Lord has burdened our hearts to bring witness to you," the tall one says.

"Amen," says Jennifer.

My ribs hurt. My legs are cramping. I am a sweaty mess and hungry. "Damn you, Danille," I mutter.

On the way home I stop at McDonald's.

•

That weekend is July 4th. I get some make-up: eye shadow and blush. I buy high heels (they're size 10 wide; the kind that stay on the shelf until some oversized drag queen needs them). I put on a skirt and pull a wide-necked leotard down on my shoulders. My cleavage is soft and full. I think about getting a perm, covering the gray strands.

I go to the bar.

"You look *different*." The bartender sets up the usual draft beer.

"A new look," I say.

"So femme..." He flashes a smile.

My toes hurt. My crotch feels sweaty and on fire. By the second dance I've kicked off my shoes and have a run in my panty hose.

Around eleven a group from the bar sits on the curb, by the corner church, to watch the fireworks.

My old friend Grace is next to me. She has been painting children's faces at the festival all afternoon and has bits of bright colored paint on her loose fitting summer shirt. Her hair looks different. A new cut has left her red curls looking tossed—frantic, the carrot color faded.

The sky is filled with spiders of light. Ozone. Loud booms.

"I'm going into therapy," she says.

I turn towards her and try to size things up. She is ten years older than me (she and Jane Fonda—though Jane looks better than either of us). She's lost some weight since I've last seen her. I've heard she's been depressed.

"You okay?" I ask.

She nods. "I find myself wanting to go backwards, wanting my

23

ex. But when we were together I was crazy, and so was she."

I sigh. "Relationships are hard."

"Being alone is hard," she counters. "I'm fifty years old and tired of playing the dating game."

There is a loud boom and a whistle. The sky lights up. She looks up and watches the fireworks.

I alternately watch the sky and watch her. Against the night I see her profile—her perfect Susan Hayward nose.

We hear the whoosh of the next rocket.

She turns, faces me, and says, "Besides, the woman at the store is starting to give me strange looks every time I buy C-cell batteries."

"Vibrator addiction." I laugh. "Spread it out. Buy them at more than one store."

"I do." She chuckles, and I don't know if she's kidding.

"Come home with me," I say. Just like that. I don't know where it came from or when I got the idea. I'm not even sure if I really want her to. I look around. Everyone's watching the fireworks. It *was* me who said it.

She looks at me. Her chin is resting in her hands, her elbows on her knees. Her lips form a slow smile. She nods.

It occurs to me then that I've been seduced.

•

A window fan is blowing warm air across the bed. The night is muggy—only slightly cooler than the day.

"Are you cold?" Grace tugs at the sheet I have firmly tucked under each arm.

I consider saying, 'Yes,' but instead confess, "I feel shy about my body. I've gained some weight."

She leans towards me, kisses my shoulders, strokes my breasts through the sheet. My body tingles. Each spot she touches feels on fire. "I always feel shy about my body," Grace says gently, "with someone new."

"I haven't been with that many women. I never slept around on Danni."

"I know." She works her hand beneath the sheet and strokes my nipple. "I feel honored."

I sit up. The sheet falls to my waist. "I didn't mean it that way. I only mean..."

"I know what you mean." Stroking one nipple she presses her lips to the other. "Now hush."

I lay back across the tangled sheets. Her fingers and tongue seem to be everywhere, leaving moist trails of heat.

I shake off thoughts of Lilith. I wonder if I'll come, wonder if I can make her come. Often Danille hadn't wanted my reciprocation. When she did, it had been over quickly. I wonder how strong my neck muscles are, how long I can last, what a different woman will taste like.

"Wait," I say.

"Am I doing something wrong?"

"Let me do you first." I have remembered that when I go first I am stimulated and don't need Lilith.

She looks worried. Her faded jeans and summer shirt are laying beside the bed. "I think I should shower first. It's been a long day."

"Maybe we both should—come."

•

We take turns with the soap as steam fills the bathroom. She washes my back, slides soapy fingers between my legs. Rubs and rubs. She soaps my belly, my breasts—kneading my nipples. They are hard. Despite the steamy bathroom, the hot, wet needles against my back, my nipples have drawn tight, as if there is a draft. She pulls me close, her hands rub gentle circles on my shoulders.

We kiss.

She passes me the soap. I start at the back of her neck and lather her wet skin slowly.

I lather her soft mound of Venus.

She places her hands on my shoulders for balance as I separate her labia and with a slippery finger stroke her vulva.

"Oh." She takes in a breath and holds still.

I touch her, gentle and slow, the way I haven't the patience to touch myself.

"Let's go back to bed." Her voice sounds hoarse.

•

I have trouble getting comfortable. She is bigger than Danni. It feels different. When I have my tongue in the right spot I can't breathe. I feel real scared.

The pillow is her idea. She slides it under her bottom.

25

Suddenly everything is in the right spot. I hold her firmly and run my tongue over her vulva. She is wet. My tongue flicks her clitoris. It is standing firm now.

She starts rocking her hips and I start sliding off the end of the bed. I raise a knee and try to brace my other foot on the floor. It works. My neck muscles are fine. I could do this forever. My own cunt is wet and throbbing. I think I might come before she touches me.

She moves suddenly and gives my head a hard push. I land on both knees at the foot of the bed.

"Grace?" I whisper.

"Huh?"

"Did you come, baby?"

"Ah huh." She starts to giggle. "Sorry, it's been a long time."

I crawl back on the bed beside her.

"Just let me catch my breath,"she says.

My own hand slides between my legs. I am wet. On fire.

"Stop that." She pushes it away. "That's mine."

Minutes later her wet curly head is moving between my thighs. Her tongue is working slowly. She pushes two fingers into me, meeting the rocking motion of my hips.

'How does she *do* that?' I wonder. 'What is she balanced on?'

Then all I can think of is a tingling that spreads through my body and centers on my throbbing cunt, as Grace's tongue and fingers push me over the edge.

•

The sheets are damp and tangled. The fan blows warm air that cools our sweaty bodies and diffuses cigarette smoke into the room above the bed.

My head lies in the crook of her arm.

"Tell me something." My voice is low. Sleepy.

"M-mm?"

"Do you think I'm pretty?"

Gently, she pulls her arm away and raises on an elbow.

'Give it up,' I think. 'How much more do you want?' "Do you think I'm pretty?" I repeat.

She throws her legs over the side of the bed and stands. Her soft fleshy bottom is eye level.

26

"No," she says, then pads to the bathroom.

I lie on my back, stunned, and stare at the ceiling. 'You're a masochist,' I tell myself.

I hear her peeing. She's left the door open.

"Intelligent. Witty," she calls. "Sensuous." The words come slow.

I hear her flush.

"Articulate. Interesting."

I hear the water in the sink run.

"Beautiful."

She's standing in the doorway, the bathroom light is behind her. Her nipples are round. And her pubic triangle is a dusky contrast to her pale skin.

"What kind of lesbian," she asks, "would want a woman who's pretty?"

Eighteen Weeks

by M. L. Head

M. L. Head subsists on a teacher's salary. She, her life partner of nine years, and numerous critters live in urban Florida and intend to run away to the country in the very near future.

After years of searching for the cosmic giggle she firmly believes that any escape from reality—good books, music, or friends—is a trip worth taking.

Eighteen Weeks

On Monday they went bowling. On Tuesday they played doubles tennis. Wednesday's was softball and on Thursday they usually stayed home.

On Friday they went out to dinner, Saturday was for house and yard work and on Sunday mornings, while Janna and Dawn played golf, Lauren and Camie were busy making love to one another. Of course, it hadn't started that way.

●

Janna and Lauren had been together four years when they sat down for a long anniversary talk. Over drinks and a fine dinner they reviewed the past, individually and as a couple. They laughed over the good times, reminding one another of their favorite stories, memories stored for just such cherishing. The bad times, of which there were few, were brushed over. It was a night of celebration: a night meant for future dreams to become a reality.

Lauren, being the romantic, once again proposed to her lover, not of marriage, but of a far more concrete symbol of their commitment.

"I think we should start looking for a house."

"To buy?"

"Of course."

"To buy together?   Do you think we're ready?" asked Janna, being the practical type.

Lauren smiled her most beguiling "I adore you even if you are practical" smile and replied, "I want to spend the rest of my life with you. I want a home of our own: a place that is ours alone, a place that will reflect our personality, a place that shelters us, but most importantly one that nurtures us as we grow old together."

As was usually the case, Janna was knocked silly by Lauren's romantic nature, her way with words. As usual, Janna responded not with words but with a grin that threatened to split her face side to side.

That evening Janna noted the specifics of their desires in a prioritized list:

1. Large rooms
2. Trees
3. Fenced yard
4. Garage
5. Fireplace
6. Pool

They began their search the following week with the location of a realty agent, and many long drives through areas of interest. By the second day they'd discovered their price range; the last two items from the list were dropped.

Still, in less than a week, after having seen dozens of houses, they found their home. They were able to tell from the outside, their noses squashed against the windows; once inside they were sold. Despite someone else's furniture, the tacky choices of drapes and linoleum, they knew that *this* was the structure that would house their future.

That evening, after putting a contract on their dream house, Janna and Lauren tried to recall every detail of their fifteen minute tour. There was a certain amount of disagreement: "There were two hall closets." "No, I'm certain there was only one," and there were areas that were grey for both women: "Did you ever see the water heater?" "No, was there a big window in the kitchen?"

Of course it didn't matter one bit. Nothing much mattered that night; they were too happy, too excited about the future. For a second time that month they celebrated, this time with a bottle of wine and an extra early bedtime. With luck, and a certain amount of scrimping, they would be moving in a month.

•

The first to share their good news were their neighbors and closest friends, another established couple who shared the majority of their leisure time.

As would be expected of good friends, Dawn and Camie were at first enthused over the announcement, but later, alone, they experienced conflicting emotions. Camie bemoaned the loss of their neighbors before realizing that she was actually feeling a seldom experienced envy. Dawn took the broader view; Janna and Lauren's good fortune was indicative of an overall upward mobility for lesbian couples. If they could do it then it was only logical to assume that their own time was to come. It was a confusing evening for Dawn and Camie: far too many changes to comprehend in a few short hours.

On the designated moving day the strong backs and pickup trucks of the lesbian community were put to work. By mid-afternoon, Janna and Lauren's possessions were engulfed by the square footage of the new house and the first case of beer was in serious decline. By early evening the four friends were alone amid the squalor, none interested in making order from the mountains of boxes. Instead they devoted their attention to serious drunkenness and conversation.

"I'm going to miss you," Camie moaned dramatically as she toppled her beer.

Janna uprighted the can, dabbing away the spill with her T-shirt and patted Camie's leg. "We'll still see each other."

"Not like before," Lauren intoned.

"Of course we will," Dawn assured. "We still bowl. We play tennis and softball together."

"But, what about the colander?" Camie asked, a reference they all understood.

Dawn smiled indulgently. "I'll buy you one, honey."

"It won't be the same," Camie insisted sadly.

Lauren crawled toward the kitchen and began ripping open Janna's carefully taped boxes. In the third she found the aforementioned colander and presented it to Camie with a grin. "You can have custody."

Camie took it, solemnly clutching it to her chest. Dawn and Janna exchanged looks of maternal understanding as Lauren and Camie hugged, further denting the already abused colander.

The evening digressed from that point. Janna and Dawn found spare pillows and blankets and dragged their respective mates off to sleep.

•

The hangovers of the following morning were bypassed with

frenzied activity. Janna and Dawn went to work organizing the kitchen. Camie and Lauren lost interest in their assigned task of hanging curtains and began ripping out the bathroom floor. Halfway through, sweating noxious beer fumes, their knuckles bleeding, they realized the ridiculousness of their endeavor but kept at it; both were unwilling to admit that fact to their more sensible halves.

It was during the second beer break that someone noticed the For Sale sign—it was only two houses away and, after initial inspection, Lauren declared it virtually identical to their recent acquisition.

"But sweetie, we can't afford a house," Dawn insisted in an attempt to dispel Camie's rising enthusiasm.

"If we can, you can," Lauren assured.

Dawn shook her head sadly.

"If you consider it as an investment," Janna, being practical, began, "then you really can't afford not to."

"And what a neighborhood," Lauren added cheerfully.

Camie went for her traditionally most successful argument; she hugged Dawn tightly, nibbled her ear, and looked pitiful.

Dawn responded by asking, "And how will we come up with the down payment?"

"Borrow from my father," Camie answered honestly.

"The first year's tax break should cover it," Janna informed.

"I'll go get the number." Lauren slammed out the door, ceasing further discussion.

•

It was in the spring, five months later, that Janna and Dawn took up golf. Camie and Lauren amused themselves, initially, with a friendly competition: the search for the perfect lawn. They spent Sunday mornings madly power-raking, fertilizing, mulching, edging, and, inevitably, mowing. Camie maintained the upper hand for the first month (something they agreed was due to a better foundation) until Lauren began her watering binge. Every morning, every evening, she put out the sprinklers and in six weeks surpassed Camie's efforts with sheer water power. That was until the mole crickets caught wind of her swamp and in a matter of weeks had reduced her lush, green, St. Augustine to brown patches of mud. Lauren, dejected, dropped out of the competition.,

During Lauren's postlawn depression Camie, a faithful friend, searched for other forms of amusement, forsaking her own lawn in favor of Lauren's emotional well-being. In a few weeks Lauren had recovered and they devoted their Sunday leisure to the beach. A new competition evolved, the perfect tan, and their closeness grew.

It occurred to both women, at approximately the same time, that a potential for additional closeness existed. This revelation did not catch Lauren by surprise; she was very accustomed to finding herself physically attracted to others than Janna and had, in fact, acted on several such attractions in the previous four years. She had never actually told Janna about the specifics of her affairs, but Lauren had warned her of the possibility when they were still dating. Janna had accepted it gracefully, with the understanding that she viewed Lauren's free time as her own—as long as it did not interfere with their time together. Camie, on the other hand, was quite shocked by her growing fascination with Lauren. She was not, and never had been, the promiscuous type. Dawn was her third lover and, as far as Camie had ever been concerned, her last.

Camie judged her attraction to Lauren as temporary insanity and attempted to let it go at that. What she did not anticipate was her inability to control her desire. Before long Lauren became the object of fantasies—first while masturbating, later during sex with Dawn. The latter began to bother Camie, enough that she considered discussing it with Dawn, but she found herself incapable of finding the right time or way. Instead she attempted to cleanse her guilty conscience by bringing it out in the open, to Lauren.

Lauren had lain back, the sun etching itself on her chest and face, and patiently listened to Camie's bumbled confession. She suppressed her natural desire to grin, maintaining an emotionless mask, as Camie eased herself of her torment and confusion. Finally, when Camie had run out of steam and ways to repeat herself, Lauren rolled casually to her side, faced her friend, and asked, "And what do you intend to do about it?"

Camie stammered, sputtered, and managed to mumble, "I don't know."

Lauren smiled, rolled to her back and remained silent.

"I feel awful," Camie revealed in obvious frustration.

"You haven't done anything to feel awful about," Lauren assured quietly. "Not yet."

33

"Not yet?" Camie repeated.

"If it's any consolation," Lauren began, turning her head to face Camie, "the feeling is mutual."

"Oh, shit."

"Indeed." Lauren sat up and glanced at the sun. "It's almost noon, we should get home." She stood and began gathering her things. "Should we forget this conversation?"

"Only if you want to."

"What I want is seldom tempered with reason or long-term considerations," Lauren sighed.

"I have another week to think about it?"

Lauren laughed. "Another week? Of course you do."

•

"Would you be terribly upset if Janna and I went to Haven Beach next weekend for the golf tournament?" Dawn asked Camie.

Janna asked Lauren precisely the same question, at almost precisely the same time.

Camie and Lauren assured their respective mates that neither would mind and that each felt chasing a little white ball around acres of grass to be a silly sport.

"Then you wouldn't consider coming?" Janna asked Lauren as Dawn asked Camie the same.

Both replied they would not.

So it was decided. Dawn and Janna would go to Haven Beach, each secure in the knowledge that Camie would take care of Lauren and vice versa.

•

Their affair began, expectedly, on Sunday morning. It took all of Saturday evening and night for them to work their way into bed. For the record, their first kiss, one Camie registered as a six on the Richter Scale, was a little before midnight but that hardly mattered as it took another two hours to get off the couch, undressed, and between the sheets.

Lauren awoke, as expected, disappointed. Three months of semi-serious flirtation had resulted in clumsy sex. Something Lauren was incapable of deducing was the equation that linked good sex to familiarity. Lauren believed that passion should equal good sex. As a result, she lived life disappointed.

Camie awoke racked with guilt. In her panic she chose to flee before realizing that her bed was the scene of their crime. That option closed, she concluded she could be, at least, a congenial host to her nude guest. "Would you like a robe? A cup of coffee?"

Lauren laughed, not unkindly.

Camie sank back on her pillow and stared at the ceiling imagining that it was Dawn beside her, wishing for that sense of ease.

Lauren lay still and did not imagine Janna. If it were Janna she'd be rising to fix coffee and fetch the paper. If it were Janna she would not feel desire rising within her body. Janna hated sex in the morning. Lauren loved it.

Lauren rolled to her side and found her mouth within close proximity of two very soft breasts. She flicked out her tongue and let the nipple rise to meet it. With one hand she pushed aside the covers to expose Camie's nude body.

Camie lay stiffly and tried to summon the courage of her guilt. But as is the way with most things in life, the physical overcame the mental. Without wanting it her body opened up to Lauren's aggression and, very simply, she forgot Dawn in favor of more immediate pleasure.

By that afternoon, after several practice sessions, Lauren found her disappointment fading. The sex had improved considerably and her desire had not diminished in the least.

Camie's guilt had subsided during the practice session, but had risen in multiple proportions as the hour of Dawn's return loomed ever closer. By the time she ushered Lauren to the door, with a last kiss on their already bruised lips, she was reaching a state of near panic and planning a full confession.

But Camie did not confess and, more importantly, she was able and quite willing when Dawn initiated sex that night.

Lauren did the initiation at their house and was very pleased when Janna responded with the enthusiasm that even a short-term separation is capable of arousing.

The week following Camie and Lauren's twelve hours in bed was, outwardly, no different than any other week in their long friendship. The four continued their routine, although Dawn and Janna had far more to say about their weekend, including a stroke by stroke account of the tournament. Camie and Lauren feigned interest but both found their minds wandering elsewhere.

Despite her attempts at sanity, Camie found herself consumed with images of her twelve hours with Lauren. By Thursday, imagination had turned the experience into the highpoint of her life. By Saturday she was anxiously anticipating Sunday morning.

Lauren found herself enjoying the rushes that Camie's memory evoked. She did not deny herself the pleasure, especially at work or other moments of sheer boredom. Lauren expended her excess energy in the only way she knew how; she and Janna made love three times that week—the first time in several years.

•

In about four months Lauren had begun to lose the desire that had excited her about Sunday mornings. Her longest previous affair had lasted less than two months; by week five she had fallen in and out of love with those women. By week seven she had been more than anxious to end the involvements.

This one had lasted almost sixteen weeks, barring rain delays, and Lauren had long since fallen out of love. As in the past, her affection for Janna had risen in direct proportion to her failing affair. The difference, this time, was that she liked Camie, still valued her as a friend, but no longer needed or desired her as a lover.

Camie was surprised to find her anticipation of Sundays turning to dread. It wasn't Lauren, it was the predictability. For the four months they had been lovers they had done nothing on Sundays but make love. It had been exciting, then fun, then, gradually, an obligation. The obligation was too much; Camie wanted out.

On week eighteen a stalemate occurred. Lauren, less than anxiously, waited for Camie. Camie, a nervous wreck, waited for Lauren. They had both chosen the easiest way out, to do nothing.

The following week progressed normally and they found themselves more comfortable both within their respective couples and within the foursome.

On week nineteen they waited each other out, again. The pressure finally got to her, and Camie made the first, and last, move.

"I can't handle this face to face," Lauren heard as she answered the phone. "I can't handle any of this," Camie hurried to explain. "It's messing up Dawn and me; it's messing up you and Janna."

"I think," Lauren corrected, "the real issue is that it's messing up

36

me and you."

"Yes," Camie sighed. "I love you, but not like Dawn; do you understand?"

"Honey, we're better friends than lovers. Quite frankly, it was getting rather boring."

Camie laughed, relieved to find it so simple. "Do you suppose we should tell them?" she asked quietly.

"That is pointless."

Camie thought for a moment and said, "It's something I may need to do."

"You do whatever is best for you and Dawn," Lauren replied. "Listen, I was thinking about the backyard, don't you think a deck would be great?"

"Yeah, we could have cookouts."

"I figured on a picnic table. Why don't you come over?"

"I'll be there in a minute."

"Bring your tape measure," Lauren reminded. She hung up the phone and went to the garage in search of her circular saw; things were back to normal.

•

Camie and Lauren, after a couple of weeks caddying, concluded that chasing a little white ball around acres of grass wasn't completely stupid. For Christmas each received a starter set of clubs from their respective lovers and began spending Sundays on the greens. Camie took a sincere liking to the game; Lauren contented herself with the fun of driving a golf cart.

In the five or six days a week they spent together, Dawn and Camie and Lauren and Janna became closer friends. Ultimately, they spent twelve good years as neighbors. Camie finally told Dawn what had happened those eighteen weeks and was surprised that Dawn had known from the start—but had thought it was a necessary phase in Camie's life. Lauren never said a word to Janna and if Janna suspected she never mentioned it. In the end it never really mattered.

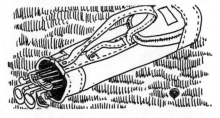

Layaway

by Shelly Rafferty

Shelly Rafferty: I am a working class white woman, native New Yorker, and I've been writing for many years. I am a non-biological parent to Rachel, and hope to provide her with a sibling soon.

Layaway

Clyde tossed his boots up onto the corner of the rickety plank table we kept on the porch and ground his sixteen-year-old backside into the seat of his ladderback chair. The newspaper (*The New Iberia Journal*, circulation: 16, 240) flapped open loudly.

I went on sweeping. The dust, what little of it there was on our houseboat, still had the power to irritate. I stifled the urge to sneeze.

"Twenty more rigs shut down last week," said Clyde, looking up suddenly. He paused to spit over the rail, an action rewarded with a kerplunk. "And today a barrel of oil dropped another dollar."

I kept on sweeping, pushing the tiny particles of grit over the transom, their little cloud slowly being eaten by the dirty water that lapped at the stern.

"You worried, Mom?" Clyde asked me.

I grimaced under my smile. "Don't do no good to worry. What's going to happen is going to happen."

Clyde pulled his curly head back down and buried it again in the pages of the front section. On the back, Dunphy's A&P was showing a sale on Tide; maybe I'd get Clyde to take a load to the washerette before Sharon got home. I wanted clean sheets on our bed.

Clyde put the paper down again.

"Shar's gonna get laid off, Mom. You know that."

I didn't say anything. I could see the concern in Clyde's serious face, the way he set his jaw and pushed his eyebrows together in a downward knot.

"Then what will she do, do you think?"

"Well, first off, she can have a vacation," I answered.

"Sure, but what kind of a job will she get?"

"Sharon's a hard worker. She'll find something. Besides, she could always just stay home with you and me."

Clyde shook his head tiredly. "And do what? There's nothing

around here," he muttered resolutely. "How will she keep herself busy?"

"Shar's never at a loss for something to do. She'll find something," I repeated. I'd meant to sound encouraging, but I knew I hadn't.

I stopped my sweeping and stuck my broom up in the rafters next to the long-poled scoop nets.

"I'm leaving in August."

"I know, son."

Clyde reached in his pocket and lit a cigarette. I felt like having one too, but I mumbled something to myself about being stronger than nicotine and pushed the thought away. I reached over the side rail and fingered the crab trap line.

"I'm going to start the pot boiling. Why don't you pull supper up?"

Clyde had returned to the news.

"In a minute, Mom," he replied.

•

In the kitchen I fired up the propane stove and started dicing some onions and peppers. Eventually I heard Clyde pulling up the traps and shaking the skittery creatures into the ice chest.

I thought about what Clyde had said.

What would Sharon do when the layoff came? There wasn't a job to be had anywhere in the whole parish. We hardly knew a soul who was still working. Sharon was as handy as anyone, but it troubled me to think of her as idle. I feared Clyde might be right; when the first days of idyllic rest passed into the common knowledge of everyday life, how would Sharon find her place? Even Shar had a limit to her tolerance for quiet fishing and contemplation. I couldn't imagine what she would do.

For as long as I could remember, Sharon had been working in the oil fields. Two weeks on, then two weeks off, that was the routine, and our lives had settled into a comfortable rhythm around it.

When folks would ask what she did for a living, she'd answer simply, "Wildcatting." Around us, everyone knew that meant hard, physical labor on an oil rig. You could say foreman, or engineer, or mechanic, but nobody gave a lick. Everybody worked hard. Sharon always came home dog-tired, a little bit thinner, but harder, and her skin was a deep, ruddy brown.

She gave most all of her money to me ("Can't spend it in the Gulf of Mexico"), after putting some of it in the bank for Clyde's college. She didn't care much about it herself.

On her two weeks off, she'd fish with Clyde, drink a few cases of beer, and we'd all usually run over to New Iberia to catch a movie and eat in a real restaurant. And then, when Clyde was at school, Sharon and I would spend most every morning making love, lazy and slow, like the bayou around us, rocking the little houseboat as gently as a hammock.

Sharon had been with us since Clyde was a baby. I met her in the hospital the day I'd had him; she'd been in a car wreck on the Old Spanish Trail, and had her leg broke when Henry Jeanerette rolled his pickup into her dilapidated Buick. (Henry only got a bump on the head and a week in the police jury jail.)

My mama liked Sharon fine, especially after Shar helped her write some letter to the utilities and Montgomery Ward. Mama told her to come home with us to let her leg mend. Sharon said she wasn't expected anywhere, so why not?

Sharon just loved Clyde. She's always said she's wanted a child of her own; Clyde filled the place. She'd spend hours and hours rocking him and bouncing him up and down on her cast, cooing in his little face and tickling him behind his ear. I liked seeing them together. Sharon had a way of being with Clyde that seemed so connected and natural. I couldn't be jealous; it was so easy to share him with her. Besides, I knew I'd have Clyde the rest of my life, so I let my new friend spoil him some; I figured she'd be on her way soon enough.

One evening we were out on the porch swing, swaying quietly in the gentle breeze, Shar's leg propped up on an old peach crate. We'd already put Clyde down for the night. Even then, after knowing her just a few weeks, our lives had found their way into a comfortable easiness, a pattern of ways that seemed natural and balanced. We didn't say much to one another, just listened to the cicadas and the cars passing on Highway 29.

Then Shar told me she wanted to kiss me.

I let her.

Soon after, we started sleeping together. I liked it so much I knew I'd have to get out of my mama's house. Sharon bought the houseboat for me and her and Clyde, and we pitched it in the sidewaters of the Bayou Teche, near the Chitimacha Indian Reservation.

Things had been steady ever since.

I never gave much thought to our lives being different. I hadn't worried about how our lives would change when Clyde went off to school or if Sharon lost her job, or if I couldn't keep up my own business, repairing nets for the shrimpers over in Delcambre. I was beginning to feel uneasy that somehow all of those things might happen at the same time.

Celery chop, parsley. Clyde dragged the ice chest in across the wooden floor. The crabs were clamoring to get out.

"Got a dozen and a half."

"What are Shar and me going to eat?" I teased him.

Clyde just smiled. "Do you want anything in town? I thought I'd go in to see if the crewboat's here."

I went on with my little knife, mincing up the fresh parsley. "Clyde, you know that boat doesn't come in until six."

"I just thought I'd wait."

I jerked my head back a bit, indicating the little bedroom where Shar and I slept. "The laundry basket's full."

"OK."

A few minutes later, he banged out the screen door and tossed the dirty clothes into the back of our pickup. "See ya, Mom," he shouted. "We'll be home later."

I watched him pull off our gravel pitch, the Ford spitting some loamy stones into the water.

•

We would sorely miss Clyde when he went off to school; in a way he had provided that third point in the map maker's scheme, necessary for orienting. With him around, Sharon and I had always known what we needed money for, how we would spend our time, where we were going.

Damn Shar. She wanted Clyde to go to college. But she'd end up paying more than money for her ambition, just like I would. Now there wouldn't be any fishing partner, no one to play poker and share basketball scores with. Clyde's graduation was only a week away, and the days of parent's meetings, school plays and football were soon to be a thing of the past.

When Clyde went off to school Shar and I would be alone with each other.

If she lost her job, could our aloneness turn to boredom? How could I be everything after Clyde was gone?

We didn't have any friends to speak of, least of all ladies like us, only people we said "Hi" to or nodded at in Dunphy's or the Dixieland Grill. Neither one of us had any family left, outside of Clyde. After he was gone, would I be enough?

I foraged in the potato barrel and found six, little fresh ones. I drew some water off the standpipe and scrubbed the skins over the side of the boat. When I cut out their eyes I nicked myself with the knife.

I strayed some cayenne pepper into the cook water. The spice made my eyes burn.

I knew Sharon loved me, though. Neither of us had ever been with anyone else, although sometimes Shar would say what a pretty girl she'd seen over in New Iberia and that would make me feel lost and kind of jealous. Sometimes she did unpredictably romantic things, like picking wild berries for my pancakes, or bringing me flowers when she came from the oil field. And she was a good lover, too, always leaving me with that feeling of a sunrise: clean and perfect and finished every time.

Jesus, what was going to happen to us?

I grabbed my long-handled tongs and pulled a fat female out of the ice chest. Her front claws were big, and they wavered and wiggled, grasping for any foothold in the air. I wondered if she, like me, had any idea of where she was going. Numbly, I dropped her into the stockpot.

•

Later that night, I found the layoff notice in Sharon's shirt pocket. She was already asleep, the result of some twelve-year-old Scotch she had emptied after dinner. She hadn't given away a thing while we were eating; she and Clyde had swapped the latest dirty jokes, as usual, as the pile of crab shell grew into a small mountain in the center of the table. We'd all drunk beer with dinner, and once, in the middle of it all, Shar had leaned over the table and kissed me, and told me she was glad to be home.

43

It never bothered Clyde.

I hung her shirt on the corner of the chair and tossed her dirty jeans into the empty laundry basket. Her socks followed, and her boots got set out on the deck for shaking off the mud in the morning.

I undressed and crawled into bed beside her. I laid my cheek on her dark, dark arm.

She woke up a little and pulled me closer.

I stared into her brown eyes and they struck me then as the prettiest eyes I'd ever seen. I kissed her mouth sweetly, and she answered me back, reaching into my hair, opening her mouth, tasting my tongue. She pulled me on top of her, and my hair hung over her face, but she didn't brush it away.

"I got laid off today," she whispered.

"I know."

I felt her hands on my lower back, kneading my skin just below my ribs. I laid my head on her shoulder, and we were still for a long time, conscious only of the likeness of our bodies: our stomachs, breasts, hair.

"Does Clyde know?" she asked a while later.

"I thought you should tell him."

"I don't want him to worry. We saved enough for his school."

I slid to one side of her, leaving a hand resting on her stomach.

"They might call me back," she continued, but her voice was heavy with a kind of tired enthusiasm. "Anyway, until they do—and it could be a long time—I need to do something different."

"Don't worry," I said. "We'll be OK. You need to let me take care of you for awhile."

Shar looked puzzled.

"You know what I mean," I went on. "You've always given everything to Clyde and me. We have enough money to last. You deserve a vacation." In my heart I felt my resolve on unsteady ground. This was new for me. I'd never had to be responsible for anyone, really. Shar had always taken such pride in being able to care for me and Clyde.

I struggled for something to say.

"We've taken good care of each other," Shar offered softly. She smiled. "And Clyde."

"Yes," I said.

"He'll be gone soon."

Shar turned her head to the window. Outside, ghostly clouds hung just above the trees on the opposite bank. Above them, the moon was full and bright. Sometimes, when she wasn't paying attention, I caught her in this peaceful attitude and I would look at her beautiful face, all of the oil rig washed off of it, in the gentle moonlight. I could see then that she was pretty, soft, woman. Tonight, she was all of those things and more; she had a look of anxious dreaminess in her eyes and she seemed to be hesitating when she spoke. I felt uneasy. I pulled myself closer to her, praying silently that she would always love me—never go—not be bored with me.

"We'll have lots of time now," she said.

"I suppose."

"And we can do what we want."

I waited. What was she leading up to?

All at once my heart seized up. It was a funny feeling, not knowing what was coming next. Our lives had been all predictability: pattern and routine. I had known from week to week and year to year what to expect from the steady timetable of work, school, fishing and weekends—from love and arguing, from the loneliness I felt when Sharon was gone, to the joy and contentment I felt when she came home.

Did she want to change all of that?

I kissed her breast, lingered on a nipple, and let my fingers trail lazily to the hair between her legs.

She pushed my hand away, and lifted herself to her elbow.

"Wait," she said.

I frowned.

She pulled me into her arms and I could feel her warm breath in my hair.

"Listen," she whispered. "There is something I want to do."

I felt myself inhale, bracing for the words. Oh God, I thought to myself, would she be telling me that it was time for her to go now, since so many things had changed forever? My heart was shaking.

She pulled back just slightly, and stared into my eyes.

Don't leave me, Shar, I begged silently. I love you.

"I want to have a baby," she said. "It's my turn."

There was a certain rightness in her wish that caught my heart then, in the sudden moment, and I felt my fears slip into the cradle of her strong embrace. Her thought filled me. It would let us keep on being what we were, and still let us change: slow, new, unhurried.

I kissed her.

"Yes," I whispered, a thousand times, until sunrise.

After The Rain

by Carol M. Bundy

Hi. I'm Carol Bundy, a white femme, forty-six, and doing life in prison. After The Rain *was written shortly after the death of someone I loved deeply. She knew she was dying, and for fifteen months I watched her tremendous fight against death. "When you are dying," she once told me, "every second of life is precious."*

This story reflects her heart, her strength and her love. She wanted only to go home for her last Christmas, one she wanted to spend with her family. She would've paroled on Dec. 17, 1987, but failed to make it by only seven weeks. I can't imagine a lonelier death than in prison, only fifty-seven days away from home. After The Rain *is my last gift to her. Merry Christmas, Pretty Lady.*

After The Rain

"Mama," Margaret said as she touched my shoulder. "Jonathan has got to get to work. He needs to know if you're ready or if we should come back for you later." Her concern warmed me. She tried not to look around the dimly lit slumber room. Her sense of discomfort was evident. "He's waiting in the car now," she said.

I felt a tear slip down my cheek as I studied the time-created lines etched into the face of my friend and lover of sixty years. "I know, dear. I'll be there in a minute. I just want to say good-bye to Miss Emily."

Miss Emily. How peaceful you look. Pretty, actually, in the rose-colored, cable knit sweater I made for your birthday, next week. You would have been seventy-five. I wish you had made it.

Pretty Lady, do you remember so many years back, our days of girlhood? Oh, how daring we were, defying our fathers, wanting to be teen-aged flappers wearing lipstick and chasing boys. Then it was "twenty-three skiddoo," "Oh you kid!" and doing the Charleston that mattered. A lifetime ago. Do you miss the innocence of that lost time? In a way I do, yet I would not give up a moment of the years we've shared in our sixty years together.

We graduated high school at a hard time, only months before the Great Depression began. I immediately married Howard, and you were lucky to find work at the telephone company. Then my twins Billy and Margaret were born.

You never married. It would be years before I understood why. You were so beautiful with your bouncy, red curls and deep dimples. I never told you how jealous I sometimes was of your emerald-green eyes that promised men so much but gave so little. Except to me. Those eyes were mine and I never knew, never realized their loyalty to me until Howard's accident that killed him at twenty-seven. I think you took it harder than I did.

I was so glad you were with me that stormy night Howard's supervisor from the electric company stopped by. I was bathing the twins, so you answered the door. Your stricken face was ashen when you came into the bathroom to get me. "I'll take them," you said, and took Billy from my arms. "Mr. Fletcher is here."

I playfully swatted Margaret's bare, two-year-old bottom and went to see what he wanted. His expression said more than his words. "Howard is dead, Gladys. He was repairing a high voltage line and the wind blew him against a hot wire. He fell from the pole..."

You and I cried buckets together after he left. Holding me tenderly, gently, you crooned soothing words and stroked my hair all that night. Later, it was you who made the funeral arrangements, took over the house and kids until I felt stronger. It was you, always you, who was there when I hurt, and you who took the pain away.

For months I had an awful time making ends meet. I couldn't pay my bills and fell behind on my rent. You rescued me when you moved into my big barn of a house, helping with expenses and child care so I could find a job. Most importantly, you gave me the companionship that had come to mean so much.

Oh, Emily, how you lightened my world. Like my twenty-fifth birthday that you wanted to make so special; it turned out to be the most special birthday I've ever had.

After feeding the children and putting them to bed we curled up on the sofa as we often did to listen to Jack Benny, some Benny Goodman music, and all those wonderful, old-time radio shows that we loved so much. Sometimes one of us would grow sleepy and lay her head in the other's lap. It was okay—*we were best friends*. But this particular night, as you lay in my lap, you had the softest look in your eyes. Your hand reached up and stroked my cheek, a touch so light I might not have felt it if my eyes had been closed. Fire shot through me, surprising me nearly to death! "Emily," I managed to croak, "Emily, I..."

You sat up, surprised as I was; I guess you felt it, too. Soon we were kissing. Passions were growing that neither of us quite understood. It took much fumbling and experimenting before we learned what we were doing, but neither of us ever looked back or felt regret.

Of course, concerned friends and relatives felt sorry for "those two lonely spinsters, Miss Emily and Miss Gladys," but we'd smile knowingly at each other and tend to our own home. We were happy, and our children thrived.

I think you had more fun raising the twins than I did. When Billy came home with a football trophy you fairly exploded with pride, and you tried so hard not to miss any of his major games. But "pride" doesn't even begin to describe the glow in those fiery, green eyes of yours the day Margaret came home from school and told us she was the valedictorian of her graduating class! You and she spent hours writing her speech, together choosing each word with the singular precision of a master speechwriter.

Then World War II broke out and eventually, right before its end, Billy joined the navy. Once again you were my tower of strength when that disastrous telegram devastated us by saying Billy's ship had gone down in the Pacific Theatre. My son, my beautiful teen-aged son was gone. *But you weren't.* You rocked me through those nights just as you had sixteen years earlier when Howard died, and I don't even remember you complaining of your own grief. Again you held me and softened my pain. Oh, Emily, what did *I* ever give to *you?*

Margaret married a nice boy who worked in his father's grocery. Now he owns a chain of supermarkets and treats Margaret as a queen. I don't think she would've even considered him if "Miss Emily hadn't approved." Now their eldest son, Jonathan, is waiting for me in the parking lot. I guess mortuaries make him nervous and he'd rather wait outside.

Johnny was quite the boy, wasn't he, Emily? So many nights you coached him in his math and algebra. He never seemed to catch on. By now you and I were getting on in years, and your job as the night supervisor at the telephone company had you tired to death. Yet you persisted for the boy's sake. You worked and drilled until you both were ready to drop, but he finally grasped those elusive concepts you were committed to teaching. Now he's grown and is a district manager for his father's market chain. He's worked hard and I'm sure much of his tenacity and motivation came from you.

Oh sure, in all those years you and I had some spats. It wasn't always tea and roses. But you know something, Emily? Even the fights felt good. And we never went to bed angry. Never. We stayed up until all the issues were resolved.

Somehow those years slipped by and age started to show itself. I developed grey hair and double chins; you grew bags under your green eyes and your once melodious voice grew husky.

The doctor said you had a little polyp on your vocal chords, probably nothing to worry about, but a year later you were spitting up blood so he did a biopsy. When the report came back the doctor shook his head. "Even with chemotherapy there is little hope. I'm sorry."

Months rolled by and I watched you tragically drop from 140 pounds to 92. Your throat was closing up and you couldn't eat. With all my heart I wished it was me and not you. I felt as helpless as you did.

Margaret and her children were there for us, but there was little I would let them do. I wanted to care for you myself. You were my world and I wanted every minute with you I could have. Margaret watched us both and worried silently. I started to lose weight myself. Just as I rarely left your side, she was always near me to take over when I simply had to rest. "Mama," she'd say, "I've made Miss Emily a little soup," and would place a tray before me with two steaming bowls on it. I'd try to feed you a little and then take a bite or two myself. Margaret would pretend to fluff your pillow and would stuff one behind my head. Then I'd doze in my chair holding your hand.

Soon pain took away your smile, and Demerol dimmed the pain. You still laughed when you could, but even the agony of cancer could not diminish the courage I've admired in you for sixty years.

Was it only Tuesday when you slipped into a coma, your ragged, tortured breathing tearing apart my heart? Margaret never let go of my hand and I never let go of yours all that afternoon. I looked down at our two hands, each wearing the same simple bands we gave each other over half a century earlier. You and I, Em, we were more married and happier than anyone else we knew, only we did it when it just wasn't done! Our two hands touching was the only wedding we could have, but I guess it was enough.

It was past sundown and I guess I was dozing in my chair when your fingers went limp. "Mama," Margaret said sharply. "Mama, she's stopped breathing!" I looked quickly to your face and I could

51

see your pain was gone.

Emily, do you recall one talk we had about dying? You said that you believed that when someone dies, the spirit of a loved one comes and escorts them to Heaven. Honey, did our Billy walk you home?

Margaret's back, Emily. Jonathan needs to go. He's probably getting impatient.

I can't help but smile. As they went out to the car earlier, Johnny's wife made some kind of remark in the vestibule about "those old Lesbians."

He snapped, "Those ladies are my grandmothers and I love them very much. If you can't respect them then shut up. OK?"

Well, Pretty Lady, we did get old, and maybe we were Lesbians, but I'll bet anything that they won't have half the love and respect we've shared for sixty years.

When Margaret was cleaning your room and packing your things away the other day, she came across that lovely Madalyne Denton poem you've always loved. It was tucked away among your hankies. I memorized it last night because it reminds me so much of you and I never want to forget it. You know the one:

> It seems my rainbows always fade away
> When the sun shines too long where I play.
> Then clouds roll in where love once was alive,
> And it makes me so lonely and empty inside.
> They say time is a healer,
> That it changes things.
> I say it destroys mountains,
> It brings death to kings.
> But when shared with someone
> Who loves you deep in their heart,
> It can create a bond
> That nothing can part.
> I dreamed of someone
> Very much like you.
> She didn't toy with my feelings,
> And her love was true.
> When you care for someone
> They can bring the worst pain.

➤

52

Or they can become your rainbow
After the rain.

Pretty Lady, you were.

Telling Mom

by Karen Dale Wolman

Karen Dale Wolman is a nice Jewish lesbian who teaches writing in an all girl Catholic college. She moved to Los Angeles four years ago after too many New York winters and subway train break-downs. She lives in the gay city of West Hollywood, with no lover and no cat, just an IBM-PC, a lot of unfiled paper, and triple stacked paperbacks from Random House and William Morrow as well as Naiad, Alyson and The Crossing Press.

She likes her life exactly how it is: writing novels, travelling to distant places, listening to decadent rock music and howling at the moon. Her only wish is that there was more time to do it all. About one hundred hours a day would do it.

Telling Mom

I pick up the phone for the fourth time, but this time I dial. My darling Renee smiles reassuringly and flashes a "go for it" sign across the room.

The numbers flow easily from memory, but I still haven't gotten used to dialing an area code to reach Queens from Manhattan. It makes it seem so far away.

The ring still sounds the same. I remember the high-pitched jingle from my teenage years, calling home to ask can I go to the movies after school, can I stay over Cindy's house, can I stay out later, can I please?

Mom, as always, answers on the second ring. Never answer on the first, Gail, she has been telling me for years; it might be a wrong number and this will give the person a chance to hang up without getting charged for the call.

"Sweetheart," she says, "I knew it was going to be you. I could tell from the ring." Another thing about Mom. She claims that she can tell from the ring who is calling. I didn't believe her until I was fifteen. What else but telepathy could explain her knowing when I was lying about where I was, who I was with, what I was doing? Moms know a lot that can't be explained by rational means.

"Aunt Josie was here yesterday," she says. "Your cousin Joanna is getting married. Her Ralph is a nice man with a good job. And not bad looking, I should add. That'll be the third wedding in the family this year. And all the Bar Mitzvahs. So many dresses." I roll my eyes and Renee smiles. Mom keeps talking as I hold the phone away from my ear. Renee hears about cousin Marcie's pending Bat Mitzvah, the new living room furniture and my brother Ben's new girlfriend.

"Speaking of girlfriends, Ma," I say as I hug Renee to me. She squeezes my shoulder muscles, then gives me a silent kiss. "Good luck," she mouths as she lets go and busies herself toward the bedroom.

"And how is Susan?" Mom asks, changing the subject so deftly I don't even realize she's doing it. "You hardly mention her anymore."

"She moved to Boston last year; you know that."

"So you can't visit her?"

"We grew apart after college."

"Friendship is important, Gail, you have to work on it."

I breathe deeply, exasperated. This is not what I want to talk about. I hear Renee in the bedroom. I long to be in there with her, stroking her silky skin, getting lost in her softly flowing hair. "Ma, the reason I called—"

"Okay, you're an adult; it's none of my business."

"It's not that, Ma, it's just that I don't want to talk about Susan." Again, I realize; she did it again. I call to tell her about me and Renee and we wind up talking about everything else. How does she do it?

"Your cousin Joanna will be calling you soon. She wants you to be one of her bridesmaids." Maybe if I let her talk herself out, I'll get my chance. It's tempting to just gossip about the family, then hang up, but this has been going on for too long. I need to let her know.

"She picked baby blue for the dresses. It will look good on you, bring out your eyes."

I realize she's mentioned my cousin's wedding twice without asking me if I have a serious boyfriend yet. I take it as a good sign. I listen to her with half an ear, wondering exactly how I'm going to tell her: Ma, I'm in love with Renee, Ma, I'm gay, Ma, can I bring my girlfriend home for Sunday dinner?

None of them seem right, so I stall.

"The wedding's not for eight months, but there's a lot of work to be done. You have to try on dresses, go for fittings. Do you want to bring a date with you?"

I go for the opening. "You remember Renee who I keep talking about, Ma?" Renee sticks her head out of the bedroom and gives me a thumbs up and bright smile. I fall in love all over again every time I see that smile.

"The writer, you mean? The one who does magazine articles?"

"Yes. That's her." I am surprised she remembers, surprised that she had listened so closely when I talked about Renee.

"We're living together now. Renee moved in with me." I hold my breath, waiting for the fireworks.

"I never did like the idea of you living alone in the city. Your rent is so high, maybe now you'll be about to save some money."

I never imagined that she wouldn't understand. Mom has always been very astute, very quick to grasp what hasn't been said.

I try again. "We're sharing the bedroom." Still no reaction.

"Mom, she's very important to me."

"Good, good. Is she a nice girl? I never did like your friend Wendy. She seemed like trouble right from the beginning."

Wendy hasn't been mentioned in years. Does Mom know she was my first girlfriend in high school?

"Renee's not like Wendy, Mom. You'll like her." Renee is still standing in the doorway, questioning me with her eyebrows. I shrug. I'm not sure if Mom understands.

Before I know it, Mom's back to talking about the family. I can't let her do this. I'll never get the nerve to tell her again.

"I haven't finished telling you about Renee yet." I take a deep breath and oxygen blasts the words across the wires. "Ma, I love Renee."

"That's good. She sounds like a nice girl. You'll have to bring her to dinner one night."

I hold the phone between my shoulder and my chin as I shrug at my mother's incomprehension.

"Does she like brisket or should I make chicken? So many people won't eat red meat these days I never know what to cook for company."

"Ma, it doesn't matter what you cook. It's not important."

"You don't want your mother to make a good impression on your friend?"

Why this time do the subtleties of my words escape her? When I try purposefully to be vague she cuts right to the point, but this time, when I need for her to know, she refuses to understand.

"Does she like salad?"

"Mom, stop talking about food. Can't you understand what I"m trying to tell you? Renee is my girlfriend. We're lovers. I'm gay."

    She doesn't even pause for air. "So," the words come across the wire, bridging the miles and the years, "is she Jewish?"

    "Ma," I say, before hanging up, "make the brisket."

Wishful Thinking

by Amanda Hayman

Amanda Hayman is a thirty-seven year old Lesbian Separatist who lives in a funky old wooden house in Tokyo, Japan, with her lover of eight years. She adores being a dyke, and puts all her energy that isn't taken up by writing and teaching into the tiny but dynamic Tokyo Lesbian community. Being British with an American lover, her ideal future would include Lesbians being given the right to work and live in the countries where their partners were born. She also dreams about a shopping mall where all the clothes are made in size XXXXXL, so that she can have as much choice as anyone else.

Wishful Thinking

Thelma lowered the eggs into the boiling water and made a mental note of when six and a half minutes would be up. She poured more boiling water into the brown teapot, and set it on the table under the cat-shaped tea-cosy her granddaughter had given her last Christmas. Then she shifted Kipper, the real cat, off today's newspaper, and put it next to Ivy's plate. Ivy was quite finicky about routine; a day that didn't start with the headlines and the post could be fraught with problems.

Speeding up a little now, Thelma turned the toast over, and then nipped along the passage to pick up the letters lying on the mat. Oh dear, here was the electric bill. That one must be from Ivy's son, and about time, too. But what was this? Curiously she turned over a large, white envelope, which was addressed, in a beautiful gold script, to her. Mindful of the toast and eggs she didn't stop to open it. Brrr! It was chilly in the hall. Thelma pulled her green mohair cardigan around her ample front and hurried back to the kitchen, which was heating up nicely. Quickly she buttered the toast, and was just putting the eggs in their special, china egg cups when Ivy came yawning through the kitchen door.

"Morning," she mumbled, in a tone that some might have considered a trifle brusque. Not so Thelma, though. Over the years of living together she and Ivy had arrived at many compromises, not the least important of which was respect for their different morning personas. So Thelma made no comment about this seemingly unsociable start to the day, the same way Ivy wouldn't when Thelma was what she considered horrendously chirpy.

Kipper mewed a greeting, and Ivy moved forward to stroke the animal's pretty grey head.

"Electric bill's come," said Thelma, pouring milk into the mugs, and giving the tea a stir. It was brewed to perfection, strong and black, just the way they liked it.

She smiled fondly at Ivy, who was carrying out her ritual morn-ing search for her glasses. "They're on your head, dear," she said softly and as tactfully as she could. Ivy harrumphed, pulled the spectacles down from where they nested in her silver hair and settled them onto her nose.

"Well open it, then." Ivy motioned towards the brown window envelope which was crouching between the jam and the milk jug, glowering at them ominously.

With a sigh of relief Thelma showed Ivy the slip of flimsy paper. They would be able to pay it, after all. Now they could enjoy their breakfast, and before the eggs got cold. Carefully, Thelma removed the shell and dug in her spoon eagerly.

Ivy had finished her egg, and the foreign news page, before she noticed that there were other letters. "What're those?" she asked shortly.

Thelma started, drawn back from a contemplation of the C.R. group she had taken part in the night before. She followed the di-rection of Ivy's gaze, and reached across the table for the envelope. "Oh my, I must've forgotten. Here. One each. Yours is from Simon, I suppose; at least it's got a Canadian stamp." She handed over the thin wisp of aerogram and Ivy eyed it distastefully; she didn't really have much time for her elder son, who had been married twice and had abandoned families in two countries.

"That all?" She was clearly disappointed, and made no move to open the communication. Ivy obviously felt Thelma's letter to be far more worthy of attention, for she did not return immediately to her newspaper, but waited with an inquisitive air for it to be opened. "What did you get? Fancy envelope, isn't it?"

"Well, I'm sure I don't know what it could be." Thelma stared again at the elegant writing, and fingered the fine vellum on which it was set out. Carefully, so as not to tear it, she opened the envelope and took out a single,pale blue card, which was scalloped and edged with gold.

At the top was a labrys embossed in gold leaf, and the word "Congratulations."

"Well, I never!" exclaimed Thelma, almost too taken aback to speak. "Just listen to this, Ivy." She read aloud: "Congratulations.

You are the lucky winner of this year's Star Prize, the granting of three wishes. On each of the attached gold seals you may write one wish. This you must then burn, scattering the ashes upon the earth. If you follow these instructions precisely your wish will surely come true. Believe and be empowered."

By now Ivy was peering over Thelma's shoulder and the two women looked at each other, puzzled. The note was unsigned.

"It must be a joke," said Thelma, turning the thick card over to look at the back, but her tone was not convincing.

"But supposing it isn't?" suggested her lover, her morning lethargy miraculously dispelled. "Just imagine! Three wishes. What would you ask for?"

"Oh, don't be ridiculous, Ivy, it's not possible." Thelma gave her a gentle nudge with her elbow, and stared again at her prize. The 'gold seals' looked like the kind of tin-foil that commonly wraps chocolates with gooey cherry-flavoured centres, but Ivy was right, you never knew.

And what *would* she ask for? There cannot be a woman in the world who has not, at some point, asked herself that question. Thelma had always wondered about the ethics of asking for purely selfish things, and even as a child, making a secret pact with the fairies, had taken good care to include at least one wish that her sisters could share.

Then she'd wanted a new party dress with a blue satin sash (instead of the hand-me-down pink muslin which both Clara and Beattie had already worn), a summer holiday by the seaside (that was for everyone), and to sit next to Ada Gold, the prettiest and smartest girl in her class. Yes, she'd liked the girls best all along, though it had taken nearly half a century for this preference to reach its obvious manifestation.

Had those wishes come true? They *had* gone to Broadstairs in June, but this was a yearly occurrence, the pattern of which had not yet been clear to a five-year-old Thelma. She'd not got a new dress, though the pink one had been refurbished with a new white sash, an attempt on her mother's part to lessen the disappointment. And she'd never managed to sit next to Ada all through infants and junior school, though she'd admired her from afar for the whole six years.

Thelma smiled to herself. Here she was, nearly sixty years later, and she could still recall those childish desires with sharp-edged clarity. Funny how some memories stick in the mind, and others drop away into oblivion. Who knew how the mind made its selection—was it totally random, or did a kind of pattern emerge?

She ran her fingers over the delicately bevelled and gilded edges of the card. Who was it from—she couldn't remember entering any competition, except the one on the back of the soap flake packet, and the prize for that had been a Caribbean holiday. But if it wasn't real, then it must be a hoax, and why should anyone go to so much trouble to trick an old woman in such an unlikely way? What was it they said? That the truth was stranger than fiction? She had a funny feeling that this might just turn out to be a prime example.

Feeling eyes upon her, Thelma turned towards Ivy and saw that she was smiling.

"And where did you go, my love?" asked Ivy. "Decided what you want already, have you?"

Thelma shook her head. "I didn't really think about it that specifically. If I *was* going to give it a try (and I haven't made up my mind either way yet), d'you think it should be something just for me?"

Ivy shrugged. "Your guess is as good as mine. Why?"

"Supposing I asked for a Lesbian-only world, or no more war? Would it work?"

Ivy's face was a study, and she snorted with laughter before replying. "Thelma, I am not an expert in the psychology of wish-granting, but I suggest that if you're going to kill off all the men you might want to wish for a crash course in parthenogenesis as well."

It was Thelma's turn to be entertained. "There's obviously more to this wish-making than meets the eye. What would *you* ask for, Iv?"

"Well, off the top of my head, and at the risk of sounding selfish, I'd say a million pounds, a more functional body, and three more wishes." Ivy replied in an extremely matter-of-fact manner.

"Oh Ivy, you are a card." The two women smiled at each other affectionately, as they held hands and enjoyed the shared moment. "I could do without the arthritis, too, if it comes to that, but if we could get improved health for *all* women, wouldn't that be better?" Clearly Thelma was becoming intrigued by the myriad possibilities and, with a view to lubricating the workings of her brain, she picked up the teapot again and poured them both another cup. Then she looked at her watch and decided two things. Firstly that she *did* have time for some more toast and jam, and secondly, this wish thing could not be decided before she went out.

She spread butter lavishly on the last piece of rye toast, and watched Kipper rise from her post on the dresser, stretch, and then pad towards the back door. The cat stood in front of it for a moment, then leapt onto the draining board. "Mee-yout," she repeated, insistently, so that Ivy was obliged to lay down the paper, which she had just resumed reading, and open the back door. A blast of icy air rushed into the room causing Thelma to curse the British weather in general, and today's in particular.

"You could wish for a Mediterranean climate, I suppose," suggested Ivy helpfully, but not without a hint of sarcasm. "But seriously, Thelma, are you going to do it?"

"You know, Ivy, I think I need help with this one. First of all to decide whether or not to take it seriously, and if I do so, how to get the maximum possible benefit for the greatest number of dykes."

Ivy nodded her head in agreement. "We could ask a few women over this evening, if you like."

This was just what Thelma had been thinking about. "Who would be best, do you think? I don't want anyone who will laugh at us, *or* who might get carried away by the 'spiritual implications.'"

They talked about it for a few minutes, while Ivy cleared away the breakfast things and started to wash up and Thelma got ready to go out, and eventually settled on five women they both liked and trusted.

"Right." Thelma pulled a striped hat she had knitted herself over her wiry grey curls and buttoned her duffle coat. "Are you sure you don't mind making those phone calls, Ivy?"

"Of course I don't mind—there's no guarantee that you'll get time, is there?"

"True enough. And don't forget that a woman from the building collective will be over sometime before twelve to look at the guttering."

"I'll bring my typewriter downstairs so I can hear the bell," Ivy promised.

"OK then, see you at four. I must get off, or there'll be a queue of women wanting information all the way to the Town Hall." Three days a week Thelma worked as a receptionist at the local Well Women Clinic, handing out leaflets and doing her best to reassure anxious patients.

"Bye love, take care." Ivy put up her face for the goodby kiss without which they had never yet parted.

•

Ivy looked at the women sprawled around the long, double living room, and thought for the fiftieth time how right they'd been two years ago to knock that wall through. Not only was the whole place lighter, but whereas the seven of them today would have been squashed before, it was now possible to fit in twice that number, if the occasion called for it. She caught Milly's eye across the room, and smiled warmly.

"What's going on?" mouthed Milly elaborately, but Ivy shook her head, pantomiming that her friend must wait until they were all settled.

Milly knew better than to argue—she hadn't been friends with Ivy for forty years for nothing—and contented herself with rolling another cigarette. She frowned, adding to the myriad lines of her big, handsome face, and took a deep drag. This wasn't exactly a gathering of Ivy and Thelma's nearest and dearest, nor yet any sort of affinity group that *she* could think of; in fact, they seemed a pretty mixed bunch. She was the only smoker, which meant she'd have to go through the motions of asking permission to continue. Oh, for the good old days, when we all trampled on each other's needs without so much as a by-your-leave, thought Milly cynically to herself.

Two women sat close together on the old grey sofa. This was actually the most comfortable way, for if you sat at the ends the sag in the middle would get you both before too long, and you'd inevitably end up in each other's laps anyway. For Anna and Marguerite this was just fine—as far as they were concerned the closer the better.

Anyone seeing them for the first time might, however politically incorrectly, have assumed them to be mother and daughter, not because of any similarity of look. The Lesbian community had rocked with gossip when Marguerite, soon to retire from her job as a social worker, had come back from a women's spirituality weekend wildly in love with a woman nearly forty years her junior.

And the whisper had gone round: "What *can* Anna see in her?" For the younger woman was a passionate beauty of Italian extraction, with flashing black eyes and a body that drew the gaze, whilst Marguerite, well, they used to call her 'poor Marguerite', because of her lumbering, twenty stone bulk. Of course the gossip had reached the pair concerned, and in fury and exasperation Anna had announced over the P.A. at a Winter Solstice disco that she and Marguerite were destined to spend the rest of their lives together— she had seen it in their astrological charts—so would everyone please shut up and leave them alone. And P.S., Marguerite was far and away the sexiest woman there.

There had been no doubt that she meant what she said and so they had been accepted, more or less, as just another couple since then. And everyone took care not to anger Anna, for she had a redhot temper that could take the skin off your psyche.

The door-bell rang, and Thelma was heard bustling from the kitchen to answer it.

Milly raised her eyebrows as she recognised the high, breathy voice that was apologising for being late. Cerise was twenty-two, and a real will-o'-the-wisp. She based herself in their small town at the times she wasn't visiting her many friends on women's land. Milly had asked her once why she didn't just live in the country all the time. Smiling gently, Cerise had explained that she wasn't sure yet that cutting herself off from the political scene was exactly the right thing to do. Then, in a low voice, with many shy glances from under long lashes, she had confessed to hearing voices in the countryside, a phenomenon to which she was not entirely reconciled. In the town these voices seemed to leave her alone, and so when she became afraid she returned here.

Milly had done her best to reassure the young woman, though she had hardly known what to say, but clearly Cerise had been grateful to have someone to talk to about it and had offered to do Milly's Tarot for her.

Cerise herself was surprised at being invited tonight. Of course she'd met Thelma and Ivy lots of times, but she'd never been to their home. She looked around the room with interest, amazed that so many different knick-knacks and posters and photographs and other assorted affirmations of love could be fitted into one space. The furniture was old, and didn't have much in common, whilst rugs of several hues had been thrown over the bald patches in the carpet. But despite this mis-matching, and all the clutter, Cerise decided that it was a room in which she could be comfortable.

Thelma came in with a tray of mugs and passed round tea. It was too strong, of course, but with the exception of Cerise everyone was prepared for this.

Following behind, with plates of biscuits, was a tall, thin woman, whose long brown hair was coiled neatly on the back of her head. Karen enjoyed great popularity in the Lesbian community, and every woman there had, at one time or another, benefitted from her great common sense and unerring fairness. There could be no doubt, whatever the purpose of this get-together, why she had been invited. Sometimes Karen complained that younger women tried to treat her as a mother, a role which she had absolutely no wish to play, but as Thelma had pointed out, it was probably because she looked just like their mothers did. Karen had laughed more than anyone at this, but the pale blue twinset and tartan slacks she wore tonight bore out the truthfulness of that remark.

When they'd all settled down, and finished saying how nice it was to see each other again, Thelma spoke.

"As Ivy said when she rang you, I need your advice. This arrived in the post this morning." She held up the pale blue card. "And I want to know what you all think about it." Karen, who was nearest, took it from her, and examined it in silence, though her expression was puzzled.

The prize was passed from woman to woman, and each in turn studied it carefully. No one said anything, though Cerise went pink with excitement, and Marguerite looked questioningly in Thelma's direction.

Eventually it was returned to Thelma, and she fingered it tentatively as she talked. "I have two questions. Should we take this seriously? If the answer is yes, then what should we ask for? I say 'we' because that is how I view the situation—I do not believe that this is something that I alone can, or should, decide. Please don't be

67

afraid to say exactly what you feel, although of course we will try and respect each other's beliefs."

"What a wonderful chance for all dykes." Cerise spoke out immediately.

Thelma looked at her affectionately. "That's what I thought too, dear, but we don't want to raise false hopes."

"What does your instinct tell you, Thelma?" asked Marguerite, seriously.

"To tread very, very carefully."

Marguerite nodded. "That's wise. Did you receive any vibrations when you first held the card?"

Thelma thought for a minute. "I liked the smoothness of the surface and the lettering. It felt... solid. And, oh yes, I remembered three wishes I'd made when I was a small child..."

"You surely don't think this is for real, do you?" Unable to stand it any longer, Milly burst into the conversation. "It has to be some kid playing a joke on you."

"But you don't *know* that Milly," objected Anna. "Supposing Thelma doesn't act on this, she might be throwing away a once-in-a-lifetime opportunity."

Milly sounded disgruntled. "So you think maybe Thelma has a fairy godmother?" A titter ran round the group.

Despite herself, Anna smiled. "Well, maybe she has," she said. "And maybe you're right and I'm wrong. But one thing I do know," here she paused and shook back her mane of glossy, black hair, "there are forces around us, maybe even emanating from ourselves, of which we know nothing. Me, I would prefer not to risk displeasing these spirits, or sprites, or fairy godmothers, if you like, by scorning their gifts."

"But she doesn't believe in spirits and sprites and suchlike," Milly tried again. "Do you, Thelma?"

Thelma shook her head slowly, struggling to be as honest as possible. "No," she said, "I don't think I do."

"But it seems that only makes it more credible," put in Karen, joining the conversation for the first time. "I mean, if it had been sent to Marguerite, or Cerise, or even Ivy, there might have been a chance for the joker to have been taken seriously and achieve the desired affect, but with Thelma there was a very good chance she would have put it straight in the dustbin."

Ivy nodded in silent agreement. She had often been troubled by Thelma's persistent refusal to become involved in matters pertaining to the spiritual.

Here Thelma laughed. "That's quite funny, really, because you know, I never even thought of this being a spiritual dilemma. I suppose the tradition of three wishes must be pretty deeply ingrained."

She looked at Milly. "What do you think I should do, Mill?"

Milly shrugged. "Quite frankly, Thelma, I think you *should* put it in a dustbin, and then just forget about it. You and Ivy have a good life together, though you aren't rich and are getting on a bit. Why spoil it by dreaming about the things you can't ever have?"

As she heard this Thelma knew she would *not* throw away her prize. At least she wanted to give it a go. Now she saw how clever Ivy had been in insisting that Milly be included in this group. She got up and walked over to where her lover was slouched in her favourite armchair and knelt beside her. "You crafty old thing," she whispered, as she kissed the soft silver hair.

Ivy gave her hand a squeeze, and then Thelma straightened up and addressed the group.

"Alright. So if I decide to go ahead with this what do you think I should wish for?"

At this question the women started to chatter excitedly, rapidly throwing out ideas and then discarding them almost as quickly. All except Milly, who sat smoking sullenly.

Ivy slipped into the chair next to her. "Come on, Milly, we need your ideas, too. Supposing it worked and we used up all three wishes on communing with the spirits. Think how you'd kick yourself then."

Milly grunted, and scowled at Ivy, but that remark had been well-placed, and it was not many minutes before she made her first suggestion.

Eventually Karen called a halt to the discussion. "I have a suggestion. Well, two, actually. Firstly, that we all write down our ideas for Thelma to think about later," here she waved aside Thelma's protests. "And secondly, despite what she said earlier, I think Thelma should make the final decision. If we're going along with

with this at all it seems we should accept that there was a reason it was Thelma who received it. What do you say?"

Everyone eventually agreed, even Thelma, whilst Ivy immediately went in search of pens and paper. Soon all that could be heard was the odd rustle or sigh, as they attempted to cull the very best of their brainwaves.

•

It was the next afternoon, sunny for once, when Thelma and Ivy sat in their favourite places at the kitchen table, the heap of papers in front of them. There really hadn't been time to read what everyone had suggested before; the last visitor, Milly, hadn't gone home till after midnight, and Thelma, as usual, had had to go to work that morning.

But now there was nothing to stop them, and it was with a good deal of anticipation that Thelma, at Ivy's insistence, reached out her hand for the first slip.

" 'A new set of laws to give dykes a decent life,'" she read out, after scanning the paper briefly.

Ivy chuckled. "I bet that was Milly," she said.

"Ivy!" warned Thelma reprovingly. "You know we said we weren't going to guess who wrote what—even if it was obvious."

Ivy smiled apologetically and opened the second wish, which turned out to be for a 'Lesbian-only planet,' and was quickly followed by 'complete freedom from worry.'

They were going to be dealing with a pretty mixed bunch.

The fifth piece of paper Thelma read made her gasp. One of their friends had written, 'I want an enormous political, cultural and social upheaval, but totally without the shedding of women's blood. I want every man to become aware that his presence on this planet will not be tolerated unless he undergoes drastic reform of his basic nature and sex-drive.'

"There's a lot of anger there," she remarked.

"And why not?" Ivy retorted. "We all have good reason to be angry with men, both as individuals and collectively. Anyway, it seems to be a recurring theme—someone else has written 'an end to violence against women', and you had 'all living things being equal, and able to communicate' a moment ago."

She picked up another paper. "See, here it is again, though in a rather watered down form. 'I don't care who lives on this planet as long as they get along harmoniously. I have straight women friends: if men would get their act together I'd welcome them into my life too.'"

Here Thelma laughed. "And in brackets underneath she's written 'though I'll always be a Lesbian', No prizes for guessing whose this is. Ooops!" She clapped her hand over her mouth and looked futiley at Ivy, who shrugged.

They went on reading together, and this further investigation yielded 'several million pounds', perpetual youth,' 'the total development of our psychic capabilities,' 'an end to disease, famine, capitalism, yuppies and everything else which means some people are more equal than others'.

Thelma pushed back her chair. "How many more are left, Iv?"

"Only a couple. Why?"

"I feel like my brain's overloading, but I think we'd better finish the job. Here . One for you and one for me. You go first."

"'In the wonderful, new peaceful, Lesbian world that you are all no doubt envisioning I ask that all women, no matter how they look, are seen to be equally beautiful and worthy of being loved, and are never made to feel any other way.'"

The two women exchanged glances. They knew full well who had written that, and the pain so exposed was uncomfortable to acknowledge.

Thelma went on to the last slip. "'I want women to have the option for parthenogenesis within themselves, so that if we find the biological male is *really* incapable of change, it can be dispensed with.' This has to have come from the same woman who wanted the revolution—she's certainly thinking of consequences."

Ivy was looking dreamily at the pile of wishes. She seemed lost in thought.

"It was *you* wasn't it?" exclaimed Thelma in amazement, grabbing her lover's arm.

Ivy put her finger to her lips. "No guessing, remember." She then proceeded to change the subject. "Has this lot helped you make up your mind?"

Thelma allowed herself to be led away from the subject of Ivy's potentially budding anarchism. "Not exactly," she said musingly.

71

"But I think I've got a clearer idea of the direction I want to go."
Here she paused, and wound one of her wiry curls round her finger.
Her next remark took Ivy completely by surprise. "Let's have a go,
then," Thelma declared. She went to the dresser drawer where she
had yesterday laid her prize.

"What. Now?" stuttered Ivy.

"Why not? No time like the present, eh!" Thelma grinned
broadly, and then turned her attention to studying the directions once
more, though she already knew them by heart.

" 'On each seal write one wish,' " she read aloud, and picking up
a biro prepared to write.

"B-but what are you wishing for?" cried Ivy, feeling as though
she'd missed out on some vital step in the decision-making process.

Thelma laid down the pen. "I reckon that it'd better be something concrete for a first try, so that we can see results, you know. If
we wished for a revolution we'll never be dead sure that it was my
wish that caused it..."

"So what are you writing?" By now Ivy appeared quite exasperated. "For heaven's sake, woman, don't keep me in suspense."

Thelma smiled mischievously. "Money," she said simply.

"Money? How much money?"

"I thought I'd just write 'several very large amounts of cash'.
After all, I don't want to limit our options, do I?" With this, Thelma
carefully wrote the words on the seal. Then she fetched an old
saucer from the cupboard and took the matches off the refrigerator.
The gold paper caught light immediately, and, it seemed to Ivy,
burned for an inordinately long time, and with a queer, purple flame.

As soon as it died away Thelma took the remaining ashes outside
and spread them on the earth, just next to the lavender bush, being
careful to brush every last particle off the saucer.

Neither woman spoke until the saucer had been washed and put
away, and a fresh pot of tea was on the table between them.

"Now how about a nice bit of swiss roll with this tea?" Thelma
asked, and she went to get the cake tin.

•

A week or so later Marguerite was rudely awakened by the
shrilling of the telephone.

"H'llo," she slurred into the receiver.

A torrent of words fell into her ears, and she held the instrument gingerly away from her.

"Thelma? Is that you? Slow down for goodness sake. What time is it?"

"Eight-thirty. LISTEN, Marguerite. Something amazing has happened. My wish! It came true! It really did! Oh Marguerite, it's not possible! I can hardly believe it, but like Ivy said, never stop hoping and..."

"What wish, Thelma?" By now Marguerite was wide awake and sitting up in bed, though Anna was still sleeping by her side.

"On my first gold seal I wrote 'several very large amounts of cash', and this morning I got a letter saying my premium bond's come up, and I've won 850,000! What do you think of that?" Thelma had to stop for breath.

"My dear, I'm absolutely delighted. How very exciting. I don't want to be a wet blanket, but it couldn't be a coincidence, could it?"

A deep laugh met this suggestion. "Marguerite, I don't *have* any premium bonds."

"Oh! So it really works?" A million possibilities were going through Marguerite's head. "What are you going to do with the money, have you any idea?"

"Not yet, but I've got some ideas. At least we'll be able to pay off the mortgage, and at last this town will have a Lesbian Centre. Look, I must go—I just wanted to let you know the good news—but really I'm all of a daze."

"Of course. I understand. Ring me again when you have time. And give my love to Ivy."

Marguerite put the phone down, and sat thinking for a moment or two. Then she shook the woman slumbering beside her.

"Hey Anna, Anna. Wake up. You'll never guess what..."

•

For the next couple of months Thelma and Ivy were much pre-occupied by how to best use all the money, especially after Thelma dug up a large hoard of King Charles I gold coins from their back yard while simply attempting to move an old rose bush that needed more sun. Neither gave more than a passing thought to the two remaining wishes. But at last there came a time in late Spring when the new Lesbian Centre was more or less on its feet and the future financially secure, thanks to the consciously invested trust fund Thelma had set up.

Thelma and Ivy were walking along the bank of the river, a little way out from the town, enjoying the longer evening and the fresh smells of the almost-countryside. Their progress was somewhat halting, as Ivy's arthritis was playing up, thanks to a series of showers that morning. Eventually they stopped and sat on a patch of grass to watch a family of ducklings have a swimming lesson. Ivy produced an orange and her penknife, and they shared the succulent fruit in companionable silence.

"Sometimes I feel like life will never be the same again," remarked Thelma, apropos of nothing.

"Oh, I don't know," Ivy objected. "We'll get used to the Lesbian Centre by and by, and though you and I will definitely be better off without the mortgage repayments, our life won't change that much."

"Ah yes." Thelma chewed thoughtfully on the last piece of orange and then wiped her hands on her dungarees. The sky was starting to go pink. The undersides of the dancing clouds became edged with a line of fire.

"But what of my other two wishes?" she asked softly.

Ivy looked at her enquiringly. "Got a plan?"

"Oh, maybe. Always, at the back of my mind. I know they're there. Although *some* people would say my winnings were just luck—like Milly—she still doesn't believe that I didn't have any premium bonds, you know."

"I know. But that's Milly for you."

"Look."

In the palm of Thelma's hand was a piece of the golden paper.

"So you *do* have a plan!" Ivy eyed her lover with interest.

"Only if you agree," insisted Thelma. "You know, Ivy, when we read all those wishes that Marguerite and Cerise and the rest wrote, it struck me that the only way women could possibly be safe was in a world without men. That idea of yours—don't argue, I know it was you—about teaching them to respect us, is nice, but I doubt it would ever work. So I've pretty much made up my mind to wish for a women-only world that can reproduce itself. What do you think?"

For several minutes Ivy said nothing. "We'll probably never live to see it," she commented at last.

"I know."

"And there are going to be some big problems until women realise they don't need men."

"Probably so."

"But all in all, I think you're right."

"Thanks, love."

Solemnly Thelma wrote her words, and then took some matches from her pocket. Ivy wrapped her hands around the wish to protect it from the breeze, but the flame had no trouble taking hold. When the flame had died away, Thelma carefully rubbed the ashes into the grass with her finger, humming softly as she worked.

Then the two women rose and lovingly embraced each other as they exchanged a tender kiss. "What about the last wish?" whispered Ivy.

"I think we'd better save that. After all, you never know what might be needed in the future."

And hand in hand they began to walk slowly back towards the town.

Bing Cherries

by   Garbo

Garbo is thirty-one years old, a Scorpio Rising with Sun in Aries and Moon in Taurus. She lives in Columbus, Ohio, where she is finishing work on her second novel: Rusty. *Her dearest wish is to do just as she pleases, all the time. And for everyone else to do the same.*

Bing Cherries

She was in Beckert's Bulk Foods, buying bing cherries. She remembered when the store had been called Long's Market. Then, the front wall had been lined with bread loaves, each wrapper bright with circus balloon spots. There'd been red-and-white soup cans: chicken noodle, cream of mushroom, beef barley. Next had come Band-Aids and baby powder and green minty mouthwash. The produce section was a long row of fresh, bright, living food: purple cabbages and green ones rolled tight against each other in the cooler, smooth, ripe, yellow bananas arranged by bunches on a hairy green cloth, with a few brown-spotty strays crowded in around the edges. Bananas had cost twenty three cents a pound at Long's, nineteen cents on sale.

Now they were thirty-nine cents on sale. The wall shelves were gone; now you fished everything out of clear plastic boxes: gum balls by the pound, white rice ready to be shoveled out. No more bread in wrappers, now there were bagels in boxes with computer-made labels: Egg, Garlic, Onion-Flavored.

Flavored? thought Christy while picking up three egg bagels, one at a time, with a pair of tongs. What does that mean? They spread onion juice on them, or what? I have to get bing cherries for Sue. Bing cherries, don't forget bing cherries.

She gave the bagel bag to the weigher, who beeped up the price on his flat, square, digital scale and twisted a price sticker around the neck of the bag. "Playing Bulk Bingo?" he said. He had a toothbrush moustache that made him look like a terrier.

"What?" said Christy, looking at the hole puncher he was holding toward her. "Oh. Um, no, don't have a card."

"Just a sec. I'll get you one," the produce terrier said, disappearing toward the checkout area. His necktie swung like a pendulum because he walked fast.

He went before she could say don't bother. Months from now she'd pull out the supermarket card, expired, with one round hole punched in square number one. Oh well, he'd gone to get it now.

"Thanks," she said, when he came back. He was pleased to have been able to do something for her. He smiled.

She walked off without the bagel bag, so he got to help her again by running after her with it. She thanked him and went to find soup. There wasn't any split pea. She had her choice of vegetable, beef vegetable, turkey vegetable, cheddar cheese, tomato. She would eat poultry, but Sue didn't, so it was cheddar, which sounded thick and gooey, and then there was tomato. Forget soup, they could have pea salad. She went to the Deli and got a half pound of pea salad, and a complimentary cup of coffee from the snack bar.

Pea salad and the bagels, and toilet paper, it never hurt to get a roll of toilet paper, and now she was getting the hell out, before the fluorescent lights completely buzzed her mind. The lights plus the color bulbs around the video display, and every three minutes the P.A. system suggested she go get a complimentary cup of coffee from the snack bar, but she'd had hers already.

Even though hot, damp air met her at the exit, it was good to get out on the sidewalk. Where was the car? Oh, over by the drugstore. She tossed the sack into the passenger seat and slid in.

Sue was cutting cored strawberries in half neatly (of course), exactly in half. She added the halves to the fruit salad bowl after every fifth strawberry. "Get the cherries?" she asked.

"Yeah," Christy said. "No, I didn't. I got bagels, and TP, and something else. I remembered the cherries, I really did, but then they didn't have split pea—pea salad, that's what I got. Pea salad." She took the bagels and the toilet paper out of the brown sack, and set them on the counter. "Can we just stop for cherries on the way, and put them in when we get there?" They were going to a potluck at five.

Sue gave her a distressed look.

"Okay, I'll go back. Give me a sec." Dammit. Well, Sue cared about her food. Christy took the pea salad tub out of the sack, and turned the sack upside down against her stomach to fold it. The Bulk Bingo card slipped out and slid along the linoleum.

"What's that?" said Sue.

"Just one of those grocery store things," said Christy. "They punch it for you, then after you get so many punches, they... I don't know, give you something, I guess." Christy picked up the car keys. "Cherries. Anything else while I'm there?"

"Want me to go?" asked Sue, without looking up. She wiped her fingers on the terry towel that was tucked into the waistband of her slacks, and continued splitting strawberries.

"No, that's okay," said Christy.

"Leave yourself enough time to change," said Sue.

"Change?" asked Christy, looking down at her pants. They were still clean, she just took them out of the drawer yesterday.

"Well, I thought you'd want to wear slacks or something nice," said Sue. "It's their anniversary."

"Only a year," said Christy. "You don't have to dress up for a year, do you?" She tried smiling.

"Well, whatever," said Sue, dumping the last strawberry halves into the bowl. She took off the towel, wiping her hands again.

Christy put her hand on the knob of the kitchen door. "Okay then, I'm going—just cherries, right?"

"Yeah," said Sue. She opened the refrigerator door and slid the fruit bowl onto the top shelf. Then she stooped down and picked up the bingo card and held it out to Christy. "Here, might as well have him punch it again."

Christy opened the screen door, avoiding the card. "I don't think they'll punch it twice the same day. Be back." She shut the screen behind her.

"Don't be silly," said Sue through the screen. She opened the door and held out the card. "You're going right over there. He won't remember you. Take it."

Christy took it and went to the car door. Once she was in, she put the card up on the dashboard, then changed her mind and laid it on the seat beside her. I'll tell her you have to get ten dollars' worth of groceries before they punch it, Christy thought, turning the ignition key.

•

She didn't see any cherries in the produce section. She went up and down the aisle, fooled by red patches which turned out to be radishes, cherry tomatos, plums. She looked at her watch. 4:14.

They were supposed to be at Betsy and Mary's at five, and she still had to change clothes. She went to the weigh station.

The terrier was gone, replaced by a very tall woman in a plaid vest, whose silvery blond hair was puffed around her face. "Cherries," said Christy. "I need to find cherries."

The tall woman leaned around her counter and pointed a long, purple fingernail. "Down there, hon," she said. "Spirit Shoppe."

"Oh," said Christy. "Thank you."

The Spirit Shoppe was four shelves of booze and mixers. Christy was confused. She started to turn away, but spotted maraschino cherries on the bottom shelf, three jars. She picked up one of them, cradled the tall, skinny glass in her palm. No, it wouldn't do. Sue wouldn't want soft, sweet cherries. Christy put the jar back and looked at her watch. 4:19.

Why couldn't Sue just leave the cherries *out*? Christy went to the snack bar for another complimentary cup of coffee. If the woman remembered her Christy would offer to pay for it.

There was no one at the snack bar. The green formica counter had styrofoam cups on it, Sweet-N-Low, and white plastic spoons in a box. HELP YOURSELF was hand-lettered on a paper napkin stuck to the coffee urn with a price label. Christy felt a little queasy already, so she only poured out a half-cup to take with her.

She bought four pounds of cat food so she wouldn't feel bad about the coffee. She put the cat food in the trunk and drove to the Eastlake shopping plaza. Her watch said 4:34 as she got out of the car. In the produce section of Thrift Foods she found two boxes of bing cherries, in between the tangerines and the nectarines. The cherries were not fresh; the bottom layers were probably completely soft, and a half-pint was $2.39. Sue would scream. Christy decided to pull the price tag off in the car. She took the better looking box to the checkout. 4:40. At least she'd found some; if Sue wanted cherries in her fruit salad then why hadn't she bought them yesterday with the rest of the stuff? Well, Sue was doing all the work, making the salad and all that. But she'd volunteered to; she wouldn't have trusted Christy to make something. And Sue was the one who wanted to go to the potluck, Christy had only met Betsy a couple of times and she didn't know Mary at all. But she'd told Sue she'd go. It would have been so nice to sit out on the porch tonight, listen to the radio or something, be home together.

Maybe she could tell Sue that she felt a little under the weather. As soon as she thought of saying it, her shoulders felt light and free, relief flowed all over her. She could stay home; she *was* tired. She might actually get sick if she had to stay up late at Betsy and Mary's. She'd tell Sue as soon as she got home; then she could go in the bedroom and take a nap.

But then Sue wouldn't be able to go, either. Sue would never go alone, and it was too late to find someone to go with her. After she'd made the salad and everything Sue would be sick if she didn't get to go. Christy's shoulder muscles knotted tight as she pulled into the driveway. Almost five o'clock: she'd better run in, change clothes, and help Sue get the salad and present into the car. Even if they flew right over, they were going to be late.

Christy got out of the car, slammed the driver's door, and dropped the box of cherries in the driveway. The side of the box exploded in a v-shaped tear, and cherries began to roll down the drive. The box was half empty now; only the soft, rotten cherries had stayed mashed together at the bottom. Christy stooped to save a few of the good ones, but already they were coated with grit and silt. She gave up, and let them roll crazily down the concrete toward the gutter.

Sue was next to her. Christy stood up, holding out the limp, paper box dripping cherry glop. "I went two places," she said in a weak voice. "And Thrift only had two boxes, and... I don't want to go to the potluck."

"It's okay," said Sue, taking the cherry box away without looking at Christy. "The salad can go the way it is. Come change your clothes."

Christy began to follow Sue into the house, but stopped after two steps. "No," she said to Sue's back. "I didn't mean about the cherries, I meant— Um, I don't feel very well. No, I'm lying, I'm not sick. I just... You can go if you want, I could call somebody for you, Cathy maybe, or somebody. Or whatever you want to do."

"But you don't want to go," said Sue flatly.

"I just," Christy began. "No. I don't want to go." She braced for the reaction.

"Oh," said Sue. "What do you want to do?"

81

"What?" said Christy. What was this, a trick?

"What do you want to do?" Sue said patiently. She was awfully sweet-looking in the face sometimes, the frown lines couldn't take that away.

"Sit on the porch swing," said Christy.

Sue thought for a minute. "Here," she said, handing Christy the fruit bowl. "Take this around to the porch and I'll get us some spoons, and call Betsy. I'll say we're a little under the weather."

"No," said Christy. "Just say we want to sit on our swing. If you want to sit on our swing; do you want to sit on the swing?"

"Only if I get to hold the salad," said Sue, taking the bowl. She reached in and scooped up a bite with her fingers.

"Hey," said Christy. "Don't eat all the pineapple."

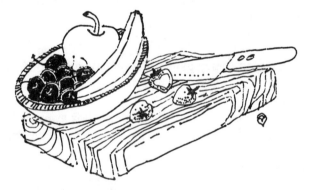

Tortilleras

A chapter excerpt from *MARGINS*
a novel-in-progress

by Terri de la Peña

Terri de la Peña considered fiction writing a hobby until two of her short stories jointly won third prize in the 1986 Chicano Literary Prize Competition sponsored by the University of California at Irvine. Since then, she has come out as a writer, and has focused her energies on Margins, *her novel-in-progress about Chicana lesbians in southern California. Between fiction projects, Terri writes book reviews and articles for* The Lesbian News *in Los Angeles and sings with the Los Angeles Women's Community Chorus. When she's not writing or singing, she's looking for the real René Talamantes (if such a mujer maravillosa actually exists!)*

Tortilleras

On that balmy summer evening, Veronica Melendez and her friend Michi Yamada were lucky enough to find a sidewalk table outside Alice's Restaurant. Westwood Boulevard teemed with noisy traffic, its rumbling sounds jarring Veronica's nerves. For most of that day, she had sat before her typewriter, struggling over the first draft of her novel. She had been relieved when Michi had phoned and rescued her, but she had not counted on dining outdoors.

Being alone so much made her cranky. And the trouble with writing, Veronica mused, was its inward focus; it intensified her reclusive tendencies and moody spells. With Michi back in town, Veronica knew her friend would not allow her to wither at the typewriter; Michi would push her into socializing again.

Veronica lifted her wine goblet. "I'm so glad you got the job, Mich! Now we'll both be on campus this fall."

Michi grinned. Her bejeweled fingers sparkled with amethyst and blue topaz. She clicked her glass to Veronica's and took a quick sip. "Course my parents'd prefer my being in grad school. But I'll be doing administrative work for a Japanese-American oral history project, so at least it'll be relevant." Michi dug into her combination salad, selecting slivers of purple cabbage. "You've been quiet tonight, Roni. Still in the writing mode?"

Veronica shrugged. "Sometimes it takes a while to snap back into reality." She rolled some garbanzo beans across her plate. "It's hard to fictionalize something that actually happened. And the more I write about Joanna, the more I miss her." She turned from Michi, watching a heterosexual couple nuzzling at the next table. The woman's hair was glossy brown, like Joanna's had been. Veronica stared for a moment, remembering, and turned away when the woman's gaze met hers.

"Maybe it's too soon, Ron. It's only been eight months since-"

Michi broke off, her face uncommonly solemn. "It might be a better idea to write about something else."

"No. I need to deal with my feelings now. Keeping a journal wasn't enough. I need to get Joanna's essence on paper, before I forget—" Veronica looked away again, her eyes wet.

"Roni, you'll never forget her. I know I won't." Michi sniffled and very nonchalantly wiped the corner of one eye in the same motion as she patted her moussed crewcut. Her black hair glistened in the streetlight's glow.

Veronica blinked quickly and tried to smile. Michi had not invited her out to talk about her deceased lover, although mention of Joanna inevitably entered their conversations. Tonight, Veronica felt she owed it to Michi—and to herself—to put thoughts of Joanna aside, to relax and have an enjoyable time.

She reached across the table and affectionately touched her friend's hand. "I'm still dealing with it, Mich, but I'm okay." She tweaked Michi's pudgy cheek. "Tell me about the student films we're seeing tonight."

Michi perked up. "After I landed the job, I swung down to the Women's Resource Center to see what's cooking on campus. According to a flyer posted there, one film has a lesbian theme." She wriggled in her chair and leaned forward, her eyes alight.

"No wonder you dragged me away from my typewriter." Veronica smiled, this time spontaneously. With typical zest, Michi had already unearthed some lesbian culture on campus.

Michi grinned. "There'll be a question and answer session after each film, but I'm only interested in the dyke flick. We don't even have to stay for the others."

They looked at each other and laughed.

•

In the Melnitz Hall screening room, Veronica and Michi selected center seats in the fourth row. The first film, a science fiction spoof, though technically superior, needed much editing. As the discussion droned on, enlivened by the witticisms of sci fi buffs, Michi scanned the sparse audience for any trace of lesbians. Veronica had difficulty staying awake. The long hours of writing had caught up with her. She soon nodded off, her curly head propped on Michi's shoulder. Her catnap was interrupted when her friend jabbed her in the ribs.

"Who is THAT?" Michi whispered harshly.

"What?" Veronica unfolded herself and frowned.

"That Latina Amazon who just walked in and brightened the scenery."

Drowsily, Veronica followed Michi's directions and viewed a leggy Chicana with a stylish haircut: short and sleek on the sides, long and tapering in back. She wore form-fitting Levis, rust-colored Frye boots, and a turquoise T-shirt with a silk-screened portrait of Mexican artist Frida Kahlo directly over her impressive breasts.

"I think my heart's stopped." Michi breathed quickly, as if gasping for air.

"She's probably straight." Veronica ignored Michi's exaggerated reaction and leaned back again. But she continued gazing at the striking woman, admiring her glowing brown skin, black hair, and ebony eyes. Keeping her thoughts to herself, Veronica considered the woman a fine mestiza dyke. Unlike Joanna's tawny-skinned delicate beauty, this tall Chicana no doubt boasted sangre de india.

Leaving a colorful hemp bag beside her notebook on the discussion table, the Chicana strode past the two friends, her long legs nimbly taking the steps two at a time, heading towards the projection room.

"She's got to be the lesbian film maker," Michi squealed, nearly bouncing off her seat. "Oh, thank you, Goddess!"

"Michi, cool it, okay?" With aplomb, Veronica picked up the one-page program and read it aloud. "The film *Tortilleras* was directed by grad student René Talamantes."

"Did you take a good look at her? Amazon City! Dyke Delight! Aren't you glad you're here, Roni?"

"As long as her film keeps me awake, I'll be fine." Veronica fluffed her hair and stifled a yawn.

•

The short film *Tortilleras* contained no dialog, but consisted of stark black-and-white close-ups of two Latinas, clad in flowing transparent robes, performing a silent but very erotic mating dance. Wide awake, Veronica gazed at the screen, mesmerized as the dark-skinned women glided in stylized movements, nearly touching, tossing their lengthy black hair over their shoulders.

In the darkness, Veronica imagined them to be Joanna and her, advancing and retreating, teasing each other with suggestive motions, fingers outlining breasts, hips and thighs. Alone in their apartment, they had often danced together, moving sensuously to rhythm-and-blues standards, falling into bed together afterwards. All those wondrous nights—Veronica longed for her Joanna, but she was gone forever. Beside her, she heard her friend's sudden intake of breath, and hoped Michi would not hyperventilate.

Communicating visually, the Latinas in the film whirled and twirled, graceful mirror images of one another. At last, they concluded their stylized dance by embracing, their lips touching and melding as the film faded to black. The audience's hushed silence was broken only by scattered applause.

"Roni, I'm ready to faint," Michi whispered. The screening room's lights flickered on and the two friends blinked dazedly.

"I'm feeling kind of woozy myself," Veronica admitted. She noticed the flush on Michi's face, and wondered if her own betrayed her. The temperature in the room seemed stifling.

They both stared at the willowy unperturbed Chicana standing at the discussion table, one brown hand casually upon her hip, awaiting the audience's remarks. A professorial-looking man in the first row wasted no time in asking the significance of the film's title.

René Talamantes' smoky voice filled the small auditorium. "In Spanish, 'tortillera' literally means a woman who makes tortillas. In the film's context, I use 'tortillera' to suggest tribadism."

Veronica felt a titillating shiver course along her spine. Talamantes' words bore a Southwestern tinge, a slight drawl uncharacteristic of local Latinas. She imagined the dark women in the film rubbing their bodies together like warm tortillas gently molded in a Chicana's hand. Veronica could not remove her eyes from the self-assured film maker.

"She actually said 'tribadism,'" Michi murmured in awe.

"I wonder if everyone here knows the definition," Veronica remarked. She could not recall having been so affected by any other film, and tried to modulate her tone. "Some of those guys in front look absolutely mystified."

"Ask her something," Michi urged with a nudge.

"You ask her." Veronica edged away and rested her chin on her hand. "I dare you, Mich, since you're creaming all over the place."

Suppressing a giggle, Michi accepted the challenge. Her right arm with its multicolored yarn bracelets shot up. Determined to be noticed, she even stood.

The film maker cooly pointed to her.

"I was just wondering why you decided to shoot in black and white." Michi's voice sounded an octave higher than usual.

René Talamantes grinned at her question. "Two reasons: first, I wanted to focus on the women's mutual sexual attraction. Color would've distracted from that, and it really wasn't necessary anyway, because both women have the same skin tones. I think black and white emphasizes their similarities. If I had wanted to show their dissimilarities—for example, if one woman were Latina and the other white, color might have worked better. For my purposes, black and white worked fine. My second reason was purely financial. Color film and processing is expensive."

Talamantes' frank answer prompted some murmuring and laughter. While the film maker responded to a more challenging question, Michi glanced at her companion. "Isn't she fabulous?"

Veronica frowned, recalling her day's labor on the novel. "What if everyone decided not to use dialog? I live by words, Michi. As much as I like the film, I'm uncomfortable with its silence."

"Tell her so." Michi gave her a teasing pinch.

Wincing from the sudden pain, Veronica moved her arm reflexively, just in time for the film maker to point to her.

"Michi, I'll kill you someday." Veronica glared at her amused friend and quickly formed a question. She felt her heart slide into her throat, but her words tumbled out without obstruction.

"I'm curious about the lack of dialog—and even of music. I think the film is unique as it is, but silents aren't too common these days. Most current films, it seems, have superfluous dialog—not like the well-crafted scripts of the classics. And recently there's been so much emphasis on technique. Was eliminating dialog and music a budgetary decision, too? Can you elaborate on your reasons for making a silent film?"

With a droll expression, Talamantes appraised Veronica before answering. Her drawl became more pronounced. "For a film student, almost everything boils down to budgetary decisions. Despite that, I really wanted to show that when a definite sexual message occurs between two people, only the basics count—eye contact, facial signals, body language. I decided to pare everything down to the bare essentials. That's why I eliminated color, dialog, and music." She paused, gesturing towards Veronica. "You seem to know a lot about films. Do you think my technique worked?"

Veronica's heart threatened to pop out of her cotton shirt. "Well—yes."

"Bueno. Quiero hablar contigo despues. Esperame."

At that personalized request, Veronica blushed, even more embarrassed when several members of the audience turned to gawk.

"Roni, you're fabulous!" Michi snuggled closer, one hand on Veronica's knee. "What did she say?"

"She wants to talk with me afterwards."

"Sounds like a 'definite sexual message.' Michi pressed Veronica's knee. "Let's ask her out for cappuccino."

"If I don't murder you first." Veronica pretended to be annoyed with Michi; yet she could barely hide her eagerness—and apprehension. "I don't even know what I said."

"Words just poured out of your eloquent little mouth."

Veronica groaned. "Michi, you're so full of it."

•

Before the next film began, the two friends scurried after René Talamantes. She stood in the film department's narrow corridor and stuffed her notebook into her hemp bag. She glanced up when they approached.

Veronica lagged behind, trying to maintain her dignity despite her nervousness. Memories of Joanna filled her mind, but she did not want to think of her at that moment. After long months of mourning, she at last felt attracted to a woman. Simultaneously, she felt disloyal. But she aimed for a calm attitude in spite of her conflicting emotions, and casually leaned against the corridor wall.

Talamantes smiled. "Thanks for your comments, women. I had a feeling I'd be crucified in there. Did you hear that one pendejo who asked why there were no men in the film?" She laughed, her teeth large and white.

"I guess the subtleties were lost on him." Veronica shrugged, hands in her jeans pockets. She noticed the film maker was about three inches taller than her and even more attractive up close.

"De veras." Talamantes' deep-set eyes surveyed her. "Vienes de aqui?"

"Santa Monica." Veronica suddenly wished she had used the proper Spanish pronunciation of her home town; she was unaccustomed to switching languages in midstream and uneasy about her rusty Spanish. She hoped the film maker would not insist on speaking it; some Latinas did as a matter of principle. Besides, she did not want Michi to be left out of the conversation.

"Yo soy Tejana, nacida en El Paso. Eres Chicana?"

Veronica nodded, not trusting her voice.

Michi cut in. "We're going for cappuccino. Would you like to join us?" Next to Talamantes, Michi seemed smaller than usual.

"Sure. Great idea." The film maker offered one lean brown hand to each. "I'm René. I didn't catch your names."

After they introduced themselves, they stood awkwardly in the empty hallway, clasping each other's hands.

Talamantes squeezed Veronica's fingers. "So you're Chicana, too. Que suave! I got jazzed seeing you in the audience. Usually I'm the only brown woman in sight."

"I know the feeling." Veronica met her compelling gaze again and did not look away. René's fingers were warm and electric.

Her free hand smoothing her moussed head, Michi fidgeted.

Talamantes noticed Michi's impatience and alternated her gaze between them. "Perdoname. Are you two lovers?"

"Friends," Veronica sputtered. She was taken aback at René's candor, but also grateful for her question.

"Since first grade," Michi swiftly added.

"Hey, that's cool." Talamantes finally released their hands, slinging her hemp bag over her wide shoulder. "Want to go off campus or over to the Kerckhoff coffeehouse?"

"Kerckhoff sounds fine," Veronica said with a sudden smile.

•

"So what brought you two dykes to my film preview?" Talamantes stretched her long legs and waited for her cappuccino to cool.

Michi raised her brows. "Are you always this direct?"

"Why not, huh?" The film maker's even teeth gleamed.

"Roni, you're blushing," Michi teased.

"That's just the reflection of my red shirt against my brown face," Veronica explained, toying with a strand of her curly hair.

"Yeah, and my eyes're slanted 'cause I'm squinting from the cappuccino steam." Michi impishly wriggled her brows.

Amid Talmantes' raucous laughter, Veronica tried to maintain a serious demeanor. "Let's get back to René's question. This Munchkin," she continued, gesturing towards the grinning Michi, "lured me over to Melnitz, and didn't even mention your film until we were having dinner in the Village. And, even though I split hairs over the lack of dialog, I really am impressed with *Tortilleras*. It's sensual and erotic—and it works."

"For her to say that's a major compliment," Michi interjected. "She's a writer, you see."

"Oh, yeah?" Talamantes leaned forward, one round breast brushing the table slightly. "Anything I'd be familiar with?"

Veronica tossed Michi a peeved glance. "I've written for *Westwinds* and *The Jacaranda Review*. And I've had pieces in *Conditions,* and in *Third Woman.*

"And tell her about your novel, Roni."

"You're writing a novel?" At that, Talamantes set down her cup, elbows on the table.

"I'm in the middle of the first draft." Veronica blew on her cappuccino to avoid looking up.

"Does it have a lesbian theme?"

Veronica nodded, finally taking a sip.

Gesturing, René's graceful hands spoke a language of their own. "Listen, we ought to collaborate. To be honest, Veronica, my weak point is structure. I do great camera work, but when it comes to structuring a story, I really have to buckle down. The writing doesn't come easily. I'd sure like to get some tips from you."

Veronica studied her, liking the way Talamantes had pronounced her name in perfect Spanish—Veh-roe-nee-ka—a verbal caress. Accustomed to "Roni," her childhood nickname, Veronica had forgotten the Latin beauty of her actual appellation. She felt herself smile.

"Well, René, I'm a grad student in the English Department, so I'll be back on campus this fall. Right now, I'm concentrating on finishing my first draft. I'd be glad to help you out, if I can, but I've only taken one screenwriting course."

"Hey, I'd be satisfied if you'd just take a look at one of my screenplays." René reached for her hemp bag and fished inside for her combination calendar/address book. "What's your phone number?"

Veronica heard herself stutter. "450-1868. It'll be Michi's, too, before long. She's moving in with me."

"We're both in states of transition, and decided we needed mutual support," Michi explained.

"Yeah. Tell me about it. I could use some supportive friends myself. I'm the token dyke in the film department, and sometimes it gets damn lonesome." René threw the book into her bag and downed more cappuccino. "Besides, earlier this year, I made the gigantic mistake of getting involved with a theater arts major. She thought I'd make her a star."

"Was she one of the women in the film?" Michi probed.

"Hell, that's what caused all the mitote between us. She's white, and couldn't understand why I wouldn't use her for *Tortilleras*." Talamantes pushed her coarse black hair from her face. "Are you two single?"

Michi sighed, playing with her ear cuff.

"Yes," Veronica said quietly. And for the first time in months, she was sure.

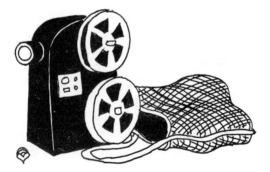

Fantasy

Once

by Andrea Siegel

Andrea Siegel is a writer who lives in Berkeley, CA.

Once

Once when you were young, but not-so-young, you had an afternoon when you were home sick, from school. This afternoon contained a dream, the details of which you have probably not remembered.

Your room, with an eighty-foot pine outside one window, was on the sunny corner of the house, north and west. You'd slept that morning, but you woke late enough to watch the sunlight, in rays, squeak through the northern window. It fell in golden morning light on your bookshelves. And in the streams of light you felt the faeries dancing.

You closed your eyes again and slept, and when you woke the sun was high. Your room was bright with the afternoon. Your nose was stuffed so you almost didn't care about the glory of being home alone at midday, but your heart was glad for the light.

You were awake enough to go off to the bathroom and then wander back into bed, so perhaps this wasn't a dream at all. But anyway, I must remind you, for at the end of the dream you made me promise.

In the twinkling of a fish coming to the surface of a pond, you were elsewhere, in the woods. It was a magic woods, perhaps, but most definitely it was a place people hadn't been for some time, if at all.

Your bed—your single child's bed—had come with you and looked very bright, unnaturally white, against the spring velvet green of the moss where it had landed. You hadn't felt that you'd flown, but there are no words, in English, for sudden appearances. Not that sudden, at least.

Somewhat timidly you stuck a toe out into the deep green moss and oooh, it was delicious. You wiggled your whole foot in it and soon found you were off your bed and dancing, cavorting about the half-shady clearing. Soon the butterflies came to join you and there must've been thirty of them, from the tiniest one: the size of a dime, bright pink with yellow dots; to a huge magenta and aqua striped one which was seven or eight inches wide from wingtip to wingtip.

This lovely, soft, squashy stepping in the moss—with these new friends flying about—might've gone on quite a long time, but for a faint whisper of new sound. Where before there had only been the song of leaves in the wind, your huffs of pleasure, and the faintest of faint joycries of the butterflies, now there was the faint whisper of a flute in the forest.

You stopped. All the butterflies stopped as well and rested on the top of your head and shoulders.

There was silence and then the faint two-whoo of the flute came again. It was a lovely sound, but troubling. Or the sound spoke of its author, who was perhaps troubled, you thought. So in a spirit of valor you decided to investigate, and perhaps, do what you could to set matters right.

In an inkling you had set off through the pathless wood, with the butterflies dancing behind you like the colorful trail of a flying kite. Your trudging brought you up a hill and over, into a valley of meadows and old oak trees. There was a stream. And then you saw her, playing the panpipes, as she rested and dangled her feet in the running waters.

You did not stop, but marched right up to her as she played her hesitant notes. She did not see you, as she was focused on the pipes before her, and you were just out of her line of vision. She trilled out a long, low, sad note. Then she stopped, looked up, and was startled by your presence. Perching on the low grass she poised herself to run, but then she noticed your train of butterflies.

She pointed, and eyes lit with some inner flame of delight, she laughed and laughed.

She was I; it was I who you saved from the enchantment of the quiet flute, on that quiet summer's day.

I was bound up in grief; it was a grief too deep to be my own. But when a traveler comes through who can fail to stop one's keening—soft and low and halting as it is?

As I stood to greet you my smile sent a greeting which, you told me later, made you understand why you had come across all barriers—past your cold and through magic—to my home place. As you walked up to me, both of us grinning like fools, the butterflies settled on our heads. Each of us could see the crown on the other's head, but not on our own.

We walked together, quite close to the stream. Eventually sitting down we gathered our stories, like schools of fish, and mingled them with each other's all the afternoon long.

Late, late in the afternoon you grew tired. You were lying on the soft ground with your head in my lap, and I was dancing a daisy across your nose. You said to me, "Promise you'll come back to me, to my home, and tell me about this. I've got a feeling I won't remember." And I promised. You nodded off quietly, and before you were quite asleep you vanished, leaving only the imprint of your body in the grasses, and the lilac smell of your hair on my soft clothes.

And so I've come to tell you again, as I promised.

What We Do In Bed

by Ruthann Robson

Ruthann Robson lives outside of Tallahassee, Florida. She's rumored to be (in alphabetical order) a computer wizard, dog groomer, gourmet cook, lawyer, teacher and xylophone player, but only some of these rumours are verifiable. This story is part of an ongoing series entitled CECILE. A collection of her short fiction is forthcoming later this year from Firebrand Books.

What We Do In Bed

One of the most salacious activities Cecile and I perform on our queen size, in full view of our combination ceiling fan/light fixture, is reading to each other. We do not merely recite provocative phrases from our separate novels or self-help books; we do not read aloud a poem or two which we consider especially intimate. We do not share portions of essays which accurately portray some facet of our experience.

Instead, after Cecile pretends to read our child Colby a story (often substituting appropriate words: there are not too many Read Aloud Books about co-mothers) and Colby slips reluctantly into sleep, Cecile gets *our* book.

It is never a classic. It is not usually a book from the "current concerns" or "lesbian interest" shelves at the small alternative bookstore almost an hour's drive from our bedroom. It is a detective novel. Well, at least it is not a romance.

Tonight, Cecile and I are anxious to spread across our earthy pink sheets, a glass of lemonade on the wicker nightstand on my side, a glass of ice tea on the wicker chest on her side. This time we are in the midst of a gay male mystery. Cecile found it in the trade paperback bookstore, not too far from the alternative bookstore.

The action in this detective book takes place in New Orleans, about a seven hour drive from our bedroom. The first time I was ever in New Orleans was a long time before I met Cecile. I was there with my friend Dulcie, who suggested we trek from our Miami shit jobs to see a Vodun fortune teller. We'd hitchhiked up the turnpike, to Route 75, and then across on Interstate 10, passing within five miles of where Cecile and I live now. Dulcie wanted to find out whether her mother in Cuba was dead or alive. I wanted an adventure.

The Vodun woman was beautifully shrouded in scarves, and many stones swinging from thin threads. Her skin and hair were darker than mine, but that was true of almost everyone in Miami; it's true of almost everyone in the world. Her skin and eyes were darker than Dulcie's, but her hair was lighter in the sense that it attracted and reflected more light in the small alcove.

Mme. Celeste told Dulcie that her mother was alive and sewing in Candeleria; at least that is what Dulcie told me the woman said. When I went into the private room off the alcove Mme. Celeste asked me for a piece of jewelry, although it was not obvious I was wearing any. I was impressed into obedience. I unbuttoned my button-down shirt and reached into the not very mysterious interior of my black leotard. I pulled out a thin silver band which usually swung between my breasts on a dirty string. I handed it to her and she did not smile. She said: "The young woman who you travel with is in love with you. You will hurt her, just as you will hurt the many women who will travel with you, most not very far and most for only a short time. But someday you will stop your carelessness. Someday you will be married and have a child."

I had wasted five dollars. Dulcie did not love me any more than I loved her. We were pals. And I could not imagine being married.

"I'm queer," I told her.

"It's your ring," she said, handing it back to me. She continued not smiling.

There are no Vodun women in the detective story which Cecile is now reading aloud. I guess a fortune teller would spoil the plot; the hero could take off his Rolex watch, hand it to her, and hear: "It is a very important man who is murdering all those men in the bathroom of the gay bar. An elected official. Like a Congressman."

Yes, a Vodun woman would taint the book. Sometimes it seems like any woman would taint the book. There are a *few* women in these pages, who either dress fabulously or drably. But however their costuming abilities are categorized, the women are invariably referred to as fish...

"You aren't going to like this." Cecile interrupts herself as she is reading, taking a slug of her ice tea.

"Oh, go ahead."

" 'What did the fish say?' " she reads.

"Oh shit," I say. "I'm getting sick of this."

"I told you," Cecile tells me.

"What does it mean, anyway?" I ask. Cecile knows a lot of gay male slang. She was once married to a gay man, but I like to forget about that.

"It means," she says, putting our book down and resting her head on my hip, "that women smell like the ocean."

I wonder how a gay man would know this, but I cannot wonder for very long because Cecile is burrowing her nose between my thighs.

"You smell like the Atlantic," she says. "At night."

"Don't you want to find out what happens next?" I tease.

I mean in the book, but Cecile answers, "This does," while her tongue separates myself from myself.

Cecile finds my wettest spot and laps it with her tongue. Then she turns, leans, and half-straddles me for a deep, long kiss. Her mouth tastes like a midnight sea. I kiss her back, clasping for a hold on the hair at the base of her skull.

"Good night, honey," she says. "I love you."

"I love you, too," I whisper.

Cecile unstraddles me and turns off the light. She tangles her limbs around mine as if we are two trees which share the same tap root.

One of the most sensual things Cecile and I do between our sheets, as the stars of the summer sky witness through our windows, is sleep together. We rarely make love at night; if making love must exclude two bodies lounging on a plain of longing; if making love must include volcanoes of orgasm.

Instead, the darkness calls us into each other. We sleep touching, always touching: our ankles wrapped, or my hand on her breast, or her arm on my thigh, or my hair trapped under her head. We sleep talking, saying: "I love you, honey," or "Are you OK?" or "Hold me," or "I'm having a bad dream."

Cecile dreams of rattlesnakes, poised and ready to strike.

I dream of Dulcie, screaming that I was a dolt not to see she loved me.

Cecile and I shake in our nightmares, waking each other. We find words for our fears and use these words to find the magic of sleep again.

Sometimes it is a barking dog which wakes us, sometimes it is

Bob the cat who jumps on my head. Sometimes Colby yells from
his bedroom. Sometimes we wake up with the sun, holding hands
like a pair of school girls who have just returned from a field trip to
the universe.

I rarely slept with women before I met Cecile. I fucked them,
went to bed with them, had sex with them, rolled with them, laughed
with them, teased, licked, and kissed them. I was manic in those
preciously dark hours between the closing of bars and dawn. But
sleep was too safe to be shared. I thought danger was the only
aphrodisiac: sex the only shelter. Love, of course, was a trap. Not
dangerous, but deadly. Not intoxicating, but addictive. If I was in
bed with a woman silly enough to mutter the word "love," I would
be back on the street so fast my head would still be spinning. I
would walk home in the night air—which would feel crisp, no matter
how hot—which would feel comforting, no matter how cold.

"I love you," Cecile says, rolling out of bed.

"Mmmmm," I say, still hugging our sleep. I hear the water running and the cabinet doors open and close. The animals scamper
across the floor. The screen door squeals. The toilet flushes. Cecile
returns to bed with two hot cups of coffee spiked generously with
half-and-half.

The mornings are our favorite time to make love. I am often late
for work, but since I have been promoted to supervisor, at the
Department of Motor Vehicles, this matters less than it once did.
Today, however, is Saturday, as Cecile reminds me, her voice lux-
urious with the uniquely extra syllable of it.

I rest my cheek against the hard flat bone between her breasts. It
smells like the white pulp of an orange rind, the pericarp, slightly
acidic and slightly sweet. As a child I used to slide that flesh between my teeth. "Don't eat that," my mother would scold. But I
always did.

Cecile's breasts are soft, and shaped like navel oranges. I lick
her stiffening nipples with my coffee-coated tongue. I kiss her eyebrows, her jawbone, and cheekbones—her mouth. She arches her
back and my fingers slide across her stomach and then under her. I
settle one hand into the mold of her back. With my other hand I
stroke her and tell her I love her, and how sweet she is, and I love
her, and how wet she is, and I love her. Cecile speaks in an un-

101

translatable language of words with vowels only, or with consonants only. I speak to her in stuttering English. I say, "more" or "deeper" or "let me." I say, "come again for me," and she does.

The air is salty with sweat between us. Cecile is thirsty; I go to refill our coffee cups. Cecile is cold; I cover her with a damp pink sheet. I pick up the detective novel, thinking to read the next chapter aloud to Cecile. I do not even have a chance to find our place from last night, when Cecile slips her leg under me. She holds one hand lightly on my wrist and the other on my face. I am still wet and open from touching her. When she enters me, I cannot be any more wet or open. Her face is close to mine. Our eyelashes touch each other, blinking their own messages. I can hear her words, feel her breath, smell the salt on her neck.

Her eyes are where I go when I come. They are not limpid pools (as a child I wondered who would want a limp pool in her head), but her eyes are more like the crystals which hang in our bedroom windows, refracting the morning sun. Her eyes are a hard, but inviting place, with every color I have ever seen/heard/felt/tasted and a few I have not. Sometimes I wander in her eyes and there are so many facets, it seems like there must be a mirror hidden somewhere. There is not.

When I return to the bed from her eyes and my knees stop shaking, I hear a voice that is not Cecile's.

"My heart is beating."

I slowly move my hand to my chest. My heart is, in fact, beating. It has not flown from between my breasts into Cecile's eyes. I hear the voice again; it is impatient and childlike. I look at Cecile. Her mouth is closed, but smiling—her eyebrows arched.

"That's good, Colby," Cecile says. "Your heart is supposed to beat"

I focus on Colby who is now standing near the bed. I did not even know he was awake, and he has already brought us his beating heart.

"He just walked in," Cecile answers, before I can ask her if Colby has been witnessing my travels into her eyes.

"Why don't you go watch TV? It's Saturday," Cecile says. Although it is the only day Colby is allowed the television, Cecile's temptation is not a success.

"I want to sleep," I tell Colby.

I close my eyes. Cecile rearranges the sheets, including fitting
the fitted sheet back onto the mattress corner. Her hand strokes my
thigh. I open my eyes.

"I have an idea," Colby announces.

Then he is gone from the bedroom. I am ready to go back into
Cecile's eyes. My tongue aches for a taste of Cecile. Cecile and I
kiss.

Colby yells, "I am back," and climbs into the bed. He has several books, one of which is sharp against my skin. He is smiling
and smiling. One of the most passionate practices Cecile and I enact
on our queen size, with our child looking from face to face, is to alter
the words in the Read-Aloud Series.

A Different Kind of Family

by T.C. Robbins

T.C. Robbins is an eighteen year old Black Lesbian. She is currently attending the University of Pennsylvania, where she is active in several campus groups. She hopes that someday it will be easier to be both Black and Lesbian on campuses and around the world.

Less globally, she enjoys reading, especially Lesbian literature, and various outdoor activities. She hopes to graduate with a B.A. in Sociology and/or English, move someplace where there are more trees and, maybe, write on a regular basis. Her dream for the future includes her lover and a house in the country.

A Different Kind of Family

"Her bath's done and she's waiting for you to come tell her a story," Kamaria said with an air of understated victory. Meg looked up from her work at the desk, faintly amused. Her eyes showed the love she felt better than words could. Even if Kamaria had not spoken Meg would have known she'd entered the room; Kamaria had that kind of presence. She had striking eyes; eyes that seemed more to reflect the deep brown of her skin than to have a color of their own; eyes that suited the tall, large woman who looked elegant even in faded blue jeans and an old college sweatshirt, with her long braid disheveled.

"Thanks, Kamaria. Looks like you got a bath, too. What story do you think she'll want to hear?" With a smile and then a laugh, Kamaria crossed the room. She stood behind the chair and placed her arms around Meg's neck.

"Oh good, a question I know the answer to. Beth asked me if I thought tonight you'd tell her the story about the party. I said I thought maybe you would." The request didn't surprise either one of them. This particular story was one of Bethany's favorites; she had had a part in it. "Meg, what did you ever find to tell her about before you met me?" Kamaria meant the remark to be flip, but her arms tightened just slightly around Meg's neck. Some days it really did seem like a fairytale, and a year—how different things had been a year ago.

Meg took Kamaria's hand and pulled her around so they were facing each other. Both women looked down at their hands. The contrast of their skin had at first seemed to be a gulf; now it united them all the more. They were still for a moment, then Meg broke the silence. "Guess I better go tend to that kid of mine. Will you take a look at the ledger when you get a minute?"

Meg accepted the other woman's nod and walked to the door of her daughter's room. The walls were a kind of pale green that only an adult would inflict upon a child. The circus accents were more in keeping with Bethany's taste; animals of all types were one of her many passions. While waiting for her mother Bethany had found something else to do. She was on the bed, dark hair flying, arms just missing lamps and other unimportant objects, bed creaking with every movement. "Hi Mommy!" the child said, then halfway through a bounce she realized that Mom was not quite as amused by this game as she was. After hitting the bed she stopped bouncing and proceeded to look innocent. "Are you gonna tell me a story now, Mommy?"

Despite herself, Meg had to laugh just a little as she rearranged the child and bed into some semblance of order before she sat down. "Yes, but you can't be jumping on the bed like that. OK?" She waited for the child to nod. "Good. What would you like to hear? Perhaps Snow White?"

"No, Mommy, I wanna hear how I got you and Kay together." Meg looked slightly pained, but settled in to tell the story. "Kay, are you gonna come listen to the story, too?" Bethany said to Kamaria who, looking rather neater than before, had come into the room.

"No," said the black woman, leaning over to hug the child, "I just came in to say goodnight. That is one story I've heard quite enough, thank you. Sleep well, little one." Though Meg's eyes were green to her daughter's brown, and her hair shorter and lighter, the mother and child still looked very much alike. Kamaria was surprised she didn't feel like an outsider, but she didn't.

"Goodnight, Kay." Kamaria always had to smile when Bethany called her by her nickname. It sounded so grown-up coming out of such a little mouth. It had originally been Meg's name for her because Meg claimed that "Kamaria" was too many syllables in bed. Bethany had adopted the name because she'd wanted to share in the special closeness between the two women. In doing so she had solved the problem of what Bethany should call her.

Kamaria and Bethany had a really good relationship. What could have been a rivalry for Meg's attention was instead a partnership, of sorts. In the time they had known each other Bethany had developed a great deal of respect for her mother's lover. In fact, Bethany had grown to love Kamaria, maybe not the same way she loved her mother, but it was love all the same. She was deeply proud of having a different kind of family and often bragged about having two mothers. She didn't understand everything, but the change in her mother had been dramatic; Meg laughed more and wasn't always so worried. And Kamaria was always willing to take the time to talk to her.

As she released the child, Kamaria hugged the other person on the bed. "Have fun, sweethearts." Kamaria laughed at her lover's helpless expression and turned off the light as she left.

In the semi-darkness of the night-light, Meg began her story. "Once upon a time, in a galaxy far, far away— No? OK, OK. I'll tell it right," Meg said, responding to Bethany's outraged look. "Let's see. Your daddy and I had been divorced for a little over a year when I decided to move to this section of town."

They had moved out of the apartment they'd lived in before the divorce. It had been a hard move, but a necessary one. Meg had still been dependent on her ex, Jim, and she'd known she needed to do something about that if she wanted to ever get on with her life. Lucky for Meg, Jim had been very supportive about the whole thing, including Kamaria, when it came to her. He'd understood Meg's need to live her life her way, but he was still very much a part of his daughter's life. He had been pleased the school Bethany would be attending was so good.

"School..." As the tail end of her thought was spoken aloud, Meg suddenly remembered she was trying to tell some sort of a story. "When I took you to your first day of school here we met Kamaria. And to tell you the truth, baby, at first I didn't really like her. She was one of those people who just seems too good at what they do. I remember her standing there in her blue dress, looking so strong, so purposeful..." The dress had been shirt waist style, made out of lightweight denim. It looked like it would go as well with cowboy gear as it did with the dark blue flats Kamaria had worn with them. Kamaria's midnight black hair, though long and soft, was extremely thick and tended to tangle if it wasn't pulled back. That time it had been arranged in a neat ponytail.

Meg's first impression was that Kamaria looked like someone out of a Marlboro ad: someone used to wide open spaces. How could she explain to her daughter how lost she'd felt and how

Bethany's beautiful new teacher had struck her. Meg had been attracted to other women before and she certainly didn't believe in love at first sight, but she'd felt an immediate connection to Kamaria. It had been more emotional than physical—that had come later. Somehow Kamaria had made her feel safe and accepted. There'd been an overwhelming desire to trust this woman completely, let her in. That had scared Meg. She hadn't allowed herself to depend on anyone in that way in a long time—trust gave the other person power. All the same, Kamaria had made her feel wonderful and horrible and just completely confused. It had brought a sense of belonging and an even stronger sense—of longing.

All this, from their occasional contact as parent and teacher. To put this disturbing woman out of her mind, Meg had decided that she disliked her, but of course it wasn't that easy. And to make it even harder, Bethany and Kamaria had quickly become great friends; every night it had been Ms. Flint this and Ms. Flint that.

"I heard about your new friend all the time, and then one day when I was out alone at the Gold Key, I met her. She was at a table with a bunch of other women and I was sitting at the bar. She saw me and after a couple of minutes she got up and invited me over to her table. I didn't really want to go, but I didn't have anything better to do so I did. And you know what?" Meg cuddled Bethany who had crawled into her lap. "It turns out Kamaria was a really nice person. I liked the people at her table, too. After a while I forgot that we weren't sitting around someone's kitchen table. For the first time in what seemed to be a very long time, I was comfortable.

"For a bit Kay and I were just friends, but that started to change quickly, perhaps *too* quickly. I guess I was scared to take a chance. Anyway, I said some things. She said some things. She is so different from anyone I've known." Meg shook her head and smiled slightly, remembering their first fight. She had felt so lost after Kamaria had left in anger. To Meg it had meant that everything was over. She and Jim had rarely fought; she'd figured if she and Kamaria could make each other that hostile, especially early on, then they couldn't possibly have a future.

"I didn't know what to say or how to say it," Meg continued. She had wanted to call Kamaria, but she hadn't been able to, not yet. "You remember those days, don't you, Beth? I was pretty hard to live with then, jumping every time the phone rang." The little girl nodded sleepily and opened her eyes just a little; this was her favorite part of the story. "My friends and even your dad said I should go ahead and try to make up with Kay. But, in the end, it was you who did something about it, huh, Beth? You kept the secret so well that I never guessed at all."

Bethany's actual contribution had been small, but it had made her feel important. All she had done was mention to Kamaria that her mother's birthday was soon. That had given Kamaria the idea to throw Meg a surprise party. It was just the type of grand gesture Kamaria liked to make; she never did anything halfway.

Kamaria had moved into Meg's apartment a month after their relationship began and it had only been another month and a half before the fight. It had started about space, but had gotten vicious when all their underlying problems had come to the surface. Kamaria hadn't liked Meg's insecurity. She hadn't liked always having her feelings for Meg questioned and she'd grown tired of having to walk on eggshells around Meg's fears.

She'd been scared, too. She hadn't been so sure she wanted to help raise a child or, for that matter, commit to a relationship. In some ways it had frightened Kamaria to know Meg meant so much to her.

When Kamaria had left the apartment after the fight she hadn't been sure she ever wanted to go back. In the end, though, she decided three things: that she had faith in their love, that it was worth a fair shot, and that she wanted to say so in a very big way. Mostly she'd invited all the women from the Gold Key, but also, through Jim, she'd gotten in touch with some of Meg's old friends.

"It was lucky Kay still had the apartment key or it would have been a bit harder for her to set the whole thing up," Meg continued the story. "I was damn near struck dumb when I walked through our door and was greeted with confetti and shouts of "Surprise!" You know what my first response was? 'What are the neighbors going to think?'"

"That figures," Kamaria said quietly as she slipped into the room. And it did figure; Meg tended to worry a lot about what other people thought. She rarely accepted things at face value, either, and she almost never thought people did things for her because they wanted to.

Kamaria could understand Meg's wariness; they'd both been hurt in the past. Bethany asked a muffled question, and it brought Kamaria back to the subject at hand.

"I came to hurry your mother up," Kamaria replied. "Maybe then I can have her back before midnight." Meg caught the humor in her lover's voice. Then she caught her eyes.

It had taken Meg a long time to learn the different ways Kamaria expressed emotions. Meg was used to talking at length about her feelings, but a touch, a hug—a smile, even—could mean more to Kamaria than all those words. Kamaria talked, especially when it was important, but she didn't try to verbalize or justify her feelings. It was easier to just let things happen, and to trust in her ability to handle the outcome.

That's what their fight had been about, really; neither of them had understood how the other communicated. Meg needed to be *told* that she was loved. Kamaria felt that her actions said enough. Meg had felt overwhelmed, and had been angry that Kamaria didn't talk to her; she'd felt that she never knew what Kamaria was thinking. Meg hadn't expected this relationship; she'd been afraid that it would end as quickly as it had begun.

"Anyway," said Meg, continuing with the story as Kamaria settled in to listen to the end, "I couldn't believe Kamaria had done all this for me; I mean, nobody had ever thrown me a party, not since I was a child. It was great; I loved the huge banner across the living room door, and the balloons and streamers everywhere. I guess it was more or less your typical birthday party, but it meant a great deal to me, just that Kamaria was willing to go to all that trouble." Meg looked up and smiled at Kamaria. "After everybody else left we tried to figure out where to go from there. It wasn't an easy conversation and we didn't figure it all out then, but we've got time. And love..."

Anything more Meg might have said would have been for Kamaria's benefit only, as Bethany had fallen fast asleep. Instead of going on, to say how wonderful the year had been or how much faith she had in their future, Meg simply took Kamaria's hand. Together they tucked Bethany in. At the doorway Meg turned and looked at Bethany, then she looked at Kamaria, catching her eyes. Once she had thought that her child was her chance, her hope, but now—now she had another chance. One that was hers and Kay's.

When She Sings

by Janet E. Aalfs

I, Janet E. Aalfs, was a shy child. Now it has become difficult to shut me up. I have been writing, seriously, since I discovered pencil and paper, and fighting, seriously, all my life. One thing I really appreciate is a sense of humor. I believe in the power of the unseen and pay attention to thumps in the night and silver stars that appear in my peripheral vision. I have been in touch with poltergeists, and kissed on the shin by a fur seal off the coast of California.

I live and work in the Pioneer Valley of Western Massachusetts and am currently commuting to the MFA Program in Writing at Sarah Lawrence College. I am a black belt in karate and in arnis (Filipino Stickfighting) and am one of the head instructors of Valley Women's Martial Arts, a school for women and children.

All six feet and one inch of my white, middle class, Lesbian body that appeared on this earth (in smaller form) in 1956 is proud to be part of a family of blood relatives that includes other Lesbians, as well as to have created for myself a chosen family of loving, diverse, and rebellious women. I hope to continue sharing my life with such feisty folks and to grow ever more exuberant each glorious day.

When She Sings

Even when I was young I knew my mother was not a saint. She had her flaws, just like anyone. Besides, the teachers at sunday school told us that protestants didn't have saints.

No, my mother wasn't a saint; she was a fairy. Even though most fairies didn't go to sunday school or church, my mother did. She was caught in an image to uphold, my father being the minister and all.

We lived in a white wooden house up the hill from the center of the town that consisted of a church, general store, drugstore, playing field, the town common, and a couple of schools. The town was just another small clearing in the midst of the the forest. The forest was the *real* world as far as I was concerned.

Fairies lived in the woods. They mostly lived in old rotted logs and deep inside the hearts of flowers. They were the ones who brought me a dime and placed it under my pillow when I lost a tooth. But I didn't tell my mother that I knew it was her who put the little white envelope in my shoe, and I didn't let on that I recognized the tiny handwriting that said:

> I hope I didn't wake you
> when I brought this
> dime in. It was so heavy
> I had to ask twelve friends
> to help me carry it
> —and we dropped it
> once!
>   We love your sweet
> heart!
>   —The Blue Fairy

I could just picture my mother and her twelve fairy friends, all

113

with pointed caps and shoes. There was the purple fairy and the pink fairy, the brown, green and yellow fairies, the red fairy, the black one, the orange one and some various shades in between. All the colors in my crayon box—that's how many fairies there were. Even then I knew it is common for fairies to travel in groups of thirteen. If the sun comes out while they are flying in the rain, they hold hands across the sky to dry their wings. Although most grown-ups only see the colors, my mother saw more.

My mother took my sister and me to visit her friends. We walked down a shaded path, beyond the old mill, next to the river that ran over a dam and on through the New Hampshire hills. Celia and I scampered back and forth from rock to rock, pretending we were elves and that these were huge boulders, knowing that if we fell, we would be swept into the current and over the dam, never to be heard from again.

When we neared the fallen tree that spread its trunk and branches across our path, my mother announced that she saw a wisp of smoke coming from one of the knotholes. The fairies were having tea; they had the fire going and the kettle on. If we were quiet, we could walk even closer without disturbing them.

I whispered, "Oh yes. I see the smoke. And I hear the voices, too. Tiny ones. Like bells. What are they saying?"

I knew my mother understood. I decided that if I listened hard enough, I would be able to understand, too. After all, I was able to read the note on the tiny envelope. Why would the Blue Fairy have bothered to write it if she didn't believe I knew fairy language?

I closed my eyes for a moment, concentrating all my energy on trying to hear. I imagined I was small enough to crawl through one of the knotholes and into the log. The fairies saw me and asked me to their table. They placed a cap on my head and fastened wings onto my shoulder blades. They presented me with shoes made of tiger lily petals and invited me to stay with them for as long as I wished. When I returned to my mother and sister who had waited for me down the path from the log, I didn't tell them what I'd seen. I feared that in the telling all that I'd witnessed would disappear, and I wouldn't be able to return to the log or the fairies or spread my wings again.

I never told my mother that I knew she was one of them—and so was I. It was our unspoken secret. I felt surrounded by the danger of someone finding out. My mother could only be a fairy at night or very early in the morning when no one else was awake, and then she could fly in the dark. I could be one whenever I wanted because grown-ups don't notice when children disappear. I took to making regular trips to the fairy world. Nighttime was the best time; I didn't have to worry so much about how long I stayed away as long as I was back by morning. Even during the day I found ways to talk with my fairy friends, ones my mother had introduced me to and others I met on my own. Sometimes I left notes for them on the top of my bedroom door-jamb where no one else would find them. These notes said things like—

> Dear Fairies—If I could disappear forever,
> I'd come and live with you.

—or—

> Dear Fairies—Thanks for the dime. I
> bought a chocolate bar.

—or—

> Dear Fairies—I'm coming to visit tomorrow.
> Around teatime.

My little sister was the only one who knew where I went. She couldn't go there alone; she needed me or my mother to take her. Sometimes I got tired of holding her hand and giving her directions. I scooted off to the woods by myself and she was angry with me when I returned. But she never told. For this I was grateful and made sure to include her enough times so she didn't get sad. My mother was too busy to take these trips often. My sister kept me company, and she usually went wherever I wanted to go. She had a fine-tuned ear and heard music the way I heard words. She knew that the places without sound were where we began our journeys—in the shadows under a log, in a grove cushioned by pine needles, in a

115

damp rock cave. Crouching in silence, we entered a whole new world of sound where my words were music and her notes were poetry. If we stayed long enough, the fairies would creep out of their hiding places and sing along with us.

My mother sang with me during naptime when the other kids were sleeping. She played the piano softly and I sat next to her on the bench, singing along, learning the words and melodies as she sang:

> "White coral bells upon a slender stalk;
> Lilies-of-the-Valley deck my garden walk.
> Oh don't you wish that you could hear them ring?
> That can happen only when the fairies sing.

In these stolen sessions when I and the music were all who shared my mother's attention, I listened carefully to her messages. It was not so much what she said to me, but rather the way she touched the keys (light but firm at the same time), the slight tilt of her head, the spark in her eyes, and the tone of her voice, that told me where she was and how to follow.

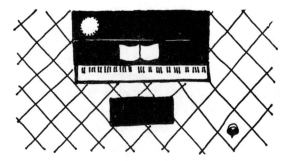

A Sleeping Cherub

By Marjorie Morgan

Marjorie Morgan is the pen name of a Jewish lesbian librarian. She is in her fifties and has had numerous book reviews plus poetry and features published in various gay, lesbian and feminist publications. Her ambition is to win the lottery and cease working for the Establishment. She shares a small condo with a mischievous stuffed pet named Creature. Philadelphia, PA is her locale.

A Sleeping Cherub

The first time I saw you you were sound asleep. You were wheeled into my hospital room, gently placed on the vacant bed and covered with blankets.

What an interesting face, I thought. Sort of like a sleeping cherub, with a high forehead, a small sweet mouth, and your hair—a mass of brown curls with strands of white. Your body was tall, I noticed, and your fingers were devoid of rings.

The nurse accompanying you said, "There was a mixup on the fourth floor. They gave her bed to a new patient while she was in the operating room."

"What kind of operation did she have?" I asked.

"Same thing you had two days ago—a hysterectomy. Will you buzz us when she awakens?"

"Of course," I replied.

Very soon after she left your eyelids fluttered. Your arm reached out and began to grope around. I flicked the nurse call then said softly to you, "What is it you're looking for?"

"My glasses," you muttered thickly. "Can't see a thing."

The nurse entered. "Well, Miss Miller. I see you've come back to us."

"Ms., not Miss!" you growled at her. "Nurse, will you please give me my glasses! I can't find them and I'm almost blind without them." She complied with your wishes, and soon you were glaring at both of us through thick lenses. "That's better," you muttered. "Thank you, Nurse."   At that moment I wondered what kind of cherub could ever seem this fierce.

The nurse brought you some ice water and you drank thirstily through a straw. Then she left the room. As the anaesthesia wore off I noticed you became more and more uncomfortable. Your head tossed on the pillow, and you bit your lip in an effort not to cry out.

118

I got out of bed gingerly (I was still feeling some pain) and went to the bathroom. I returned with a damp washcloth and went to your side.

"Here, see if this helps," I said, applying the washcloth to your forehead.

"That's wonderful," you told me, patting it into place. Your eyes closed and you looked peaceful. "What're you in for?"

"I had the same operation as you, two days ago."

"Oh, get back in bed! Aren't you having pain, standing here?"

"Just a little." I leaned over and took your hand in my own. "Helen Miller," I read from your identification bracelet. "Hi, Helen."

"Hi," you said, frowning a little behind the glasses and the washcloth. "What's your name?"

"I'm Sarah Goodman. My friends call me Sally." I slipped back under the covers of my own bed.

"A nice Jewish name. Are you a nice Jewish girl?"

"That's a difficult question. I'm not a typical one, shall we say. And I'm middle-aged, not a girl."

"I'm a middle-aged WASP," you informed me.

"I love WASPs," I responded enthusiastically. "They're so polite and gracious and self-confident!"

You burst out laughing.

"Well, it's true," I said defensively.

Just then the nurse entered. "Here's your medication, *Ms*. Goodman. And *Ms*. Miller, I have something that will make you feel more comfortable for the next few hours."

"What's *your* name?" you asked her.

"*Mrs*. Adams," she responded haughtily.

"I see," you replied, your silence saying a million things. Mrs. Adams didn't linger long. I remained quiet and soon, aided by the medication, you fell asleep.

I got out of bed and lightly removed the washcloth from your forehead. You smiled a little bit in your sleep, and I stood there looking at you, thinking what beautiful clear skin you had. I got back into bed and lit a cigarette. I smoked several before you awoke at 5:00 PM.

"You've been smoking, haven't you?" you said to me.

"Does it bother you?"

119

"We'd better ask someone to open the window," you replied. The window was near your bed; I walked over and managed to open it. "That's good," you told me.

"You're very nice about it. Some people would fly into a tantrum at my smoking."

"You must need cigarettes psychologically, or think you do, or you wouldn't smoke." You gave me a benevolent, wise smile.

"You—you're very understanding," I said softly. Just then my dinner was delivered by a young man. I got back into bed and began to eat. You just lay back, seeming exhausted.

"How about some ice water?" I asked.

"Not right now."

I thought from your expression that you must be having some pain. After I finished my supper I went to your side. "Come now, why don't you take a little sip?" I said. I managed to get you to drink some, but finally you turned your head away crankily.

"Who did all this for you two days ago?" you asked, wincing with discomfort.

"No one," I replied, not wanting to think about it.

"You're very kind," you whispered and grasped my hand. Your blue-gray eyes peered at me. "And you have pretty brown eyes, Sally."

I flushed. "Thank you. Helen is a beautiful name." I paused, self-conscious, wanting to divert attention from myself. "Tell me about yourself."

"I'm a lawyer. I specialize in cases of discrimination against women and gay people." You were still gripping my hand.

I gave your hand a little squeeze. "You went after your ideals instead of a lucrative practice."

"Yes. My income is modest. What about you?"

"I'm an editor of books for young adults, and I find it difficult to practice my lesbian feminist ideals at work without getting clobbered. It's an uphill battle." My hand was still in your larger one, and neither of us moved to withdraw.

Mrs. Adams entered with the medicine. Our hands remained clasped together. "Ah-hem!" she cleared her throat loudly. Neither of us moved an inch. "Your medicine!" she said tartly.

"Oh yes, *Mrs.* Adams," you said to her. "Just put it down, and

120

we'll get it in a moment."

She glared at you, set the medicines on our respective tables, and left. We burst out laughing. I brought you your medicine and returned to take my own.

Later that evening I had a long telephone call from my mother, then you had two visitors—two women who appeared to be a couple. You introduced us and then we were all conversing. I noticed that one of the women was tall and thin, like you, and the other short and plump, like myself. I liked that. It gave me hope.

Your visitors stayed for about an hour. When they left, you lay back on the pillow, again exhausted. "Washcloth time," I announced, bringing the damp cloth and patting it gently onto your forehead. You had tubes coming in every direction, including a catheter to relieve your bladder.

"Dear friend," you whispered, again grasping my hand and this time kissing it.

At the moment of the kiss Mrs. Adams chose to enter and once more cleared her throat. "Ah-hem!!!"

"Hello, Mrs. Adams," you said, busily kissing each one of my fingers.

"I'm here to remover your catheter," she sputtered, frowning.

I moved back to my bed and Mrs. Adams drew the curtain between us. After a short time she opened it and left.

"There you are," I said. You sighed, shifting uncomfortably.

I got out of bed again and padded toward you. I leaned over and kissed your forehead, above the washcloth. When I straightened up I saw you were smiling. We looked into each other's eyes, then I leaned down again and kissed your beautifully-shaped mouth. "Cherub," I murmured through the kiss.

At that moment there was the sound of someone entering. "Miss Goodman!"

I straightened up. There was a nurse whose name-pin included the words "Evening Supervisor." She said, "I think you'd better let Miss Miller rest. She's fresh out of surgery."

You broke in. "I'm getting the best of care from Ms. Goodman. She's been an invaluable help."

"I'm sure," growled the supervisor. "But now you'd better get in bed, Miss Goodman. You don't want to jeopardize your own condition." Her words took on an ominous meaning. I slowly returned to bed.

"Thank you, Nurse," you said in a tone of dismissal. "We'll let you know if we need anything." The supervisor said nothing and left the room.

"Word is getting around," I said.

You smiled. "Good. It'll liven up their evening. Besides, maybe they'll learn a thing or two."

I managed to give you one more kiss before we retired for the night.

In the morning they removed the rest of your tubes. At noon you were brought a light lunch, which I fed you, as you were reluctant to eat. In the afternoon you were drowsy. I tucked the blanket around your foot, which had escaped from the covers. "What pretty toes you have." I smiled at you. "I always envy people who have beautiful feet."

You reached out and pulled me right down on the bed next to you. "Come under the covers with me," you whispered.

"What if they see us?" I whispered back.

"All the better if they do."

I crept under the covers with you and we leaned together, gently, because of our delicate conditions. We held hands.

There were a few whispered sounds in the hallway, then a nurse entered. She wore a pin saying "Director of Nursing."

"Miss Goodman! she barked.

"Yes?"

"We're going to have to move you to a private room. There will be no extra charge."

"You move her and we'll both sue the hospital for harassment," you told her.

She immediately left. Ten minutes later, a young man with a mustache entered. "Hello, I'm Barry Schwartz from Administration. I'm told there is a problem here of—ah—violation of nurses' instructions—"

"Mr. Schwartz," you said from your position next to me in the bed. "How would you like to have 900 lesbians and gays picketing your hospital? And newspeople present from the major television networks, radio stations and newspapers? We have lots of contacts."

"All right, Miss Miller—"

"*Ms.* Miller."

"All right. You win. I don't see what all the fuss is about, anyway. You're just being affectionate."

"Right," I said. "It's the best medicine." He left, closing the door behind him. "You darling," I murmured into your neck, placing lots of soft little kisses on the smooth skin.

"We almost had a big do," you said, your eyes shining excitedly.

"Would you like to support me for the rest of my life?" I asked.

"You're thinking of leaving your job?"

"No, but I could get fired if we had that kind of publicity."

"I realized that at the time," you said, "but I was pretty certain that I could get them to back off."

After about five more minutes, a young woman in the uniform of a student nurse entered and said, "I just want you to know that some of us think you're great!" Others came in during the afternoon and evening to tell us the same thing.

We each spent the night in our own beds. In the morning I said to you, "I'm going home in two more days. Will you come stay with me when you leave here?' I held my breath, terrified you would reject me.

"I guess we'd better learn how to take care of each other," you said, sitting up and opening your arms wide. I climbed in.

That afternoon, Mrs. Adams again found us snuggled together in your bed. "Would you like to congratulate us, Mrs. Adams?" you asked her. "We're going to spend the rest of our lives together."

"Humph!" she exclaimed sourly. "Which one is the happy groom?"

"I'll tell you a secret, Mrs. Adams," you shouted at her. "Neither of us is the groom!"

After she left I burst into tears. You put your arms around me and tried to console me. "Soon we'll be out of this awful place forever."

"But it's all the years of all the world against us," I sobbed into your small but comforting bosom.

You kissed my face tenderly. "I wonder if you feel discrimination more keenly," you said, "being a member of a minority ethnic group." I sobbed a few more times, liking the feeling of your

123

bosom against my cheek. You held me closer, kissed me and said, "We'll make sure to spend our time among people who accept us. And as for the people whose attitudes we want to change—at least we won't have them in our own home."

•

A year later (which was just last week) we sent a note to Mrs. Adams announcing our first anniversary. "Our happiness has known no bounds," the note said. "Words cannot describe the beauty of our life together. We hope your attitude toward people of the same sex who find love together has changed."

Two days ago you came to me with eyes shining and face alight. "What is it, Cherub?"

"It's a note from Mrs. Adams. She says: 'It's a funny thing. Your note caught me at the perfect time. I recently learned that my daughter is a lesbian. I've had to cope with it and rethink some of my old attitudes. I'm sorry if I was rude to you last year. I wish you the best of luck.'"

That night, to celebrate, we made our favorite spaghetti dinner.

"When are you going to make me Jewish chicken noodle soup with knadlach?" you asked, teasing me.

"When are you going to make me plum pudding with hard sauce, like a good WASP?" I replied.

"I'll tell you a secret." You winked. "I've never tasted plum pudding and I don't know what hard sauce looks like."

"I couldn't make a knadlach or dumpling if my life depended on it."

"You are a dumpling," you replied, kissing my cheek.

We sat down to our good Italian dinner. Our hearts were light.

The Checking Account

by Roberta B. Jacobson

Roberta B. Jacobson is a left-handed lesbian who has not had a checking account since 1984. Besides her job at the daily newspaper, she freelances by writing silly greeting cards, a magazine advice column and European travel articles. Her poems and short stories have appeared in thirty-seven anthologies. Her largest writing project has been an ongoing (never ending?) dissertation about lesbians in the army, Dykes with Stripes, *while her craziest creative adventure was thinking up zany clues for a new board game. Her dream for 1989 is to edit a lesbian poetry anthology with half the space devoted to unpublished poets.*

She collects ceramic and wooden owls and enjoys her unconventional life with a lover, Susan, who collects porcelain and plastic pigs. Along with Troy-the-cat, they share sweet dreams in their apartment in a sleepy village in West Germany.

The Checking Account

The occasion of opening a new checking account was momentous for me, so I dressed in my best jeans and favorite red and gold plaid work shirt. I remember the Friday morning visit going something like this, as I sat across from a straight-looking customer service representative:

"Here you are, Ms. Jacobson, our new line of checkbook covers. This blue one is very popular."

"I'll take the lavender one, please."

"Oh? We don't get many requests for that one."

"Well, that explains why the bar is so empty on Saturday nights."

"Excuse me?"

"Nothing. I'd like to see your checks please."

"Certainly. Just look through the pages of this brochure and we can place your order for two hundred or four hundred checks. Two hundred checks cost eight dollars."

"I don't see any that I particularly like, although these pink hearts aren't so bad. Got any triangles?"

"No, only hearts, I'm afraid. We do have elephants. Would you like a pink elephant?"

"Got any labrys symbols?"

"How's that?"

"Looks sort of like a hatchet. As in chop off the patriarchy. A large one in the left corner of the check would be just fine."

"We do have this little crossed hammer and saw. It's more of a man's logo. Is this close enough to your hatchet?"

"No. It's not the same. Do you have any lambdas?"

"Pandas?"

"Lambdas. Greek lettering with pride."

"No, I don't believe we do. However, we have special printing orders available for an extra fee, Ms. Jacobson."

"Good. I'll order a pink double woman's symbol. Do I draw it in the little square here on my order blank?"

"You realize there's an additional charge for special work? Of course, you can get a discount if you order six hundred checks."

"I'll take a thousand, please. Can you add a little "Stop Acid Rain" above the women's symbol? Maybe in a nice script?"

"Certainly. Now what's your husband's name?"

"Nancy. Last name is Berry. No middle name. Can you add the Ph.D., please?"

"Nancy?"

"N-a-n-c-y. It won't run into the women's symbol?"

"You're telling me your husband's name is Nancy? I don't believe I've heard that before."

"She's actually a lot more like a wife."

"Sorry?"

"OK, spouse. Is that better for you? How about partner?"

"Which one goes on top, please?"

"Actually, we switch. See, when the role pressure is off it just isn't an issue. If one of us is tired..."

"On your new checks, Ms. Jacobson. *You* or Dr. Berry?"

"Well, she's contributing more money to our account. She should go first."

"Fine. That was Nancy Berry, Ph.D.?"

"Right. But I'm the one opening the account. Maybe my name should go on top."

"Would you perhaps like to do this alphabetically, Ms. Jacobson?"

"Yeah. Great. That sounds fair to me. Put Nan first then. What color ink are you going to use?"

"Black isn't OK with you?"

"Well, I'd prefer lavender. Or pink would do. What pastels do you offer?"

"Only royal blue and gold. I'm afraid that's it. Except for black, of course."

"Gold? Now that sounds festive. I'll take it; mark me down for gold."

"And during this month only we offer free voting logos. Would you like a free logo in the bottom right corner of your checks?"

"Sure. Why not? It's free."

"In order to participate, I'll have to ask this. Republican or Democrat?

"Socialist."

"Socialist? Oh dear. I'm afraid we don't offer that kind of thing. Not at this bank. I'm sorry, Ms. Jacobson."

"No problem. I'm used to it. I would like to special order a little <u>Down with Apartheid</u> in the lower left corner and a bold-faced **Women Rule the World** over here on the right."

"And you realize there is a printing charge?"

"Yes. And under our name can you print a little photograph? I have this special picture of Alice B. Toklas and I think she'd look great right near the top—maybe near our zip code."

"Well, this is highly irregular. But I guess it'll fit. Maybe we'll have to take off the area code of your telephone number. Would that be all right?"

"Sure. Do it. And I know. There's an extra charge."

"Is there anything else, Ms. Jacobson? I need you to look this over to check for accuracy if there isn't anything else."

"Looks fine. And that's it. Very nice."

"So that's fifteen dollars for the checks, and an additional twelve dollars for the larger order. Special ink is another three dollars. Special type is three and a quarter. The logos will cost nineteen dollars and thirty cents. Let's see, extra printing comes to another twenty dollars and ten cents. Tax is five percent. Your total is seventy-six dollars and twenty-eight cents, Ms. Jacobson. Just sign here please."

"This really looks great. Thank you."

"And how much will you be depositing in your new account with us?"

"Uh, fifty-one dollars. Can we figure this again?"

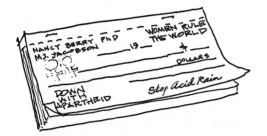

Fantasy

DRACULA RETOLD

An Inspirational Story of Wimin's Culture

by zana

zana: i've been a wife, a clerk typist, a political activist, journalist, and microfilmer. at forty-two i'm enjoying my tenth year on lesbian land—the best thing life has ever offered me. it's not utopia, but we're trying! my dream, and my work, is to make such communities more accessible to lesbians of all ages, races and ethnicities, classes, physical and mental abilities. i dream of us unlearning patriarchy and teaching ourselves new ways. and we are!

DRACULA RETOLD

An Inspirational Story of Wimin's Culture

this tale concerns lucy harker, a young womon of some spunk and intelligence who had nonetheless gotten herself married off to a duddy all-american-boy type named jonathan. it happens, even to the best of us. lucy was young yet, and being a wife was still a bit of an adventure. something new and different, you might say. the wedding was fun, playing house was fun, sex was...well, new and different. after a month of marriage, though, lucy was noticing that most of her days resembled each other closely, and that her adventures were limited to experimenting with recipes from her card file.

one day, while lucy was polishing the plastic fruit, a moving van pulled up next door. through lace curtains, lucy watched with some interest as muscular moving wimin unloaded a number of lavender packing crates.

that evening, when jonathan came home after a hard day of being a real estate agent, lucy inquired if he knew anything about their new neighbor. as a matter of fact, he himself had conducted the house sale and could tell his wife what an eccentric old biddy was going to live there. a foreigner, too—by the name of dracula.

the next day lucy prepared a tray of lemonade and cookies to take over to ms. dracula. she found her neighbor sitting under a shady tree reading a book called *sexual politics*. lucy was a little unnerved at the thought of a womon ms. dracula's age reading books about sex, and she didn't see what sex could have to do with politics, but she politely ignored the book and smiled brightly. ms. dracula smiled back—a slow, warm smile. her deep brown eyes riveted lucy's. the two wimin began to talk, and they talked of cookie recipes, the neighborhood, the institution of marriage, and wimin banding together to smash the patriarchy. it was quite a pleasant afternoon.

that night lucy tossed and turned. not wanting to disturb jonathan, she gathered some blankets and went downstairs to sleep on the couch.

during the wee hours she had a strange dream: a black cat came meowing to the open window...lucy invited it in, and once over the sill it changed form...into a womon...into dracula! but how different she looked! instead of a neat cotton shirt and slacks, she wore a long black velvet garment embroidered in silver with many symbols. her silver hair, which had been twisted in braids around her head, now flew loose and long. lucy was impressed.

and those eyes again—they were mesmerizing. dracula glided over to the couch and bent over lucy, maintaining eye contact the whole time. "woo-ee," thought lucy. "this sure feels real for a dream!"

in the morning jonathan grumbled and sputtered when the alarm kept ringing. lucy was always the one who quickly shut it off and hopped out of bed to fix breakfast, while jonathan grabbed a few more winks. but she was not in bed.

he stumbled downstairs. lucy was sitting on the couch writing in her journal. she didn't look up. she was wearing a light cotton nightgown, but had a wool scarf wrapped around her neck.

"where's breakfast?" jonathan demanded. "and why the hell are you wearing a muffler in the middle of july?"

lucy continued writing for a moment, then glanced up as if her attention had been caught by an interesting bug.

"breakfast? oh, i'm not really hungry so i didn't make any." she fingered the scarf, hiding a smile. "i feel a bit of a chill. maybe i'm coming down with something."

a week later, jonathan consulted a psychiatrist about his wife's continuing queer behavior.

"she wears this scarf constantly," he related. "while she was asleep i pulled it down and found two red dots on her neck. looked like a cat bite."

"*very* interesting!" cried dr. van helsing. "and you say she refuses your sexual advances? hmm-*hmm* !"

he produced several items from a drawer.

"we're seeing more and more cases like your wife's in this city," van helsing said, "and i think your new neighbor may be at the root of it. here are some items that such wimin find repugnant. you must invite ms. dracula over and test her with these. if she reacts badly, you must kill the evil in her by driving your, uh, stake into her. then both she and your wife will be released from their unnatural compulsions."

jonathan smiled to himself as he left van helsing's office. he'd have his lucy back again, with the good doctor's help.

at jonathan's invitation, dracula appeared at the harker home on saturday night. unfortunately, since lucy had been shunning kitchen duty, the meal consisted of jonathan's grilled cheese sandwiches. with dracula all decked out in black velvet, too.

jonathan wasn't pleased with the warm glances exchanged by his wife and his neighbor, but he hid those feelings under his thickest layer of real-estate-salesman charm.

"won't you lovely ladies come sit awhile in the living room?" he invited. "i'll put some coffee on."

while the water was boiling and as jonathan was trying to figure out the instructions on the instant coffee label, he kept one ear out for what was going on in the next room. one of the items given to him by van helsing was planted there.

"yech!" dracula cried, loud enough that jonathan dropped a coffee cup.

"oh!" lucy gasped as dracula swatted at the copy of *hustler* until it fell off the coffee table in a heap on the floor. "i'm so sorry. i can't imagine where that thing came from!"

they sipped their coffee in awkward silence—jonathan smirking, dracula and lucy looking deep into their cups.

suddenly jonathan jumped to his feet. "would you like a tour of our home, ms. dracula?"

"certainly," she replied smoothly, meeting his sharp gaze with one just as steely. lucy cringed, but dracula laid a calming hand on her arm for a brief moment.

they walked in procession up the maroon-carpeted staircase. in the bedroom, jonathan quickly flung open a closet so that dracula's image was reflected in the door-mirror. in that reflection, her plain velvet gown was covered with odd symbols, and her neatly done-up hair flew wild around her face. aha! a clear case of the hidden perversions that only a mirror could reveal. once more, dr. van helsing was proven correct!

as they left the bedroom, jonathan casually picked up a can of hairspray. dracula shrank back in horror, fleeing as he sprayed her.

"i know your secret!" he shouted, pursuing dracula from room to room. "i'm supposed to drive my stake into you and save lucy and all wimin from your perverted influence!"

just as he cornered her, dracula let out her best cat-in-heat cry. immediately the room filled with wimin wearing flowing purple gowns. as dracula greeted her sisters, jonathan gasped to see that lucy was now floating in lavender swirls instead of her patchwork hostess dress.

jonathan was easily subdued. the wimin formed a circle to decide what should be done with him.

"he knows our secret," began dracula, "and has threatened me grievously. surely we can't let him go free."

"right!" agreed a sister. "for all these centuries you—and some of us, too—have had to keep a low profile because of men like him. i'm damn sick of going around like zombies during the day with our sappy little smiles and shaved legs and bras, working at dumb jobs for peanuts."

"yes," said another sister, "but after sunset we do get to go out looking like ourselves. now we've got our wimin's bars and even a few concerts, and we can always spend a fun evening biting straight wimin and turning them on. let's be careful what we do, so we don't mess up the gains we've made."

"revisionist," grumbled another. "it's about time one of these jerks got what's coming to him, no holds barred. but the point is: we can't just off this turkey. that's male tactics. we wimin have always had a bit more finesse."

well, dear reader, you don't want a transcript of their entire meeting, since it took a good three hours to reach consensus. however, the upshot was that jonathan's karma would be accelerated a tad. through a magic incantation or two, he would find himself in the middle of his next incarnation as a more useful form of life—i.e., a ladybug.

and dracula, having finally found her love of the ages in lucy harker, decided to withdraw from the recruitment end of the political scene. she and lucy (now known as amazonclitwomon) and some of the sisters formed a wimin's community in the countryside. there they are living happily forever and ever after—discussing vegetarianism, non-monogamy, and whether converting all men to ladybugs would upset the ecology.

The Katmandou

by Susan Hecht

I, Susan Hecht, just turned forty. In a salute to middle-age, I started writing Lesbian short stories. I find myself, instead of being over the hill, rejuvenated and joyful. My career life is crammed between writing, teaching and spiritual counseling. I'm looking forward to a long, satisfying love affair, travel to obscure places (on the earth and in the mind), and the time my meditations for peace will be obsolete because everyone will be living together in a vibrant harmony.

The Katmandou

I was in Paris and I was lonely. The Katmandou bar came rec-
ommended. I dressed in Spanish creme suede with ass-tight pants,
and cursed the woman I'd left behind in the States for making herself
unforgettable. Well baby (I said to her in my mind because I
couldn't quite kick the habit), here we go.

The last metro was sardined with tourists. A jazz trio jammed in
our car, keeping their balance by straddling their cases. Twelve
forty-five AM and we're all just starting the night.

I wasn't prepared for the dark street and the dark warehouse
front with "Katmandou" written in faint orange neon two stories
above me. If it weren't for the cars parked four deep in the street, I'd
have hailed a cab and gone back to the hotel. How lonely am I, I
wondered?

Lonely, I decided, and pushed the white buzzer on the left.

Hot damn, the place was a hive. I jumped on an empty bar stool
so recently vacated the seat was still warm. This gave me a vantage
point for the door to my left and the lounge to my right. Through the
crowded lounge I could barely make out couples dancing. The scene
was clouded with smoke and European perfume.

You'd love it here, I thought to my absent one. A roomful of
Parisian women dressed for Saturday night. In my enthusiasm, I
slapped my thigh.

"*Une jolie nuit, n'est pas?*" came a high French voice to my left.
Cute, but not my type. She wore a long silk scarf holding back a
wild crowd of hair, and skirts layered like a gypsy. Too artsy for
me. I like my women small, dark, and elegant. Why else would I
run to Paris?

I bought the one next to me a second Perrier and left to roam.
Lots of eye candy here and I have a sweet tooth. In fact that's what

put me in the red back home.

"I can't take it anymore," Cat had said to me. "Go play the field. You're always telling me to ask for what I want. I want a woman who wants only me."

So I ran. Give me an ultimatum and I always take the back door. Had a week coming anyway and business was slow.

The brandy warmed me up. Paris had been deluged with rain, and my fantasy for a springtime fling was turning into a wet dream. I meandered past the mirrored dividers at the end of the bar where a cutie was dancing to her own reflection.

"Hey dollbaby, shake that thing," I said to her, watching her red knit mini-dress go to the edge of her sweet thighs and back down. Her hands, covered in red and white polka-dotted gloves, blew circles in the air. She nodded to my reflection in the mirror with a suggestive grin.

Two steps up landed me in the tastefully decorated lounge done in new Art Deco, with grey modular seats and mauve carpet. The walls were alternately black and mirrored. I caught an ottoman in the aisle and ordered a drink. The place was packed.

Oh, visions of Radclyffe Hall, will you look at this! Across from me lounged a couple right out of the 1920s. There sat an aristocratic dyke in tux with short, distinguished grey hair. A princess dressed in a maroon velvet strapless dress graced her right side. Her white chest was festooned in jewels. She reminded me of a young Evita, with thick blond hair pulled back off her forehead. The blond was whispering into the dyke's ear while the other gazed serenely around the room with a flourish of her cigarette holder every now and then. At the end of each sentence, the blond took a deep breath and moved closer against the other's arm. She began to rub her breasts against the dyke with every word, and as she rubbed, her bodice squeezed her breasts dangerously close to the edge. I perched on the ottoman and watched with my head cocked and eyes unfocused so I wouldn't be staring. Then the blond stopped, sat up straight, and they ordered again. What the hell, the night was young and the Katmandou didn't close until sun-up.

I was ready for a little action. Watching the blond had made me conscious of my tight pants. While standing in the aisle, I noticed she was now puffing on a thin fag, sitting too straight in her seat,

138

and pouting an adorable pout. What a handful she must be, I thought, and gladly left the duty to the one in the tux.

Meandering towards the bar, I realized my mini-skirted treasure was no longer dancing in the mirrored entry. I found a circular staircase and an upstairs lounge where the smoke was even thicker, if that was possible. Finally seated in a chair comfortable for my 5'10" self, munching on peanuts with a view of the minuscule dancefloor, I thought about the woman back home. Damn it.

"Lee, you can't stand having it so good," Cat had said, rubbing her breasts, free under her white angora sweater, against me. That's when I named her Cat, Catherine was too long. Well, maybe she was right, and maybe she wasn't. I'm not partial to settling down, getting comfortable.

"I'm not easing into one of those convenience relationships," I warned her. "I like to court and sizzle all the time." That was at the beginning. Before my old habits got the best of us.

What am I doing up here? I jerked myself out of the past and jumped to my feet. I'd never meet anyone while sitting up in an eagle's nest mooning about a woman too far away to count.

From the balcony's view, I saw the unmistakable shake of the red gloves waving like exotic birds over the dancefloor and I decided to try my luck.

I was glad for my height and years of jamming myself into crowded elevators. A small broomstick of a woman tried to snuggle in close but she smelled of alcohol so I managed to pretend I was dancing with the woman in front of me. It wasn't strictly couples. In fact, we were squeezed together so tightly it would take an anthropologist to figure out the relationships.

The gloves circled the middle of the dancefloor as I straddled the edge; progress was slow. The woman in front of me, a Swedish-looking beauty with braids wrapped around a chignon, asked me to speak a little English to her. She must have heard me swear when an overactive dancer kicked me, and marked up my creme suede. Now that I had a goal, however, my impatience soared.

"I am moving towards the middle," I said with as much politeness as I could muster at the moment.

"*Ah oui,*" and she grabbed my hand and pushed her way through the crowd like a pro.

I was too late. The gloves had stopped waving in the air and were fondling a black leather jacket. My cutie was slow dancing with someone to a disco beat. This was serious.

"This is your date?" the Swede asked me with real concern on her face. "Too bad. Perhaps you will find someone else."

I stood and felt my defeat, then I had to admit how good they looked together. About the same size, they could've been sisters, except they were clinging to each other, and grinding. At the end of the selection they didn't stop; they didn't loosen their grip on each other. I tried to look away, checking out possibilities. The tension between these two was so intense, my gaze kept returning almost independently of my desire. I found myself burning when I realized the woman had nothing under her black jacket. She had pulled away for a second to push her long hair behind her and I saw the zipper open to her waist. The red-gloved hand traced the canal from throat to where the zipper waited and the other took her hand. Again they were locked in an embrace so tight I couldn't tell where one started and the other stopped except for the color of their outfits.

No matter what the music played, we all danced the same, a mindless jumping and swaying on our tile of the dancefloor. I noticed others begin to look at "my couple," as I began to think of them. They were making love on the dancefloor. Black leather had her hand squarely on the red knit bodice, cupped on the breast, squeezing and releasing. Red had her head back and all her curls were floating behind her as the other kissed her neck and bare shoulders and the wonderful deep indentation between her collarbones.

Then I noticed the zipper was completely undone, and the black leather jacket was flapping around the red-knit dress. Somehow they managed to stay tightly together so nothing was really showing, but everyone knew.

Even with all the frantic dancing, we could feel the energy pouring out; we could smell the sex. To my right a young punked-out couple with magenta spikes for hair started directing others over by pointing and making swooning looks. A little circle started to form and my couple went right on as if they were alone. The rest of us were panting and waiting for the shudders, the groans, the release, when management broke the spell.

The Europeans have so much finesse. Management strode

over—a large impeccably dressed woman with fists like two foot-balls—and she merely held onto the back of the black leather jacket. She was smiling, but one hand tightly gripped the leather and pulled it upward. Still smiling, saying "*S'il vous plait,*" she started the couple off the dancefloor, as if left to themselves they'd be unable to move. The three glided out of sight, and left the rest of us with the music blasting in the background and an unfinished orgasm raging between our hips.

After another half hour of jarring my body on the dancefloor, I decided to call it a night.

Outside the Katmandou, Sunday dawned in Paris. The buildings stood silent and dark with a patina from centuries of Sundays like this. A happy group of drunk revelers swayed and sang their way to a cafe. I raced and beat a young couple to a cab and instructed the driver to take the long way home, crossing the Seine.

The Bateaux-Mouches' lights reflected on the river and reminded me of a trip I'd taken with Cat, two weeks before my Paris departure. We were driving south, down the California coast, home from a romantic hideaway in Carmel. Cat leaned against me and the velvet tips of her collar nuzzled my neck. Her body blanketed my side with her hand nestling between my thighs. Late at night, the cypress were darker than the sky. For no reason, I felt sad, just as we passed Pismo Beach and those eerie, gold street lights. It was a deep sadness, more than the Sunday night blues. I'd felt lost and alone and far from the crowded, smoky piano bar where we had spent the evening.

Cat soothed and calmed me with her talk and now I realized that I trusted her like I've trusted no one else. Her white hands had rubbed my neck and they were like signposts against the long darkness of my sadness and fear, which had risen so swiftly and without warn-ing. Not that I was like that very often, or wanted to admit it, but that night she wrapped me in her capable hands and helped me feel safe. Just as soon as I'd felt like myself again, the old restlessness had returned and I confessed my plans for Paris.

The driver crossed the bridge with the sun coming up behind the city. God, Paris was beautiful! I wondered what I was doing here alone, with no one but myself to exclaim to in English. We passed the Gare d'Orsay with its round clock and I thought about booking an early flight home and calling Cat. What the hell, we've been through this much together, maybe she'll just shake her head and give me a mega-hug.

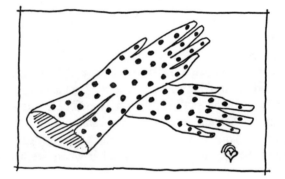

Fantasy

Mamugrandae

The Third Tale

by Merril Mushroom

I am a tall, myopic, middle-aged hot Jewish mama of Ashkenazi Russian heritage. I live in the woods and love writing for lesbians. I am all my characters and am, otherwise, very shy. I wish all of us sweet dreams, whatever they may be, and realities that are individually satisfying.

Mamugrandae

The Third Tale

"**I** am the wild thing!" screamed Vildachaya, reaching for Mamugrandae's hair to grab her by it, but Mamugrandae whirled out of the way.

"So what?" Mamugrandae yelled back. "I can be wild too!" and she roared a terrible roar and gnashed her teeth.

Now Vildachaya really went into a frenzy. She threw her body onto the floor. She flailed her limbs. She screeched and she yelped. She did this until she had finished, and then she stopped.

Mamugrandae was watching her and frowning. "That was the last straw, Vildachaya. I know you are a wild thing, but this is getting ridiculous and a little out of hand. I cannot put up with this fighting any longer. I am going away from here. I will see what I can find."

"Goodbye then," responded Vildachaya, not looking at Mamugrandae. "I shall stay here and see what comes to me." Then she muttered, "I am the wild thing."

"Well," huffed Mamugrandae, "I certainly wouldn't leave my soul with *you* under the circumstances." But she didn't really want to take it with her, either; so she stashed it behind a rock and set out upon her way.

Hum, she thought fretfully, as she crossed the meadow that lay between their home and the road to the forest. *That was a little too easy for my liking. Vildachaya didn't even try to stop me. Well,* she frowned, *if she doesn't want me, then she just can't have me.*

Mamugrandae was so deep in thought that she didn't notice the woman who was sitting by the side of the road until she was almost upon her. Mamugrandae stopped short and stared. The woman was enormous—a giantess, a monolith. She looked like a massive statue roughly carved from granite, great feet and thighs and buttocks sup-

144

porting her breasts, arms, and head. Mamugrandae began to think that she might, indeed, be made of stone, she was so still; but, as Mamugrandae watched, the woman moved. She raised her right hand, tipped her head to the right and said, "Blah, blah, blah." Then she raised her left hand, tipped her head to the left, and said, "Blah, blah, blah." Then she lowered her right hand, tipped her head to the right and said, "Blah, blah, blah," then the left, repeating the cycle over and over.

Mamugrandae watched for a while, but as the woman paid her no mind, Mamugrandae decided to let well enough be and go on her way. She passed in front of the woman and stepped onto the road; and as she did so, with no warning whatsoever, without a sound nor even the flicker of an eyelid, the woman reached down and grabbed Mamugrandae.

Mamugrandae was taken quite by surprise to be suddenly scooped off her feet by such a huge hand, then clasped in the crook of an enormous elbow and pressed against the side of a gigantic breast. *Well,* she thought, *if I must be caught, I could easily be in a worse place than this,* for she was being held gently, and the woman seemed not to mind when Mamugrandae leaned a bit more firmly against·the side of her breast.

Then the woman held Mamugrandae upon both her palms and away from her body. She looked her over slowly, opened her tremendous mouth, and asked in a deep, powerful voice, "Who are you?"

"I am Mamugrandae, and I am beautiful. Who are you, and what, please, are you doing?"

The woman grinned, showing all her teeth. "I am Azeesatookis, and I am doing nonsense. Doing all this nonsense has made me hungry. You are a lovely morsel, so I shall eat you right now!" and she opened her mouth wide and prepared to pop Mamugrandae in.

But Mamugrandae did not have a mind to be disposed of right then, nor in such a manner. "I am no lovely morsel for *your* eating," she said; and she grabbed Azeesatookis' nose in both her hands and tweaked until it was red.

"Ouch!" yelped Azeesatookis. She dropped Mamugrandae who immediately went scurrying away into the underbrush at the other side of the road. By the time the tears of pain had cleared from

Azeesatookis' eyes, Mamugrandae was gone and safe. But Azeesatookis was angry. "You'll be sorry for this!" she bellowed into the forest. "I'll get you for this, Mamugrandae, and I will make you sorry!"

•

Meanwhile, back at the house, Vildachaya was sitting alone and brooding. "Cluck, cluck, cluck," she muttered to herself. "I am who I am, and I will be that." Then she sighed, "but I do miss my Mamugrandae." She leaned back. "However," she commented, "it *is* rather nice to have all this peace and quiet with no one to nag me all the time about the way that I am." Then she sighed again. "Although I must admit that I *am* rather lonely without my Mamugrandae to talk to." About this time there came a knock at the door. "Who's there?" called Vildachaya. She was not particularly interested in getting up to see.

"It is I," a strange voice answered. "Open up and let me in, you wild thing."

Vildachaya sighed one more time. When she went to the door and opened it she gasped with surprise. Standing there was the most beautiful woman she had ever seen. "Who are you?" Vildachaya stammered.

"I am Shaynapunim," the woman replied. Then she turned, and the light from outside seemed to go right through her; her form became indistinct. Vildachaya rubbed her eyes. "Well, are you going to ask me in?" said Shaynapunim.

"Certainly," responded Vildachaya. She moved her head to the side and squinted, peering at Shaynapunim through her lashes. Shaynapunim's form seemed to be flowing, shifting slightly around itself; Vildachaya wondered if her vision might suddenly be deteriorating. She looked over at the trees and the rocks. They appeared clear, firmly outlined, easy to distinguish. Vildachaya wondered, then, if the problem could be with Shaynapunim herself. "Are you disintegrating?" she asked the other woman as politely as she could. "I seem to be having a bit of difficulty differentiating you from your space.

Shaynapunim laughed. "However you experience me, Vildachaya, is exactly how I am. You get what you let come to you."

146

"Well," said Vildachaya petulantly, for she was beginning to feel cross, "that is certainly stated vaguely enough. So, precisely what is your purpose in coming here, such as you are?"

"I have come to help you clarify your desires," Shaynapunim explained.

"Oh you have, have you? You certainly are presumptuous, Shaynapunim, aren't you?"

Shaynapunim smiled slyly. "And where is Mamugrandae?" she asked.

"Oh, um, she's busy right now," replied Vildachaya evasively.

"Where is Mamugrandae?" Shaynapunim repeated.

"None of your business," Vildachaya snapped. It was certainly none of *anyone's* business as far as she was concerned.

"Where is Mamugrandae?" Shaynapunim asked yet again.

Now Vildachaya felt very, very sad. "She has gone," she answered at last, "and I do not know where."

"So what, then, do you want, Vildachaya? What do you really want?"

Vildachaya watched Shaynapunim flicker a moment. She looked down at the ground. She looked at the door to the house. Finally she said in a tiny voice, "I want my Mamugrandae to come back. I want my Mamugrandae here with me." For a moment she was very still. At last she nodded her head decisively. "I shall go and find her," she announced, "and I shall fetch her back!" She roared a terrible roar. She gnashed her teeth and jumped up and down.

Shaynapunim watched her, somewhat amused by her antics. "*Fetch* her back?" she murmured. "You certainly are a wild thing, Vildachaya."

Vildachaya quieted. She looked at Shaynapunim. A large tear filled her eye and rolled down her cheek. "I shall then," she said almost in a whisper, "find her, and with all my heart sincerely request that she return to me."

"Then I wish you all the very best, you wild thing." With these words, Shaynapunim's form shimmered until it seemed to be one with the leaves fluttering on the trees, and then she was gone.

Well, thought Vildachaya, turning up her nose, *that was rather show-offy, I'd say.* But she had liked Shaynapunim, and she forgave her. Carefully closing the door behind her, she stepped outside

147

and set off across the meadow.

•

Meanwhile, Mamugrandae was sitting by a waterfall waiting to achieve peace of mind. She had arrived there some time before, but she was not feeling very much better. *Fooey on Vildachaya,* she thought. *She is just going to have to stop being so wild all the time and give me more space to express myself, too.* Mamugrandae thought and thought, about all the things that Vildachaya was going to have to stop doing and start doing; and the more she thought, the sadder she became. She thought about all Vildachaya's defects and deficiencies, climbing down complaints as though they were the rungs of their relationship, until her considerations took her right down into the pits of her mind; and when she reached the bottom, there was nowhere left to go. Then she held her thoughts quiet, and watched the waterfall.

At last Mamugrandae's mind began to stir again. *Hum,* she thought, *I wonder if perhaps I might at all have been the least bit overly demanding.* The possibility that maybe she herself could have had some part in Vildachaya's displays intrigued her at first; but the more she thought about it, the more she tended to decide that this was not in fact the case. *There is no sense in trying to figure this out alone,* she mused. *I would be much better off going home and dealing with Vildachaya directly.* As soon as she thought about going home, she was overwhelmed by a rush of love for Vildachaya which was swiftly followed by a deep sadness and missing of her; then Mamugrandae knew only that she wanted to be back with the one who loved her enough to send her to find her soul in the first tale, and whom she loved enough to have left it with in the second. "I am what I am, and I have what I have," she said aloud, "and I will want that and love it." And Mamugrandae stood up and turned toward home.

Just then, who should come by but Azeesatookis. She appeared on top of the ridge behind the waterfall and glowered down at Mamugrandae. "Well, well, well," she chortled, "look who's here." Mamugrandae leaped back and made ready to run, but Azeesatookis did not seem at all inclined to give chase. Instead she smiled, almost benevolently. She looked down at something she was holding between her two hands.

"Mamugrandae!" came a shriek. "Help me! Please help me!"

"Quiet!" roared Azeesatookis, closing her hands together.

Mamugrandae frowned. "Azeesatookis," she demanded, "what have you there in your hands?"

Azeesatookis' smile became not very nice at all as she purred, "Why Mamugrandae, don't you know? Can't you tell? I have your soul."

"What? What did you say, Azeesatookis?"

"I have your soul."

"And just where did you get it, Azeesatookis?"

"Oh," Azeesatookis said very casually, "I happened on it behind a stone. 'Could this be Mamugrandae's soul?' I said to myself as I spotted it, 'Why sure enough, it is.' And so, Mamugrandae, I took it; and now I have it."

"Well give it here, Azeesatookis. Give it back to me!"

"Oh no. Of course I shall not."

"And why not, then? Why not?"

"Because I have got it. I took it, and now I shall keep it." And so saying, Azeesatookis clutched Mamugrandae's soul tightly to her breast and casually strolled away.

Now Mamugrandae was the one to give chase. All other thought vanished from her mind. She knew only that Azeesatookis had got her soul, was running off with it, and that she, Mamugrandae, must somehow retrieve it. She must get it back! "Here! Here!" she called. "Return to me my soul! Give it back!" and she chased after Azeesatookis with all her might.

But Azeesatookis was very fast and she knew the forest well. She eluded Mamugrandae. She escaped. Mamugrandae lost all trace of her soul, and she felt a great sore fear happening inside her. Deep in the forest, Mamugrandae wandered aimlessly among the trees. Her soul had been taken and she did not know what to do. Despair filled her, and she sat down on a stump and leaned her face into her hands. She sighed, and she sighed, and she sighed.

"Hello," said a voice nearby. "What's the matter?"

Mamugrandae looked up. Before her stood a woman of medium size and ordinary appearance, but as the woman moved, light seemed to go through her, and her form became indistinct. "Who are you?" Mamugrandae asked, somewhat annoyed at being interrupted from her sighing, especially by so nebulous a figure.

"I am Shaynapunim."

"Well, I am Mamugrandae."

"Yes, I know."

Mamugrandae felt a surge of anger. How dare this stranger know who she was without being told? "Then you must help me," she demanded, deciding that Shaynapunim owed her at least that much, for knowing.

"Oh must I, Mamugrandae?" Shaynapunim replied.

"Yes, you must," insisted Mamugrandae, nodding her head.

"Very well, then. I shall. What must I do to help you?"

"Azeesatookis has taken my soul," said Mamugrandae, and suddenly she began to weep.

"Oh?" Shaynapunim responded, seeming to be not in the least concerned.

Mamugrandae stopped weeping. "What do you mean, 'Oh?'" she said, indignant over Shaynapunim's display of insensitivity.

"Well, so, Azeesatookis has taken you soul. So what?"

Mamugrandae felt her anger rising. "So what? She *has* it, that's so what, and I must get it back!"

"Why?"

"Because it is my soul, and I must have it!"

"Mamugrandae," said Shaynapunim patiently, "do you remember how back in the first tale you went on a quest to find your soul?"

"Yes," shouted Mamugrandae.

"And you succeeded, correct?"

"Yes," agreed Mamugrandae, becoming somewhat calmer.

"Well, once you have found it, it is yours, and it can never be gone from you again."

"You speak nonsense, Shaynapunim," Mamugrandae snapped. "How could it not be gone? Azeesatookis has taken it."

"Souls are peculiar that way," Shaynapunim explained. "In fact, Mamugrandae, you always really had your soul, even before you found it; and when you gave it to Vildachaya, you still kept it. So just because Azeesatookis has got it does not mean that you have lost it."

"I did not give it to Azeesatookis of my own free will,"

Mamugrandae argued. "She took it, and now she has it and I must get it back!"

"And if you do not? What then, Mamugrandae?"

Mamugrandae was quiet for a long while. She thought about this, and the changes that she went through showed on her face. At last she sighed deeply. "I suppose, Shaynapunim, that if such turns out to be the case I will not have it, and I shall just have to give it up." As soon as she said this her head and body felt very light, and a sense of relief filled her. Shaynapunim disappeared.

Just then there was a noise in the underbrush, and who should step into the clearing but Vildachaya. She stopped and stared at Mamugrandae. "Well," she said at last, "there you are, Mamugrandae. I am very glad to see you."

"I am very glad to see you, too, Vildachaya," Mamugrandae admitted, hanging her head just a bit. She swallowed hard. "I missed you."

"I missed you, too, Mamugrandae." Vildachaya swallowed hard also. "I have come to humbly request that you return home."

Mamugrandae felt a trickle of suspicion. "That was very nicely said, Vildachaya, but it is not at all like you. What's this really about?"

Vildachaya felt very awkward and embarrassed. "I came looking for you, Mamugrandae. I came this far to find you and to ask you to come home, and I think you could be a little more receptive to my efforts."

Mamugrandae slowly smiled. "You're right, Vildachaya, and I apologize. I am very glad that you are here," she took Vildachaya by the arm, "and I want to go home again with you."

•

Meanwhile, Azeesatookis was sitting under a tree waiting for Mamugrandae to come after her, so that she could run away again. She placed the slightly tattered soul on her knee, and the soul shook itself and began to fluff up a little. "You wait now," Azeesatookis told the soul. "I am sure that Mamugrandae will be right along after you any time, and then we shall have our merry chase once more." They waited and they waited, but Mamugrandae did not appear.

Azeesatookis decided to take a little snooze. "Maybe Mamugrandae will come upon me while I sleep," she said hopefully, "and then I can awaken just in time, leap up, grab her soul, and run away again." She entertained herself until she fell asleep with sweet thoughts of Mamugrandae chasing her through the forest, begging for her soul, while Azeesatookis kept ahead of her always, strive as she might to reach her.

Finally Azeesatookis awakened again, but there was still no sign of Mamugrandae. "I wonder where she could be," she muttered. She was becoming highly impatient and somewhat frustrated. At last, she stood up. "Come on, soul," she said, perching it on her shoulder. "Let's move around and try to attract her attention." She wandered through the forest, shaking bushes loudly and stamping her great feet to make noise, but no Mamugrandae did appear.

At last Azeesatookis could stand it no longer. "I am terminally bored!" she announced. "This is no fun for me at all, and I may as well be done with it. Come on, soul, I'll take you home." Then she carried the soul back to where she had found it and stashed it behind the stone again.

And when Mamugrandae and Vildachaya happily returned home together, their arms wrapped around each other's waists, they were very glad to see Mamugrandae's soul, right where she had left it.

In the Dark

by Barbara Harwood

Barbara Harwood is a fifty-two year old playwright/actor/director who lives contentedly on the coast of Northern California. This story is her first attempt at writing prose. It is one of a group of similar stories she is writing for a book to be titled: Lesbian Love Scenes.

Barbara graduated from reform school, spent six years working in various factories, worked her way through college, became a relationship counselor, entered the world of theater late in life and is presently finishing the rewrites on a play about Lizzie Borden.

Barbara dreams of a world where the creative genius of each individual is encouraged and financially supported. Most specifically she wants to encourage lesbians to write. Her advice is don't talk about it, don't take a class, don't read a book, just do it. If you have something to say, say it. Only by writing will you become a writer. Trust your own beautifully unique voice and just start putting it down on paper.

In the Dark

Rachel punched in at the time clock and headed for the break room. One more quick cup of coffee before facing those long eight hours. She was already tired and the shift hadn't even started. Working nights and going to school days was becoming a real drag.

Hell, factory life wasn't so bad. She could transfer to days and get some decent sleep—quit the whole business, dump the books, and get on with some civilized living. Photo finishing was, after all, an honorable profession. Nothing wrong with the pay, either. What did she need with a silly piece of paper telling her other people thought she was educated?

It was the envies. She got those goddamed envies, every time she corrected prints of fancy rich folks standing in front of the Eiffel Tower or tooting around in those weird-looking gondolas. Hell, she couldn't even afford to go to Yellowstone, not that she'd want to. Not on your life. Not after seeing four million pictures come through of those stupid tourists feeding the poor bears. Dumb assed tourists! They buy those expensive thirty-five millimeter cameras just so they can go to Europe and take blurry pictures. After a full night of that her lousy little paycheck seemed like the greasy leftovers after the turkey's gone.

•

The coffee was freshly brewed. Her own cup was sitting on the warmer, filled to the brim, and just the right color, telling her that Mara had seen her come in. Rachel smiled warmly. Goddam, there goes another lousy mood down the drain. Seemed like anymore, her mouth would just sort of turn up at the corners when she'd think of Mara. Since Mara joined the work force six months ago they had become good friends—not just good friends—great friends. They never socialized away from work though. Rachel was busy with school and Mara's husband would never tolerate her hanging out with a dyke. Work was where they found time to play and make each other laugh. They had good, warm times together.

Mara was thirty-six. She had two teenage kids. Her cropped brown hair, small framed body, and over-abundance of energy sometimes tricked people into thinking she was close to being a teenager herself. She was a declared Democrat with fantasies of someday being a radical. Just waiting for the kids to get grown, she'd always say.

In contrast, Rachel had never entertained the thought of marriage or children. She was twenty-nine, tall, with the body of a natural athlete, and methodical in the way she dealt with life. She wasn't exactly a Republican, but seemed to suffer from a similar disease of conservative origin.

Rachel sometimes wondered how she and Mara could be so different and yet so close.

•

Rachel turned as she heard Mara come bouncing into the room. "What ya got for eats tonight, you gorgeous broad?"

"Tuna," Rachel answered. "You?"

"Donkey-dink sandwich and a jug of panther piss. Wanna trade?"

Rachel cracked up. She would never get used to the crazy things that spilled from this woman's mouth. "What, no dinosaur dong?"

"That was last night. Can't have the same shit two nights in a row, gives ya brain damage," Mara playfully poked her finger into the dimple she had created in Rachel's cheek.

Rachel quickly moved away, sitting down on the other side of the table. Even though it was just a playful poke, she felt a sense of intimacy that made her uncomfortable. They were close, they cared a great deal, but they had never touched before.

"Oh, we're going to play separate tables, are we?" Mara said teasingly as she moved around the table and started poking Rachel in the ribs.

"Stop it." Rachel laughed nervously as she tried to wriggle away.

"And what will you do if I don't?" Mara began poking her all over.

Enjoying the sensation of Mara's touch, but still wishing she would stop, Rachel pretended playful outrage. "Stop it, you crazy bitch, or I shall leap to my feet and ravage your sweet body."

"You and what army?" Mara said, standing back with her legs spread, hands on hips, her small breasts thrust forward.

Rachel was caught off guard for a moment as her eyes focused on Mara's firm nipples pressing though her T-shirt. "Ah hah! So it's armies you want now."

"That'll do for starters," Mara teased, as she began to strut around the room, her back to Rachel.

Rachel, now potently focused on Mara's firm round buttocks, joined in the teasing, "How about a whole Amazon nation? Would that satisfy your wanton lust?"

Mara stopped dead, turned slowly, and looked with unflinching seriousness into Rachel's eyes. "How about just one Amazon?"

Rachel wanted to stop playing. Mara was not playing fair. She had never challenged Rachel or come on to her before. Mara was straight. Rachel had a hard and fast rule: no affairs with straight women; the complications were always devastating, the responsibility monumental. And besides, you could get a social disease.

Mara stood staring seductively, demanding a response. "Well?"

Rachel sat for a moment, totally confused, not knowing what to say. "I..."

The loud piercing sound of the work bell chopped into Rachel's reply. Relief filled her voice as she said, "I think we better get to work."

Mara couldn't help grinning as she noticed Rachel's relief. "Saved by the bell, you turkey." She walked out the door and into the main plant.

Rachel grinned and followed.

•

Normally, Rachel and Mara spent most of their shift working across from each other at the print inspection table. They could seldom resist the temptation to play while they worked. Sometimes they created little comedy routines that kept the rest of the crew in stitches. At their very best they would make up crazy songs about the management. The fun and games never interfered with work though. They were the best print inspectors in the plant.

Rachel was relaxing into the rhythm of the work, enjoying the constant visual stimuli as prints of flowers, deer, cathedrals, babies, sunsets, and families passed before her trained eyes. A color correction there, a density correction here, the work was easy and allowed for lots of free mental energy.

She began to reflect on what had happened in the break room, feeling the ambivalence of pleasure and concern, as she remembered the look in Mara's eyes. It was confusing. She didn't know what had caused Mara to make this sudden change in their relationship. Had she inadvertently done something to cause it? No! Rachel was always careful to blunt her sexual energies around straight women. But what about the times when Mara would stand or sit very close to her, always brushing against her as they passed? Sometimes she would catch Mara watching her. Rachel had never thought much about these potential intimacies. But now, she realized, they had been happening more and more often. Like how Mara always seemed to reach across her for the cream or sugar during break, her breasts almost brushing Rachel's face.

Suddenly a paper clip hit the side of her face. Looking up, she saw Mara prepared to throw another. "Are you solving the problems of the universe?" Mara asked.

"No, just thinking about a paper I have to write when I finish work," Rachel lied.

"Well, you better adjust your automatic cutter, you just chopped up half a role of prints."

Rachel looked to her left and saw the prints in a pile with neat slices through the middle. "Oh shit, shit, shit!" she exclaimed loud enough for the whole plant to hear.

"Quiet down," warned Mara. "You want Lady Stinkum to see what you've done?"

Rachel couldn't help grinning. Only Mara would have the daring to refer to the plant manager as "Lady Stinkum," even though it was true. That rancid ancient perfume she embalmed herself in was enough to gag a maggot. It came in handy though, you could always smell her coming.

Rachel threw the prints away and made out a repeat order to send back to the printer. She knew that Mara must have been watching her again. She felt uneasy as she resumed her work. She finished three print orders and then glanced up at Mara.

Mara was staring right at her. Rachel instantly pulled her eyes back to her work, then stole a quick glance up to see Mara still watching. The bold little bitch! Rachel decided she'd stare her down. She raised her head and looked directly into Mara's eyes. But her plan backfired; Mara didn't look away. She kept her gaze steady and increased the intensity as she allowed Rachel to look into her private thoughts. What Rachel saw was clearly more than friendship. The wanting that was there seared into Rachel's senses and she felt a warmth flood through her body. God damn this woman! What was she doing?

The intensity of desire that Mara's look was building in her was more than Rachel could handle in such a public place. "I've gotta go pee," she announced as she stood up and headed for the bathroom.

When she got back, Mara wasn't at her work station.

•

At least two hours passed before Mara returned and sat down to work. "Where've you been?" Rachel asked.

"Stinkum sent me back to run the printer," Mara replied. Then, teasingly, "Saved your hide, didn't she?"

"You keep this up and you're the one who's going to need saving," Rachel retorted.

"What if I don't want to be saved," Mara said, looking at Rachel with even more seductive fury than before.

Rachel spoke to Mara with a serious sense of concern, "Damn it, Mara, do you know the kind of fire you're playing with?"

Mara spoke with clear and serious intent. "I know I'm not playing...and as for the fire..."

Just then Stinkum came into the room and asked Rachel to go to work at the printer. Rachel didn't respond. She was momentarily stunned by Mara's statement. Stinkum had to tell her again.

•

Sitting at the printer, Rachel's thoughts returned to her earlier concerns and confusions. What in hell was she going to do about this? Bad enough that Mara was coming on to her, but much worse that she was being turned on by it.

She made up her mind to find a private place during break where she and Mara could talk.

She settled down to accomplish the volume of work she was capable of. She took pride in the fact that she was good at everything she did. In no time at all she had finished a hundred roll batch and was ready to take them to the darkroom for chemical processing.

Rachel hated the color darkroom. It was jet black, not like the black and white ones where at least you had a dull red light to see by. In color, any kind of light would ruin the prints. To prevent any possibility of a light leak, there was a strict routine for entering. You opened the first door, closed it, then opened the second and entered quickly in case someone else accidentally opened the first.

It was damned spooky being in that dark place, your entire focus on getting the print paper connected to the conveyer without getting your fingers pinched. It made you feel totally vulnerable. Dave, one of the guys in Processing, sometimes got his kicks by hiding in the darkroom and scaring the shit out of everyone. He only did it to Rachel once. She'd reached out instinctively and slapped him across the face. He'd learned quick.

•

Rachel entered the darkroom with her usual sense of dread. Moving quickly to the left, her hands reached out blindly to find the feeder end of the conveyer. She began to connect the roll of paper with quick, sure movements. She didn't want to be in there any longer than she had to.

Just as she was close to finishing, she heard the door click and knew someone had come in. "Who's there?" she asked warningly, as much for the other person as for herself.

No answer.

"Dave, if that's you, just remember my hand's real good at finding your head in the dark."

Still no answer.

"Dave, I better hear your voice damn quick, you son-of-a-bitch!"

Again no answer.

Rachel could sense that someone was moving toward her. She couldn't turn around because her hands were engaged in finishing the paper connection. If she let go now it would all go through crooked and ruin the work, so she just focused on refusing to be scared. She wouldn't give that asshole the satisfaction of hearing her scream when he touched her.

159

"It's me," Mara said quietly.

Rachel jumped slightly but breathed a sigh of relief. "I'll be through in a minute."

"No need to hurry," Mara said as she moved closer.

"It's OK. I'm almost done. But you'll have to use the other conveyer. This one's full."

"I didn't come in here to mount prints," Mara whispered seductively. "I've come to ravage your body."

Rachel thought she was joking until she felt Mara's body pressing up against her. The pressure of that small, taut body against her back told her this was no joke. Mara's arms slowly and deliberately circled her. Rachel's knees grew weak as the intensity of arousal spread through her body. "I'm almost through..."

"I want you," Mara whispered huskily as her hands moved to cup Rachel's breasts.

Rachel moved away a few steps but was stopped by the wall. "I can't," she whispered futilely as Mara pressed with more intensity.

Rachel could hardly breathe as long-denied feelings came surging to life. This couldn't be happening, Mara was straight! They were just friends. But the warmth and passion building in her forced the veil of denial away. It was true. She had always wanted Mara, maybe even loved her.

"Yes..." she said in surrender as she turned to embrace her friend whom she now desired with her whole being.

Mara's hands moved up to Rachel's face, pulling it down to where their lips could meet. "God how I love you," she said as her mouth reached passionately for Rachel's. Their bodies pressed together in a special, sensuous rhythm as the passion of their kissing intensified. All thought of where they were or who might come in was driven from their consciousness by the frenzied passion that was building between them.

Rachel's hands began stroking Mara's body, touching everywhere with a sense of urgent pleasure, discovering the hills and valleys and secret indentations. Little moans came from Mara each time Rachel's hands touched a special place. Rachel could smell Mara's wetness. She yearned to touch it, though she feared she would faint if she did.

Mara must have sensed her desire. She took Rachel's hand and pressed it firmly to her crotch. Rachel could feel Mara's trusting wetness through the cloth of her pants. She began to move her hand sensuously against the cloth, enjoying the excitement that a barrier sometimes inspires. Her hand moved more frantically as excitement mounted. The barrier became intolerable.

"I need to touch you," she whispered desperately into Mara's ear. "I need to be inside you."

Mara fumbled quickly with the zipper of her pants. Rachel expertly slid her hand into the private place, her fingers warmly enveloped by Mara's wet labia. Mara moaned deeply as Rachel's finger began to move lovingly in and out. She moved excitedly against Rachel's thrusting, her movements punctuated with deep, guttural moans.

Rachel drew in her breath as Mara reached for the front of her blouse and ripped it open, her mouth searching frantically for the tip of Rachel's breast. Finding it, she sucked it in greedily. Rachel had rarely felt such a powerful sensation. She wanted to feed this woman her life's milk. She wanted Mara to drink from her until she was empty.

Suddenly they froze as they heard the door click. Someone was entering the darkroom.

Both women trembled as they stood absolutely still and held their breathing to a minimum. Who the hell was it? Slowly a familiar smell greeted their nostrils. They both had to stifle a laugh as Lady Stinkum moved toward the conveyer. They could hear the tearing of paper. Rachel must have mounted the paper crooked and Stinkum had seen it when it came through the wall into the light.

Moments went by. It seemed like it was taking her forever to fix it. Typically, Rachel's nose began to itch, but she was afraid to move. Just as she thought she couldn't stand it any longer, she could hear Stinkum moving away toward the door. At the same time she felt Mara's hand finding and teasing the nipple on her breast. What in God's name did this crazy woman think she was doing? Rachel grabbed Mara's hand and held it firmly. The door clicked and they had the room to themselves.

"You bold little bitch," Rachel breathed lovingly into Mara's ear. "You trying to get us fired?"

"Fired up, my dear woman, fired up," Mara whispered back.

Rachel felt herself begin to melt again. "We've gotta get out of here."

"Only if we go someplace else," Mara said seductively. "I'm not through with my ravaging."

Just then the dinner bell rang.

"You go out first," Rachel said. "I'll wait two minutes and then leave. I'll meet you in the parking lot."

"What about your blouse?"

"What about it?"

"Well, my dear woman, it seems that some little cunt tore all your buttons off in a frenzy of passion."

"Oh God!" Rachel's mind raced for an answer. "If anyone notices I'll tell them I got it caught on the conveyer.

"Sounds like a cover-up to me," Mara teased, as she ran her fingertips gently across Rachel's lips. "I love you," she said as she moved away toward the door.

•

When Rachel entered the parking lot she saw Mara sitting in her car. Rachel opened the door and slid into the driver's seat. "Where to?" she asked.

"Sure as hell not my house," Mara teased, "though it might be fun to make love under the bed while my dear husband snores his life away."

Rachel didn't like Mara making reference to her husband. She didn't want to be reminded. She didn't want to think about anything except where they could go to be alone together. "We could go to my house," she said, "but it's a half-hour drive. We'd just get there and have to come back."

"So let's not come back," Mara said as she began stroking Rachel's leg.

"Oh sure, you really mean that, don't you?" Rachel countered. "You really want to get us fired?"

"We could say we had a flat tire," Mara pleaded as she let her hand rest warmly on Rachel's crotch.

"Now that's original." Rachel laughed nervously as she worried that someone might notice. "OK, maybe we say we got stuck in the mud and couldn't call 'cause there wasn't any phone."

"Sounds great," Mara said as she pushed her hand up inside

162

Rachel's blouse. "Now start the car and let's get out of here."

•

Stepping inside the front door, Rachel reached to turn on the lights but Mara quickly put a hand to her arm and stopped her. "Don't," she said. "We do very nicely in the dark."

Rachel removed Mara's hand and pressed the palm to her lips. They embraced slowly, gently, enjoying the feeling as their passion began to rekindle this passion that did not obey any rules about straight women. Mara pressed the fullness of her body into Rachel's. She began to nuzzle her face inside the torn blouse, while rubbing the side of her cheek sensuously against Rachel's breast. Reaching to pull the blouse off, she dropped it to the floor, her hands trailing down to unzip Rachel's pants, pulling them down below her hips.

Rachel stood still, enjoying the sensations moving through her body as Mara continued to pleasure her. Her burning crotch begged for Mara's touch.

Mara knelt to pull Rachel's pants to her ankles and helped her step out of them. She wanted Rachel completely nude. That done, she pressed the side of her face against Rachel's soft, silken public hairs. Rachel pressed herself forward against Mara's face just as Mara turned her head and opened her mouth to received the soft fullness of Rachel's vulva. Mara's tongue expertly stroked as if she'd been a lesbian all her life, exploring sensuously and deliberately, making little moans as she went.

Rachel's body surged with excitement. She fell back against the wall for support as she moved quickly toward climax. Too soon! Too soon! She grabbed Mara's hair and gently pulled her to a standing position. "Together," she said, as she began pleasuring herself in removing Mara's clothing. She didn't rip the blouse, but slowly undid one button at a time, making herself wait making Mara wait. Unzipping the pants, she knelt and pulled them off. She remained there, pulling Mara down to her.

Rachel's lips pressed warmly against Mara's neck, nibbling their way to her mouth. She ran the tip of her tongue across Mara's soft lips, teasing them open. Rachel's tongue entered Mara, whose body responded instantly. "God, how I want you," Mara sighed as she pulled her mouth away, lay down, and pulled Rachel onto her.

Rachel's mouth searched for the succulent part of Mara's breast. Her tongue stroked it quickly as her hand reached down between Mara's legs. Mara groaned and thrust herself hard against Rachel's hand, forcing the fingers into that soft, wet, love place. Rachel's own excitement matched Mara's. As she thrust her fingers wildly, she could feel Mara building toward climax. Mara moaned as she pushed Rachel's finger out of her. "Together," she pleaded.

"Together," Rachel said as she gently positioned herself over Mara, taking care to make sure their bodies touched in all the right places. Mara began to move rhythmically and sensuously as Rachel pressed down on her with matching movements; their bodies began to act as one, bonding in that special way that only happens when there is deep-felt love.

A sense of warm, liquid gold washed over them as their bodies spilled into each other. A cry of ecstasy came from Mara's lips and her eyes filled with tears as she experienced the fullness of her first complete sense of loving, and being loved.

•

The sheets were cold and soothing on their hot bodies. They lay on their sides in the moonlight, holding hands and looking into each other's eyes just like young innocents.

"I've wanted you from the first moment we met," Mara said.

"From the very first moment?" Rachel questioned teasingly.

"Well, maybe the second," Mara teased back.

"I never knew," Rachel admitted.

"I didn't want you to know. I just wanted to enjoy the feelings, the fantasies. I thought that would be enough."

"But it wasn't?" Rachel said, smiling.

"It was until I realized I was in love with you."

"And when was that?" Rachel asked, pretending disbelief.

"This morning, at six forty-five." Mara grinned.

They both laughed with the wild and free pleasure of it.

"What're we going to do?" asked Rachel.

"I don't know," Mara answered. "I just know I'm not going to give you up."

"And I'm not willing to share you," Rachel said firmly.

"Then we'll just have to run away together," Mara teased.

"You'd leave your husband?"

"You dear, wonderful woman," Mara said reassuringly, "the moment I first touched your body I left my husband."

Rachel suffered a moment of breathless pleasure as she experienced the love that emanated from Mara's eyes.

"What about your kids?" Rachel asked.

"They can come or stay. They're old enough that I'll respect whatever choices they need to make."

Rachel had one last moment of disbelief. "Are you sure you really want...?"

Mara's lips pressed against hers with a quick, tender kiss, cutting off her words. "I'm sure of the want, my darling woman, I'm just not clear about the how. Now let's go to sleep. I have to tell you that one of my finer fantasies has been waking up in your wonderful arms." She pressed a gentle kiss against each of Rachel's eyelids as she rolled onto her side and pulled Rachel's arms around

Rachel fell asleep, feeling loved, and wondering about the beautiful futility of making hard and fast rules.

Surprise

by Estrella Root

Estrella Root is a healer who wears many hats. As a word artist, she offers her writing as a balance to life and the destruction on our Mother Earth. As a performer, she heals the ravages of the dysfunctional patriarchal family thru her songwriting and music. She is also a closet channel. (Look for her to come out soon around these psychic transmissions from the Star Beings!)

The piece included here is an excerpt from a work in progress entitled The Dinosaurs Could Come Back, *which is a hopeful blend of nuclear humor and peace activist cheerleading for our troubled times.*

Let visions of a peaceful future dance in your head!

Surprise

The day the men disappeared was certainly a turning point in the whole thing.

We woke up one morning and check it out! They were gone. No notes of sweet goodbye; no trace of them anywhere. And just when we were calling around and figuring out that this was a universal predickament, a ghost-like rainbow presence on the tv announced in its smooth calm genderless voice that extra-terrestrial forces had intervened on behalf of our survival.

Yes indeedy, they had removed the warlike element of the population—all males over ten—to another solar system to be deprogrammed to a more pacific nature. We would have to make do without them for awhile.

This left us wondering what to do next; we were alone on the planet. Well, not exactly alone. There were millions left with the world in our hands. But these were hands used to labor, not authority.

First, we had to deal with an attempted coup on the part of the older white american boys, But it was quickly snuffed by their mothers and sisters who said, *Wait a minute! You can't even clean your room and you want to run the world?*

The lesbians, who were the last to find out that the men were gone, were also the first to act. While the other women were weeping and wailing, the womanly-oriented were drinking mineral waters and celebrating and having meetings about what to do next. When some of the more politically astute hetero sisters discovered this, they crashed the meetings and included themselves in the proceedings. From then on, all the women worked together. The wives of the former rulers and such females who had connived their way into the circles of the former male elite were small in number and deflated in spirit, so opposition to the social changes initiated by the broader consensus of women was easily dispatched.

As the real work of creating a new peaceful world began in earnest, the new rulers, finding themselves in charge of all institutions, proceeded to abolish them.

The women decided against capitalism and communism and all male philosophies, in favor of a practical, democratic and consensual approach, based within small regional councils that emphasized communication and coordination. The morning coffee clatch or tea time became the main gathering of energies, where women decided what needed to be done and the priorities, etc. Then, after a nutritional breakfast, everyone just went out and did it. It was amazing, all that could be accomplished with just a little cooperation and elbow grease.

At first many of the women were holding some resentments for the lesbians, presumably because most of them had been celebrating when the non-lesbians were weeping and wailing. But after a few weeks, most everybody could start to see their point.

Yes, after a while, those lesbians began to look real good—so handsome and intelligent—as the general tone in society transformed from mourning to conscious appreciation of the present. Peace on earth was well worth celebrating and it was quite clear that the new and good could not have happened without the absence of a certain element and the presence of another.

It was the feminists' finest hour. And the lesbians did have a slight edge: their previous knowledge of sexual independence, which grew less and less esoteric with time.

The younger boys were not enjoying the implications of growing older and having no models to follow, so they elected to join the others in the deprogramming place. Though this made the mothers and sisters sad, the aliens explained it was all for the best. Plus, the population being cut in half and a more egalitarian social system had instantly relieved the world from hunger, a problem that never returned.

But this made it even more imperative that this parthenogenesis business (that some radical lesbians had been yammering about for many years) really get into gear. And some sisters did focus on doing it, until the danger of species extinction from population dwindle blessedly disappeared.

Dividing ovum with sheer energy did limit the making of babies, however. So more of the earth returned to wilderness, the animals flourished, and the plants grew abundantly in the new eden.

With all these improvements, the men and boys were not missed so much as at the beginning. Still, the women resolved to welcome them back with open arms and hearts and integrate them into the new world whenever they returned.

But no one knew when that would be. They weren't due until the whole lot could come back together, after the most severe cases had been brought to awareness. Thus it might take awhile.

And nobody was holding their breath. Running the world was a pleasure, actually.

Love Letters

by Suzanne Zuckerman

Working as an actress and teacher of English, Suzanne Zuckerman has traveled throughout Europe, the Middle East and Northern Africa, but she always returns to the rent stabilized Brooklyn, NY apartment from which she cannot afford to move. For the past two years she has been working on the collection of short stories of which Love Letters *is a part. Naturally, she looks forward to the adulation, fame and fortune that will be forced upon her after its publication.*

Love Letters

My Darling Rosemary,

June at last! The end is in sight! I know this will seem the longest month in recorded history. Jim Miles has a calendar on which he counts down the days. Crass, but effective. The kids don't even know enough to find it insulting.

The staff thinks I'm terribly diligent writing full lesson plans this late in the term. They don't realize I'm actually communing with the holder of my heart.

Darling, I miss you terribly! I don't expect you to write every day, but I long to know how you are. You've been gone three weeks! I realize the people of California need to know your televised predictions for the future, but I need to know what you're doing in the present. I will try not to write again until you do. If I send fewer letters will you send more?

It's been the usual sort of day. An aide interrupted my first class for me to read—and sign to prove I had read—a notice directing the staff not to interrupt classes in progress.

Third period, my most polite student—the only one who can read at grade level—was taken through the halls in handcuffs by two burly cops; she's about 4'3" and skinny. It seems she was carrying a knife that her mother gave her. If I had a child that had to come here I'd give her a shotgun!

Joe, nineteen years old, fifth grade reading level on a good day with the wind behind him (I don't expect you to remember when I'm so anxious to forget), discovered he was in imminent danger of passing his classes and possibly graduating. He immediately removed all his clothes.

As none of the other students found this an attractive enough activity to join in, I shall not count it against him. Why should the

171

Board of Education provide two more years of entertainment when he tells me he has a VCR at home?

I have another swell evening planned at the laundromat. Edna, Joan and I are becoming a regular threesome. I'd be surprised if the neighbors haven't begun whispering. The only good thing about your absence is I've finally been able to empty the hamper.

I found a pair of your socks near the bottom. (No, I'm not wearing your clothes, although I would if I could fit into them; they'd make me feel less abandoned!) One had a hole, so I imagine you left them on purpose. You know I'll have them darned and cleaned in time for your homecoming (which can't be too soon for me!)

Lea left a message on the machine; she's found someone to sublet our apartment. She's determined to get your occult sensitivity into that cottage of hers which, ghost or no, sounds like heaven—organic garden, grassy meadows, running brooks, pine forests, no near neighbors. Let me know what you want to do! Summer is coming tra la, tra la!

Of course my mother wants us to keep her company in Huntington. She'd prefer to have me alone, but knows I'll hang up if she says so—I remind her regularly that even though you're not a doctor you are my first "nice Jewish girl."

She called at dawn this morning, having waited for daylight in deference to your comments during our only visit, and I picked it up because you weren't here to tell me not to! She intoned the weather report—hot, hotter, hottest—and reminded me that my father let the ledgers of the the Long Island Railroad work him into an early grave so I could have an air-conditioned childhood.

She says she's lonely, but I begin to agree with you that it has become both her choice and her habit.

I don't want to pressure you. But I'd be happy to come to San Francisco. As an ex-hippy, I've often regretted not making the pilgrimage to the Mecca of Flower Power that would guarantee me a hereafter at the feet of Baba Rum Ball.

I love you. I adore you. I need you. I want you. I'm told TV stations in New York City are just as nice as those in San Francisco!

Kiss, Kiss, Kiss, Kiss, Kiss, Kiss, Kiss, Kiss, Kiss, Kiss,

Laura

•

June 9

Sweetest Rosemary Dear,

Hearing your voice on the phone was a joy and a torment. How can I listen without wanting you near enough to touch? To hold? To kiss? To stroke? You know where we go from there—don't tell me you've forgotten.

Lea's friend's name is Mary. She lives upstate near our haunted cottage but wants to spend this summer in The Big Apple. The possessor of a recently broken heart, she's confused higher population density with greener pastures. I liked her enough to warn her about New York's famous muggy heat that seems to generate muggy smells and muggers. Somehow I didn't convince her.

Outside of this strange obsession, she seems a lovely and responsible person. She promises to take good care of my plants. She brought written references!

We made a solemn ceremony of it. I put the "Trumpet Voluntary" on the ghetto blaster, and sitting at the oak table we passed the papers from hand to hand. Mary signed our lease and wrote me a check, which I signed over to Lea after signing her lease.

It was, of course, necessary to use an official signature pen—I retrieved your forgotten bon voyage gift. The reversible naked ladies were deemed most appropriate. (If I send it to you will you use it?) Then we shared that bottle of champagne I bought for our second anniversary before I found out you wouldn't be here. A lovely time was had by all!

The kids are enjoying end of term fun too. There was a riot on the fifth floor. Someone figured out how to hit the hall fixtures and shatter the tubes. It rained fluorescent glass for fifteen minutes before security arrived—where do they hide? My students were desperate to join in the fun. I put my body in front of the door then regretted the effort. Amazingly, no one was hurt or caught.

I continue the daily business of filling out green and yellow forms, dotting the computerized attendance sheets, writing up official complaints, all the while knowing I'll pass any kid who came and made an effort. Of course, those seventeen or older who read at a sixth grade level and don't drive me crazy pass automatically. Look into my chart and tell me why I'm doing this.

No, don't bother, I don't really care. School gets out in two weeks and your return makes everything else unimportant.

I know you're disappointed that "Astrology On The Air" didn't live up to its potential. But it was only a two month contract. Whether your appearances were too brief to be adequate indicators or your air time was disadvantageous, there's nothing you can do and no reason to blame yourself for not being extended. Even the most scientifically correct charts offer only possibilities; how much more accurate can a Nielson rating be?

I, as a poll of one, will be delighted to have you home. (Did you notice that I have not written for over a week? It's been very difficult and I want my restraint to be appreciated.) Let me know the day and time—leave a message on the machine, I'm spending the weekend at Mom's—I'll meet you at the airport.

I embrace you with my astral body while awaiting your flesh.

Laura

•

July 4

Darling Rosemary,

The cottage is everything we've hoped; I can hardly wait for you to see it! (I can hardly wait to see you!) We have two large rooms and an attic loft furnished in early flea market, with views of wild flowers, trees, and water.

You will not believe the garden! Lea must have planted it three months ago. There are vegetables that even the strictest lezzie-veggie would be hard pressed to identify. Our rental obligations include eating as many as possible!

I arrived around four yesterday, Independence Day traffic being anything but free! But emptying the car went so easily it was as if half the things moved themselves. After that endless drive any change of activity was bound to be a delight.

Actually, I guess there wasn't all that much in the car. Towels and dishes and all that survival stuff, the very best quality of mis-matched church bazaar, were promised in our lease. So although I boxed up all our breakables—not because I don't trust our tenant, but I wanted to avoid any problems beginning with "Ooops!"—I took

174

only my clothes and toiletries, some books and tapes and staples I didn't expect to find growing in the garden.

I opened your closet and was surprised to discover there was nothing of yours to pack. Of course you need all your summer things in sunny California. When you arrive here I expect to confront some serious laundry! The choice will be between dropping it into the nearest washing machine, which is about seventeen miles as the roads meander, or beating it in our stream, which is abundantly supplied with rocks.

The windchime has suddenly gone mad. It is sending out a jangle reminiscent of that awful class trip to the piano factory. Most of the time it's soft and lovely with a haunting echo-like quality, very soothing. I've searched briefly but haven't located it—probably up in some tree and hidden by the leaves. If this racket occurs with any regularity I'll have to remove it! For now I shall escape by relocating to the hammock by the lake.

This is one of the absolute glories of our new home: a moss floored grove perfect for morning Yoga and close enough to the water for a rewarding swim after meditating. If we walk around our private cove to the dock, which is really a half beached float where the sunfish is tied, we can see the town pier. Perhaps I can sail our wash to the laundromat? There's supposed to be a regatta and fireworks tonight.

Of course my private celebration takes the form of this letter. I just wish you could be here before it reaches San Francisco.

Your post card was wonderful, although I'm surprised they let that kind of picture go through the mails! After all these weeks without any communication I was beginning to suspect that being on television was having the same effect on your writing skills as watching it has on my students'! Delighted as I was to read that you're enjoying "California's beautiful sun and sand," it's your schedule that I really need! (You'll love the "beautiful sun and sand" here, too—and I'll love sharing it with you!) I wish you'd called before I left the city. Now you'll have to write or telegraph when you're arriving because

Please excuse the punctures! (I didn't nibble the page—I'm

saving that for you!) The breeze snatched this sheet. And only my highly developed pedagogical agility and the thorn on a well placed bramble made retrieval possible.

I was about to admit to a horror that you'll fear far more than any ghost—we have no phone! The prodigious expense of running a line this far off the main road proved prohibitive.

No there is no electricity, either. Heat comes from the back to back stone fireplaces that form the center piece for each of the rooms. They are the perfect height for butch posturing; elbow on the mantle, shot glass in hand. There were lovely fires laid and ready to burn when I arrived.

Replenishing the wood pile will undoubtedly build better muscles than your Bloomie barbells. Kerosene lamps provide surprisingly decent illumination. The oil must be scented because the smell of flowers intensifies during the night. Everything here is charming; I know you'll love it.

Charm does not equal a lack of indoor plumbing! In our spacious bathroom stands a tub big enough for two (hint, hint) on ball mounted, splayed claws. There's even enough hot water to satisfy your sybaritic dissipation!

Huge propane canisters feed the heater tank and, although you'll probably never touch it, the stove. In case of storms, which I'm told are dramatic, we'll be in better shape than those who depend on wires that are frequently blown down.

If I can manage, and you know how I hate change, you'll adore it.

To tell you the truth, coming here alone made me terribly apprehensive. If the apartment weren't sublet I think I would have waited for you. The idea of the ghost was particularly unattractive. Your interest in honing your psychic abilities (and my trust that they were quite sharp enough already) constituted the only reason I considered occupying a haunted house.

Fortunately, our ghost turns out to be rather shy. I waited up for her last night but she pulled a no show. Actually, this lovely book on local history fell at my feet when I removed the fireplace matches from the shelf. I started reading and had no idea how late it had become until I noticed the logs had become embers.

According to the book, this is an absolutely marvelous area, full of the follies of private politics and legends left to us by Native Americans—the book calls them Indians.

Our particular ghost is described as a young woman named Constance. She and her fiance were building their future home on this site in March of 1843. She wandered off in search of early wild flowers and died in the woods because of an unexpected blizzard.

Noted for being not only benign, but helpful, Constance is credited by various individuals and groups for saving their lives. There are also testimonials to her abilities as a match maker. Too bad she didn't come by for an introduction; the dancing flames created the perfect environment in which to view a ghost.

Of course they also offer a perfect environment for romance! Dearest, I'm expecting you next week at the latest. Please let me know when. If you don't, I'll summon a medium to call on Constance's much touted skills!

There go those chimes again. What a racket! Even at this distance they are impossible. I'll have to go and try to do something about them now!

> I LOVE YOU,
> Laura

•

July 28

Rosemary Dearest,

We seem to be suffering from role reversal. I have read your two lovely letters. The first was such a sad postmortem on "Astrology On The Air" that I expected you on the next red eye! Instead I received your astonishing second letter a mere two days later.

And here it is more than two weeks and I've had no time to answer them! I don't know where my time goes. I'm amazed to realize that I've neglected to send so much as a postcard wishing you luck on the radio! My days melt in a swirl of activities. It is only the rain disrupting my schedule that gives me the time to write today. I can honestly tell you I don't think I've ever had such a wonderful summer. And I'm sorry that you're missing it.

I have fulfilled my intention of doing Yoga first thing every morning! The grove where I practice is so lovely that I feel deprived being indoors today, although I was very good and did not take advantage of this perfect excuse to skip. Often I arrive and discover flower petals on the moss. Occasionally a whole bud or bloom on an intact stem will be caught in the bark of the tree where I like to meditate. These bits of color are particularly lovely in this wooded place. As there are no nearby gardens or even wildflowers, this is obviously a trick wind.

Rather like the storm gusts which are now rattling the wind chimes with an ear splitting determination I haven't heard in weeks. Not only have I not been able to locate them but Lea wrote that as far as she knows they don't exist! She claims she never put them up nor has she ever heard them! She suggests it's the ghost.

I believe the ghost is a lot of wishful thinking! If you were here you would probably feel we rented under false pretenses. The summer's practically half over and she has not shown herself even once! Maybe if the storm continues into the night there will be a sudden brilliant flash of lightning that reveals a slender female form racing for cover against the violence of the wind driven rains.

To continue my usual day, after meditating I swim and dress. If I need anything or have a laundry to do, I sail across the lake to the town pier. On weekends, when the day trippers clot up the roads, it's faster than driving; mostly I enjoy it. And having a purpose reduces my sense of riding a toy boat in a bathtub.

When I return I prepare lunch and clean up the house or yard. Although I save energetic activities like chopping wood (can't wait to show you my biceps) and weeding for the sunlit evening hours when it's cooler, there is always lots to do here.

I've cleaned out the root cellar and begun canning. Lea deserves to share the incredible bounty of her garden. Some of the local dykes, friends Lea asked to keep an eye on us, have taught me how to make jelly with wild apples and berries.

We had a gala picnic and picking party. I developed a knack for finding the fattest, ripest berries—following paths suggested by the breeze. As I was the only single, the others teased me saying I must have charmed a wood sprite.

Most of the time I'm alone here, but I am never lonely. I love walking through the woods and often wander for hours.

After watching a spider, I've started an immense weaving project out of grasses and bits of wood. As I discover interesting or beautiful natural objects I add them to my creation.

This week I invited two couples to dinner. It came close to being a disaster. Everything was steaming or baking when I suddenly realized I had no tamari. We don't use it but in this neighborhood, among the veggie-lezzie set, soy sauce flows like beer. There was not time to drive to town and no phone to request a loan from one of the guests.

I was testing out the better excuses—it evaporated, the dog ate it, the ghost shampooed her hair with it—and considering the ultimate sin of using, oh no, horror of horrors, fate worse than death, SALT, when a high corner cabinet creaked open to reveal a single bottle standing like a jeweled scepter in a museum case. My dinner was a great success! Only your presence could have improved it.

Of course, I realize a syndicated radio program of your own is an improvement over a slot on someone else's local TV show! And, of course, I wish you all the luck in the world. But I am wondering if being national, perhaps, it would be possible (eventually) for you to broadcast from New York? That is if you intend to come home? Do you? I would like to know.

> Love,
> Laura

•

August 19

Dear Rosemary,

Your radio success is wonderful! I have been using precious battery power to listen. It was sweet of you to include a special "hello" just for me. It made me realize I should let you know that although the romantic prediction you made for my sign is true, you are no longer the partner to whom my chart refers.

I should have written sooner.

Like the last time I wrote, it is raining. This is not the first storm since then, but your show encouraged me to make time to respond. You know that I loved you. I wanted you and missed you. But your long silences, your empty closet, your urging that I come here while you stayed in California suggested to my totally non-psychic sensitivities that you were ready to find someone else; or perhaps you already had.

Here, alone in the woods, I did not expect to meet anyone. I was not looking for anyone. I wrote and told you how I had filled my days with projects and activities, very few of which brought me into contact with other women.

Further, very few women come to live in the country alone. It's a couple sort of thing; surely you remember how it was when we made our plans? Therefore I am as surprised as I am delighted by my new relationship. And I fully understand why you might find it unexpected.

In my last letter I made a joke about hoping to see the ghost as a figure in the storm. Imagine my surprise when later that night just as I described it, the lightning flashed and I saw a woman buffeted by the gale.

Ah ha! At last and about time too, I was thinking when she encountered my water logged weaving. Instead of passing through it in correct wraith manner, she was caught in the strands. I had no idea dried grass was so strong!

It took me a moment to realize that hers was a living body. But as soon as it penetrated my ghost bemused mind I went out, untangled her and invited her to share my fire. She had been driving on the main road when something went wrong with her steering. Her car landed in the drainage ditch which, being full of water, made driving out impossible.

The local mechanic kept her car several days but couldn't find anything wrong with it. He told us, "Maybe some water got in somewhere." His tone suggested he knew that it was alcohol and just where it had got in!

I'll skip the details. Nan's living here with me. A freelance designer can work anywhere. She chops wood like a buzz saw (and tells me the correct expression is "cuts wood"); she knows more about canning than a cookbook!

I've applied to the local school board—it's bound to be a more rational experience than teaching in New York City—and written Lea about a winter rental.

The apartment's yours if you want it. If not we'll have to wait for Mary to leave before we move our things.

It's just as well the ghost turned out to be imaginary as you never

arrived and I couldn't have stayed alone in a haunted house. Let me
know what you decide.

Your friend always,

Laura

The Dance

by Delia Cunningham

Delia Cunningham, who regularly writes about business and women's issues in addition to lesbian/feminist literature, lives in Florida with her partner of twelve years. Mothers-by-choice of three children, they are active in the Unitarian Universalist Church and participate in gay and lesbian community activities as a family whenever possible.

Facilitators of workshops dealing with Parenthood By Choice and Alternative Families, Delia and her family encourage feminists, gay men and lesbians to understand the power of defining themselves and those important to our lives as "families." They look forward to the day when intergenerational community activities are the norm and no adult event or workplace lacks quality, low cost daycare.

The Dance

The first time I saw Tricia Wilson I'm not sure what stood out more—her exuberant personality or the magnificent way her leotard framed her well-developed body. It isn't how I'd prefer to remember a woman (feminist awareness serving to remind me that sexism may be the greatest problem in the world), but the fact remains.

It was difficult *not* to notice her among that class of high school girls. I was a college student myself, continuing to study dance because it was my first love, though I never expected to make my living with it. Tricia was doing graduate work in theater, which is how she came to find herself in the Gainesburg School of Dance and Drama.

At first I had little to say to her. Tricia's vibrant personality brought laughter and a fresh perspective to this conventionally serious world of dance arts. She amazed me with her natural talent for relaxing and entertaining those around her. Super skinny teens momentarily dropped their self-conscious sophistication and allowed themselves to truly enjoy tapping their toes when Tricia showed us all how to laugh at ourselves over a missed step or forgotten routine.

She really wasn't that much older than I was, but at that time my twenty years seemed significantly less mature than her twenty-five. As an undergraduate who had recently transferred from a community college, I felt overwhelmed with the size of the university campus and intrigued at her ability to keep in step so gracefully. Quietly I observed her blonde curls, exuberant breasts and fast-moving feet, not missing the gold wedding band on her left hand.

Tricia was friends with our dance instructor, whom I liked and respected. It presented a bit of an internal conflict, because my lesbianism was a part of me that had always seemed irrelevant to dance class; unimportant and unnoticed when my inner self accepted the flow of the music and my body cooperated with my mind to translate sound into movement—mostly graceful.

It wasn't until the night I saw Tricia in the gay bar that I began to feel something more.

The smoky, dingy lounge was crowded when I noticed her from across the room. The college town was fairly liberal, so it wasn't uncommon for occasional groups of straight people to wander in for an evening's entertainment. The female impersonators drew their own following and others who joined the patrons of the gay bar soon realized how comfortable it was to be in a place that accepted them for whoever they might be. That was my first expectation of Tricia, but as I watched her that evening I realized she was accompanied only by gay men.

For awhile I considered what I should do. Staying behind closet doors wasn't my usual choice, yet my coming out to Tricia might spoil my untouched world of dance. Finally, I decided I had to approach her before she noticed me.

"Hello, Tricia," I said timidly.

"Delia! What a surprise. I haven't seen you here before."

"You've been here before?" I wasn't expecting that response.

"Sure, Honey. What do you think?" Tricia's glass of wine may have loosened her tongue, but I couldn't be sure. Enthusiasm was part of her personality.

"I thought you were married." There was no use hiding at that point, and I wanted to hear her story.

"It's what you call an open marriage. Actually, we're more like roommates." Tricia reached out to take my hand with what seemed merely a friendly gesture. "Do you want to dance?"

Going out on that dance floor gave the two of us a chance to combine memorized routines with imagination. We swept across the wooden boards toward the stage, enjoying the spotlight and truly earning the applause our friends began. Dance after dance we swung and turned, rocked and rolled with a new kind of rhythmic sharing.

Finally, the music slowed. Tricia took both my hands in hers, then pulled me close. Our bodies were damp, heat rising as the space between us closed in. Her soft breasts pushed against my braless chest, our arms fitting comfortably around each other. She led, I followed with my cheek touching hers. My entire body was awake, exhausted yet tingling at her nearness.

Later that night in my college-size apartment it took more than a warm bath and a cup of hot milk to induce sleep when I pulled the covers up on my single bed. It was one of those times I was thankful for the privacy of living alone.

It was also the reason I hesitated when Tricia asked me to room with her at dance convention several weeks later.

"I don't know, Tricia," I said. "It's expensive. And it's a long trip."

"To Miami?" she returned. "Come on. We'll find a cheaper motel on the mainland and commute to the Fountainbleu. We'll have a great time."

That was precisely what I was afraid of.

The trip down was easy. We took turns driving and talking. I learned about how she came to be married out of convenience to her best male friend, then later discovered herself in love with a woman. The affair didn't last but the marriage hung on.

"Now we're both free to see other people," she told me. "It's part of our politics. I'm a socialist, you know."

I didn't know and I didn't care. I thought she was beautiful. Usually I stayed away from women who claimed to be bisexual, finding it too difficult to deal with the relationship when a man came along. But with Tricia I made an exception: the attraction between us was stronger than my self-preservation.

"What does that mean, that you're a socialist?" I questioned.

"It means I believe in a classless society, not one based on imperialism and capitalistic values that make a god out of money, that make basic rights into privileges that come with wealth. I'm talking about things like affordable health care, regular meals."

"Oh." Her convictions brought out her passion. "Well, how do lesbians fit into all that?"

She smiled. "Did you know there are gay bars in the Soviet Union?"

"No. Come on."

Tricia nodded. "Things aren't always as we're led to believe. And of course we still have a long way to go before true political freedom exists *anywhere* in the world."

"Well, I can see you've thought about these things a lot more than I have," I admitted. "You've been solving the problems of the world while I've been concentrating on what's inside people's heads."

"Psychology is a middle class privilege. Working people don't have the time or money for analyzing themselves. They're just keeping food on the table," she said assuredly. "I'm sure you'll help people when you graduate, but I hope you decide to work for those who need help rather than for rich men whose kids are troubled because they're spoiled rotten."

Her manner was more informational than judgmental, presenting issues that years later made me continue to examine my goals and expand my consciousness.

That we were drawn to each other became self-evident. By the time we reached Miami we were holding hands. We checked into a dingy looking motel where our room offered a view of an alley. Because I was afraid to guess what I might mean to Tricia, I waited for her to make the move. But when we fell asleep that night we were still just holding hands.

The next day was filled with hard work. Dancers cannot afford to miss classes at convention if they intend to take home all they learn, and all of us at the Gainesburg School were serious. I felt wonderful, dressed like the others in matching leotards and tights, finally at home in the front row of several hundred dancers, with Tricia at my side. It was my dream come true.

By the time Tricia and I were back in our room that evening, I was exhausted. She showered first, then I did, both lost in memories of new dance steps and routines. I would have fallen right to sleep except for what happened next.

When I crawled in under the the covers of the motel bed, I guessed Tricia was naked.

"Delia, you aren't *that* sleepy, are you?" she asked softly. As we both lay on our backs, she reached for my hand.

"Tricia, I..."

"Sh," she cautioned.

My fingers opened, then shut between hers.

"You're nervous, aren't you?" Tricia whispered.

"Sure," I admitted.

"Don't be." Tricia rolled to her side, where a stream of light from the street allowed me to see her deep blue eyes. She methodically kissed every finger on my hand, causing a brief flick of her tongue to dampen each fingertip. "You're a natural dancer, you know. I was watching your body today," she told me.

Her approach was arousing, yet fear held me back.

"We dance well together, Tricia," I said.

"Ummm. I think so too." She smiled, gently rubbing my side. Then, with both of her arms, she pulled me close and held me.

I stroked her back silently, afraid to do more. This was new to me, being led into lovemaking by someone I'd fantasized about. Most of the time I only watched others meet, and then leave gatherings together. For me there had only been one woman before, the person I thought I'd love forever. When that ended, well, the time or the person had never seemed right again.

"Delia, you're so shy," Tricia breathed into my ear. "Let me help you." Her manner was seductive, yet motherly. I ached to touch her body, trembled to imagine her wanting me.

Motioning for me to lean forward, she slid my cotton nightgown off over my shoulders. We sat side by side, studying each other's outline in the streetlight that flickered through the slatted blinds.

Braver now, I reached across with my left hand to cup her right breast. The nipple was slow to erect, her fullness overflowing my grasp.

"You're beautiful," I whispered.

Tricia lowered her head to my nipples, bathing them alternately with her tongue.

I lay back, eyes closed, as she positioned herself over me and allowed our bodies to meet. She kissed me fully with lips and tongue. Rivers of emotion flooded my senses as I felt my toes tingling and my back arching to meet her.

Amazed to find myself amidst all this loving, I let go of fear and opened to desire. We formed pirouettes without motion, merging with the bonds of friendship and the tenderness of sisterhood. In my arms was the woman about whom I fantasized frequently, finally sharing intimacy.

We danced to our own music that night, hips swaying, bodies rotating. Sensitive to the muscular motion of ourselves on pointe, we stretched out head to toe. I massaged her angular feet. She drew lines of pleasure across my arches with her fashionable fingernails.

My fingers found their way between her legs, parting tiny curls

187

and swimming in the sweet fluid bathing her moistened opening.

Finally, I lay atop her. No longer inhibited by my self-conscious fear or memories of anything that went before, I parted my legs for her as I buried myself in her depths. Together we choreographed womanlove.

When we awoke the next day our sleepy eyes bore evidence to our late night workout; our muscles told of the workout of the previous day. Still, we returned to our task in full attire, hesitant to position ourselves too close to each other for fear that our lovemaking might show.

Although the others stayed another night, Tricia and I were forced by our budgets to drive back home when the last class ended. In some ways that drive was delightful, as we shared special touches and dangerous kisses along the Sunshine State Parkway. But the excitement was packaged with melancholy. I knew she would be going home to her husband and that I would be unlocking the door to an empty apartment. Our friendship may have moved to a deeper level, but the reality of our lifestyles left little time for love affairs.

Those last days of the college semester were filled with studying for exams, writing term papers and packing for vacation. We spoke on the phone and managed to arrange several lunchtime encounters, but we never again touched each other with the openness and passion of our first night. Finally, we met for a secret, drawn out good-bye kiss behind the campus cathedral. Tears touched our cheeks, but we accepted the understanding that we had different paths to travel, different priorities in life.

Over the years we did manage to keep in touch, although she had moved from Gainesburg by the time I returned in the fall. Tricia's husband left when a job offer drew him to California. She wanted to tackle the footlights of Broadway.

It wasn't without her influence that I began to see my chosen field in a new light: concentrating on working with runaway youth and troubled adolescents rather than with the brightly dressed youngsters of highly paid professionals. While my involvement with other women progressed as I matured, I was happily uncommitted years later when a professional conference gave me an excuse to travel to New York City.

That weekend was the last time I saw Tricia. She loved her

metropolitan lifestyle and was acting on a soap opera. Her politics may have been compromised somewhat, but I was sure she continued to work for social change when she wasn't pursuing her art. Officially divorced, she was living with a roommate, and dancing whenever possible.

The day after I arrived, Tricia and I arranged to meet, took some professional dance classes together and shared lunch in a little sidewalk cafe. Conventional checkered cloths covered round tables in the open air dining area. It was populated with theater people taking breakfast instead of a typical noon meal. This was the stuff of Tricia's life now, just as overactive children and overworked parents were a part of mine.

"My life's changing, Tricia," I told her with a bit of nostalgia creeping in.

"Mine too," she admitted. "I've a girlfriend now. It's serious, I think."

"A dancer?" I wondered.

"No, not at all. She's a screenwriter and a novelist." Tricia showed me a snapshot of a short, dark haired woman with wild eyes and a smile that filled her face with spirit. "We met at a support group for women in theater."

My friend seemed pleased to have met a kindred soul amid the thousands of actresses and critics who populated the city. I reflected on my own life, the women I knew and the weekend I truly came to know the woman before me.

We continued to chat about our lives and our work, leaving certain things unsaid, things even our infrequent letters had never brought into the open. Finally, Tricia looked directly into my eyes and I spotted a hint of a tear.

"What's wrong?" I asked, concerned.

"Nothing, except..."

"Except?" I reached for her hand, our fingers interlocking.

"Sometimes I wonder what might have been if we'd met in another time, another place."

I thought of the airline ticket tucked safely in my jacket, waiting to return me to my other life, my real job dealing with young people whose problems far outweighed my own. I thought of a young woman so keenly aware of political inequities that her life was dedicated to social justice. I thought of dancing in the lights of a darkened, cheap motel room.

"Don't wonder," I told this woman I cherished still. "We met at the right time, in the right place. Even though I don't write as often as I'd like, you're a dear sister and I'll always keep you in my heart. You showed me I could enjoy loving, and that I could dance through life."

"I did all that?" Tricia smiled.

"That and more."

"Then I guess it's worth it all," she agreed.

Without words we reached for each other's hands. Outside of time's restrictions, our eyes met in harmony and our hearts communicated a wordless emotion until the waitress interrupted us with the check. I took it from her and returned it with a twenty dollar bill.

"Tricia," I said, "let's dance."

She answered with a smile. Hand in hand we stood together, made our way out from the crowded tables onto the sidewalk, and two-stepped our way down the streets of New York.

Fantasy

The Story of Rhoda

by Nina Silver

Nina Silver brings her woman-identified womon perspective to her professions as song composer and free-lance writer, the topics ranging from sexuality, relationships, feminism and body acceptance to quantum physics, natural science and the new wicca. She also has maintained a ten year practice as trance medium, healer and body oriented therapist, during which time she has befriended many particles of light.

Nina's background for this story stems from her own brief childhood encounter with braces, her love of nature, and the souls who have inspired her in her work as a medium. Her vision for this life is to help empower others with her world view that combines the spiritual with the earthy and the political.

She warmly thanks Julia Thatcher for her loving assistance. Nina Silver can be reached c/o Healing Heart Music, P.O. Box 293, New York, NY 10025.

The Story of Rhoda

Once there was an ordinary garden, very much like any wild garden you might see near any rollicking stream set on the edge of a typical small meadow. It had the usual assortment of trees, bushes, flowers and yes, weeds. The garden looked like a jungle when the plants and grasses grew copiously after a long and plentiful spring rain; and then in the autumn when the earth went through her changes, the garden would make itself smaller, as if there were an invisible gardener advising the plants to cut back, so as not to take more than the elements could provide. Green things always have a way of knowing when to speed up or slow down.

Everything about this garden was quite ordinary—everything except the southwest corner. In this particular spot nothing grew—nothing, that is, until one day a green stalk poked its head through the rugged brown soil. Soon a shrub was born, proudly unfolding its treasure; the beautiful rose-like flower known as a rhododendron. This shrub was called Rhoda, although she did not give herself that name, for flowers are generally quite content to simply bloom and enjoy themselves.

From the first sprouting Rhoda jubilantly sunbathed and drank the briskly pelting rain. She soon grew tall and strong, with stunning white petals. How could she not, in all that fresh air and sunshine?

But the other plants did not like her. They did not like the fact that something could grow where they themselves had not been brave enough to even blow a seed.

The hydrangea, who, like Rhoda, was a shrub with showy white blooms, felt especially indignant. It could not grow in the southwest corner. "You're so strange!" it hissed in greenthing language. "Why don't you go back beneath the ground where you belong?"

"Yes, trot away," sniffed the zebra plant. It was feeling sorry for itself because try as it might, whenever there was a strong wind it could not hold onto its butter yellow blooms.

"Go away! We don't want you here!" rasped the horse chestnut. It had hollered this at Rhoda so many times, it now had laryngitis.

Even the weeds were unkind. "We wouldn't *think* of growing where you're rooted," they haughtily informed the hapless Rhoda. "Heaven knows what sort of flower *you* are to look so vibrant in a plot of earth that most certainly can't support life."

So Rhoda, although healthy and lovely, was very unhappy, for she had no friends. She flourished and grew even bigger, but she was so lonely, for no one would have a thing to do with her. Even the bees shunned the southwest corner. They needed the flowers for food, and if they were to continue to eat, then under no circumstances could they even glance in Rhoda's direction. They knew it would not do to make the other plants hostile and uncooperative.

One spring night, when the moon was but a shadow of itself and the clouds were preparing themselves to cover the earth the next day, something bright suddenly appeared in the southwest corner. The plants were asleep—all except Rhoda. She had been sobbing quietly to herself and did not see or hear anything approach her, not even when something appeared in front of one of her leaves.

"Hello." This was a modest but unmistakable greeting. Rhoda, startled, looked up.

The voice that was now saying hello for a second time came from a tiny spark of gold light that wiggled and writhed, pranced and pulsated, glowed and gleamed like the bounciest and happiest of suns. When it spoke, the sound seemed to come from all corners of the garden at once.

"Why are you crying?" Rhoda was so astonished at seeing this jumping little light that she just stared. She saw that this ball of energy had a pattern. The pattern shifted and whirled, depending on how forcefully the light spoke and what it said; but all the changes were beautiful. The spark reminded her of a dandelion in the symmetry and grace of its lines. Its many-dimensional buoyancy seemed to swim into itself, ebbing and flowing. Had Rhoda read quantum physics—which no rhododendron can do; only the sage had that capability—she would have understood that she was experiencing her visitor as both a particle and a wave at the same time.

"Why are you sad?" the light asked again. Rhoda finally found her voice and answered.

"The other plants make fun of me because nothing is able to grow in this soil."

"You do."

Rhoda nodded her head as if there were nothing contradictory in her statement. "So they don't talk to me unless it's to call me names—and I've been so lonely." Her snowy petals by now were quite droopy and she looked as miserable as she felt.

The light glimmered goldly and seemed to shine even more brightly, just for her. "You are very brave," it virtually hummed, "to live your life in the face of such immense loneliness."

"It is the only thing I can do," Rhoda replied sadly. "This is my home. I have planted my roots. When I was a little seed no one told me that this soil was not good for growing, that I was not supposed to become so leafy and bright. I am by nature a hardy shrub."

The little energy whirled and spinned for it could never sit still, but you could tell that it was listening very closely.

"So I did what I do best, which is to grow," Rhoda continued, very grateful and relieved to have someone to talk to. "How was I to know that my faith in the earth's support would bring me so much unhappiness?" She stopped, feeling a bit out of breath. In all her months in the garden Rhoda had never spoken this much.

The tiny gyrating ball jumped a bit. "You know better, don't you?" it said to her—and sounded as though if she didn't, she should. "Have you ever wondered how it is that you were able to survive in this gravelly spot, and everyone else had to go," the light indicated the entire rest of the garden, "—over there?"

Rhoda lifted her stamens in surprise. "No. I'd never thought about that."

"Look at all the other plants. For them everything has to be just so, doesn't it? They wouldn't have *dared* to even try sending down a single root. But you did. That makes you special. You're courageous and strong and full of spirit. Not only that, you're beautiful."

The white of Rhoda's velvet petals turned into a pearly pink. Rhoda was blushing.

"Oh thank you," she murmured. The pink misted into a deeper shade of red.

"It's true," the particle of light insisted, its wave form taking on a wide amplitude. "I never say anything I don't mean."

Something in the far corner began to stir. "Hey, who's there?" Both Rhoda and her golden friend recognized the voice. It belonged to the crab apple tree. "Who's yammering at this hour of the night? Shut up and let me get some sleep!" And of course because the crab apple tree was yelling so loudly, it woke up several of its neighbors.

"Whoever is making so much noise stop it. It's not yet time for reveille," advised the trumpet vines. "We've had a long day."

"Well, you needn't make it sound as if you're the only one," grumbled the bleeding hearts bush. "It's been nothing but rain, rain, and more rain for the last five days. I'm so drenched that if any more water gets into my roots I won't be able to hold myself up."

"It's taking a toll on us too!" added the chiming bells. "We would like to know who's making so much noise."

"Oh, I'm sure it's all right," ventured the sweet pea vine. Even though she was quite comfortable, mixed in with all the other flowers, there were times when she secretly wished she had the nerve to say a kind word to the suffering rhododendron. The sweet pea never did like conflict.

"It's not all right! I'd like you all to shut up!" snapped the impatiens. "I bet I know who's to blame for all this ruckus in the first place." And its leaves bent slightly but pointedly in the general vicinity of the rhododendron.

Everyone at once swung around to look in the direction of the lone Rhoda, who had listened to all this wishing she could just wilt away. She turned to her bright friend (hoping that it would tell the others to leave her in peace), but to her surprise the rest of the plants did not follow her gaze. It was not until that moment that she realized with amazement that she alone was able to perceive this extraordinary point of light.

"Look at her, pretending she doesn't hear us!" mocked the snapdragon.

"Crazy as always, talking to herself," added the chiming bells, forgetting that Rhoda had so rarely spoken at all.

"I don't care," declared the fig tree, restlessly moving its limbs about as if searching for a more comfortable position for slumber. "Quiet down, all of you, so we can get some sleep."

Silence spread itself over the garden like a blanket. The only sound Rhoda could hear was the stream, merrily immersed in its own meanderings, as usual. The wind was calling the clouds into a conference of even greater numbers, gathering momentum with each new surge.

Rhoda looked over at her friend, who was as bright and lively as ever. "I'm sorry," it said, "that I can't be of more help. You see, not everyone can see me. I'm visible to only the pure of heart."

Rhoda considered this, rustling her richly textured petals. "It's all right," she replied in a barely audible voice. "I'm glad that you've come anyway." She settled down, the blazing little beam appearing to rest on one of her slender branches.

The next morning everyone in the garden was greeted by a lustreless grey sky. Not even the crab apple could complain away the grimness of the day. Bees, recognizing the shift in the sultry air, hurriedly flew about finishing their pollen collections before the coming rain.

Getting caught in a torrent usually turns out all right; and it can even be delightful, particularly if the rain is cool and cleansing, more so if you see a splendid streak of lightning spinning across the sky in an overflow of light. A storm can be magnificent, especially because of what comes afterwards; the peace, the meditative stillness, the air alive with all kinds of currents dancing through and around you. Thunderstorms have a magic that few events, if any, can duplicate.

But when you're a plant in an overgrown and tired garden that no human is tending and have already had five days of continuous rain, thunderstorms are no fun, no matter how magnificent they can be. And this is what the sun finally looked at when it was all over:

Branches that had just gotten a start in the storm were torn and flung to the ground, leaving great gashes in the sides of trees that dripped copious amounts of sap. Some of the shrubs were stripped of leaves, a sight that would have been acceptable in winter but was tragic for spring. New buds, barely open, didn't have a chance and littered the ground like fallen soldiers. The bush of bleeding hearts, true to its prediction, lay on its side groaning. The crab apple tree was shorn of most of its blossoms. The ragweed and goldenrod sniffled, counting their losses. Even the dandelions, usually good-tempered and sturdy, had suffered a beating. The weeping willow tree, serene-looking and regal—well, I don't need to tell you what *it* was doing.

Rhoda, in her southwesterly abode, sighed and nursed her bruises. Because she was so isolated from the rest of the plants, the large trees in particular, there hadn't been many broken branches to fall onto her; so that was good. Her flowers, to be sure, were a bit on the damaged side, but considering how the rest of the garden looked, Rhoda hadn't fared too badly.

The golden gleaming ball alighted on all the plants inquiring if they were all right, but no one except Rhoda seemed to notice or care.

"Imagine," whimpered the snapdragon, considerably subdued, "we went to all this trouble and for what?"

"Well, at least we have the whole summer to mend." The dandelion's cheerful countenance began to reassert itself.

"We'll be able to mend, that is, if it doesn't rain so much!" the chiming bells chorused. Their cousins, the silver bells, nodded their tiny heads in agreement. A robin appeared, poking its beak into the soaked soil for a worm. The garden sighed in one breath and began to go about the task of repairing itself. The sun was warm and doing its usual magnificent job of drying out the drenched vegetation. It was hard not to feel good when all that sopping water in your pores was starting to evaporate.

Later that afternoon, the garden had a visitor.

Everyone, even the wallflowers, lifted their heads to see who could be treading the out-of-the-way path leading down to the garden.

A little girl came into view. She couldn't have been more than eleven, though there was an air of seriousness abut her that belonged to someone much older. Her body was slight, and she walked slowly as if with great effort. She wore a brace of shining metal that surrounded one leg as if the limb were in a cage. That leg dragged behind, but the girl was determined, her jaw set as if that would transform her unsteady gait into the most purposeful of steps. Even the apathetic fig tree could tell that there was something unusual about this child.

She paused frequently to rest. Behind her abruptly appeared an older boy, who followed with a brisk busy pace. Rhoda could see that the boy wasn't interested at all in entering the garden, but was there because the little girl was. He wore an uncomplimentary scowl on his face.

The little girl spoke up. "Look at this garden!" Her somber pale face lit up into a delighted smile that seemed to radiate out in all directions. When she smiled, Rhoda thought there was a lovely glow to her.

"Oh, Lilith, it's all messy and busted." There was something about the boy's tone of voice that Rhoda didn't like. Before any of the plants could say anything, the boy came right up to one of the dandelion clusters and yanked. The storm had softened the soil enough so that the roots of the dandelion plant, generally fiercely entrenched, yielded easily to his fingers.

"Look at all these weeds. There's been no one in this garden for ages." He dropped the helpless dandelion, which immediately began eyeing the ground in such a way that let you know it was getting ready to point its roots down.

"I like this garden," the girl called Lilith murmured. She looked troubled, but did not say anything else.

"You put back that dandelion!" the trumpet vines shouted at the boy. How they wished they could reach over and put their comrade back into the ground.

Lilith looked at the boy, her eyes round as dinnerplates. Then she looked at the fallen flower. He responded as though she'd actually spoken.

"It's just a weed—and an ugly one at that!" He gave the plant a kick that sent the weeping willow into a fit. Lilith cringed. "Look, I'm not gonna baby-sit for you anymore. If you want to stay, stay the whole day for all I care. Just be home for dinner, or you'll get us both in trouble." Within moments he was gone, leaving Lilith alone with the entire garden.

She immediately walked carefully over to where the uprooted dandelion lay in agony. With some difficulty Lilith knelt on the ground and, pressing in with one hand, tenderly replaced the battered plant as best she could.

"Poor little thing. Even dandelions should have a chance to grow. I'm sorry," she said softly to the plant. "I know how it is to have people not like you." She stood up shakily and surveyed the rest of the garden. "Imagine, we live so close and never knew this was here." Rhoda wondered what that strange shiny object was doing on the child's leg. Lilith didn't run and skip the way Rhoda had heard that children were supposed to.

And then she noticed the girl's eyes, inquisitive and lively, of the most pretty hazel color she had ever seen. Apparently the other plants noticed them too, for they began to chatter all at once.

"Look, her eyes are the same color as my bark," said the birch, looking pleased.

"Yes, and she's smart. She likes us." The forget-me-nots looked even prouder than the birch.

"I'm not a mere weed!" roared the dandelion triumphantly. If it were something other than a rooted plant, it might have jumped for joy.

Lilith might have jumped for joy, too. Since she couldn't, her eyes did it for her. They bounced from tree to bush, flower to shrub, ground to sky and back to ground. The sparkle in those eyes reminded Rhoda of her friend—where *was* that point of light, anyway? After considerable searching, to her great surprise, she saw her golden friend directly above Lilith's head.

Did the child see the light? Surely she was pure of heart. But Lilith didn't act as if her hazel eyes witnessed anything unusual, even when the golden shimmer bounded right in front of her face.

"Hello, Lilith," said the luminous particle, sounding for all the world like a hive of friendly bees. The little girl tilted her head but didn't answer. "Lilith, it's me." The wave form became quite fancy, darting and dipping in pretty pulsing shapes. "You're wonderful, just like this bush. Look!" And the incandescent dot floated right onto Rhoda's choicest flower, one of the blooms that was still able to hold itself up.

The little girl gazed in the direction of the rhododendron. "Why, how strange," Lilith said aloud. (The garden was soon to learn that their human friend was in the habit of talking to herself.) "A rhododendron all by itself, not even with grass growing around it. As she hobbled in the direction of the shrub, the other plants started chortling to each other.

"See, you *are* strange!" the hydrangea accused, and poor Rhoda thought that she would have to hear this all over again.

But Lilith's next sentence stopped the others cold. "How wonderful that anything, even a rhododendron can grow in this." And her slender hand reached out to the excited bush. "It means you're special."

The girl paused, those serious eyes deeply engrossed in thought. "A bush like you should have a name. I'll call you Rhoda. It must be hard for you, growing here all by yourself. Well, I've got to go. It takes me a while to get back." Lilith spoke lightly, but her lips quivered. "Bye, Rhoda. I'll see you tomorrow. I'll see you all," she called turning to look at the rest of the garden. "Don't worry, you'll be on your feet in no time"

As soon as Lilith started up the scruffy path the plants all began speaking at once, as if a spell had been broken.

"Did you hear *that?"* She *likes* that rhododendron!"

"I don't believe it. You'd think there was something special about that shabby shrub."

"Hmmph! She didn't even look at my flowers," sniffed the hydrangea, clearly jealous.

"All I know is she put me back in the ground." In the dandelion, Lilith had made a friend for life.

"Well, I'm glad she's going to come back." The sweet pea had a softly distinctive way of speaking. "And I don't mind if she likes Rhoda. After all, doesn't she like the rest of us too?"

"So you think it's all right!" snorted the zebra plant. "Next thing, you'll go move into Rhoda's corner." It was still mourning its broken buds and wondering if it would ever be able to get a blossom to stay put for an entire season.

"Look at that, sweet pea's living up to her name," hooted the hydrangea.

"Rhoda lover, Rhoda lover," chanted the tulips, sneering. The flowering sweet pea shook. Rhoda felt terrible about this.

Of course the crab apple joined in. "Wouldn't you know it, not only do we have to worry about the weather, now we have a defector in our ranks," it complained. It would have continued had there not been a disruption.

"Stop it!" yelled the dandelion crossly. "Leave Rhoda and sweet pea alone. If Lilith likes the rhododendron, let it be."

The ensuing silence was heavy. Renewing oneself after nearly a week's worth of rain is no easy task; surely they had better things to

do than pick on one bush. Subdued, all the green things nodded off
to sleep. But Rhoda didn't feel like sleeping. She was so excited
that she was trembling from twig to taproot. Where was Golden
Ball, the name she had given her new friend? She looked though the
dark in all directions. Yet tonight, she could not find that mysterious
spark. Disappointed and a little worried, eventually the rhododendron fell asleep.

The next morning began many days of welcomed sun, the garden
dwellers awakening in unusually good humor. Only Rhoda was
worried. By late morning, she still hadn't seen her diminutive companion. Had the child's praises gone to her head? Maybe Rhoda
was no longer pure of heart.

"No, silly." Golden Ball spun its way to her side in a twinkling.

The rhododendron looked up, greatly relieved but also a bit annoyed. "Where have you *been?"*

"I'm sorry," the particle of light replied, even bouncier than
usual, if that could be imagined. "I was spending some time with
Lilith. She's coming here later, as soon as she finishes some
chores." The sweet pea's rosy colored petals were fluttering in their
direction. "Don't worry, I wasn't going to leave you. Didn't you
know I'd never do that to a friend?"

Rhoda, feeling a little ashamed of herself for doubting, immediately changed the subject. "I want to know something." Rhoda
leaned over slightly, as if confiding a secret. "Why can't Lilith see
you? It seems to me that if I can see you, she should be able to
also."

The tiny beam radiated in an especially pretty way. "You have to
understand what I mean by 'pure of heart.' You see, it doesn't only
mean that someone does nice things sometimes for others. If that
were the case, more often than not I'd be seen." It stopped for a
moment as Rhoda took this in, then continued. "How do you think
you were able to take root in this spot? Tell me what you said the
first day we spoke."

"Well," replied Rhoda slowly, not wanting to appear immodest,
"I remember telling you that I trusted I'd be able to find support in
the soil." Her now white petals began dissolving into that familiar
shade of pink.

"And the other plants made fun of you because their fear told them that they *couldn't* grow here. They listened to their fear instead of trusting what their hearts could have told them. But by trusting your heart, you were able to have faith in the earth's ability to nourish you. So you received the support that was there. In other words, you did what the others thought was impossible. Fear always hides the truth from us."

Rhoda could hardly keep her voice down. "*That's* what you mean," she exclaimed, "about 'pure of heart'!" (The sweet pea politely looked away, but at the edge of her field of vision could see the iridescent drop to which she'd been listening with such fascination.) "If you can't trust, then of course you don't even trust your own heart; you're not sure of anything. And if you can't trust your heart, then how can it be pure? Everyone else's opinions and accusations and your own doubts and fears will always sneak in, and get in its way." Rhoda's twigs stood outstandingly upright. The nearby narcissi stopped admiring themselves in the stream long enough to glance, startled, at her corner.

"Your friend Lilith," Golden Ball was saying, "has been listening for too long to everyone else. She has a big heart, a good heart, but she doesn't believe enough in it to follow it the way she needs to. The day Lilith listens to her own heart will be when she discovers her true self and therefore, for her, the world of women."

Rhoda was quiet. This was a lot to think about. How sad that the lovely child Lilith, who would take the trouble to rescue a dandelion, could not trust herself enough to—well, stand up to that horrid brother of hers, for instance, or be able to see... Who or what was Golden Ball anyway?

By now, Rhoda was aware that sweet pea could see this little light, for the pink-flowered vine was outright staring at it. Suddenly, everyone in the garden turned at the sound of footsteps and clattering. The banging was of indeterminable origin, accompanied by intermittent squeaks and a whole lot of grunting.

"Hi, Lilith," called the dandelion. Rhoda had never seen the dandelion more cheery. She would even have called it blissful.

"I'd recognize those steps anywhere," the lady's slippers noted with great satisfaction. "Welcome, Lilith."

"Take your time," advised the impatiens to the amazement of everyone, even Golden Ball. "That's a difficult road you're on."

Before any of the plants could ask the impatiens what could have possibly gotten into it Lilith came into view. Walking very carefully so as not to fall, the little girl was pulling an old red wagon. In it were a shovel, several long pieces of thin wood, and some odds and ends.

Pulling and tugging, Lilith finally managed to get the wagon to the southwest corner, the only place there was room. Rhoda's heart went out to the child; if only she could help her with the wagon. The small bright beacon watched but said nothing. Lilith laid down the handle of the wagon and went over to say hello to the dandelion.

"I'm so glad you're okay." She leaned over precariously, trying to keep her balance. "I won't let anything like that happen again."

"Oh thank you, Lilith," purred the dandelion. Although the child was unaccustomed to understanding the speech of flowers, Rhoda thought she brightened nonetheless.

Lilith stood as straight as she could, which was rather at a slant, and appraised the rest of the garden. "This," she said firmly to no one in particular, "is going to be a lot of work."

The bleeding hearts needed attending to right away. "You need some of these," said Liliith, and in that plodding, unsteady way of hers, she went to the wagon and returned with some of the wooden stakes. "That's better," she encouraged in a soothing voice, after the bleeding hearts had been propped against the stake with some twine. "Sometimes we need to have help," and she looked down at her brace.

Next she turned to the zebra plant. "I see, you don't have any flowers. Storm or no, you might need a little plant food." She took out some brown stuff from the wagon and patted the earth around the zebra plant. All of the zebra's neighbors thought it looked better already, the striping on its leaves gleaming even more whitely.

Lilith looked pleased. She also looked tired and leaned up against the weeping willow. The tree, delighted at being selected, held itself at its most erect so Lilith could feel its sap run strongly through the trunk. Trees will do this when you're tired and need energy. As Lilith sat down she said, "Don't worry, you'll all get your turn."

She was going to take care of them! They had never been treated like this before. The sweet pea asked the willow, by far the oldest one in the garden, if it remembered ever having a gardener.

It thought hard. "Once, long ago, when I was just a sapling. But not since. Oh, it feels so good to get all these stones out of my toes." Lilith was clearing away some large pebbles from the willow's roots as she sat beneath the tree. She could almost see its roots wriggling.

In the weeks that followed the healing of the garden continued. Lilith shovelled and sweated, placing the torn earth back to where it had lain before the storm. She picked up leaves and sticks and broken branches, and, when her wagon was full, hauled away the debris. The girl also dug and planted and pruned. She never destroyed a single living green thing, not even what we call a weed, and when she pruned she always did it gently.

And Lilith talked—to herself, Rhoda, to the trumpet vines and the willow, the chiming bells, even the crab apple tree. She checked the zebra plant religiously (which by now had three yellow flowers on it) and pulled up stakes from around the bleeding hearts (they got to where they could once again stand alone). She also made sure to admire the hydrangea on a regular basis.

All of the plants were crazy about her. For the first time in many years the garden felt loved.

One hot day in midsummer, when Lilith was resting on the ground feasting on a ripe fig, voices were heard on the path above the garden. Lilith stopped eating. All the flowers and bushes and trees stopped what they were doing and turned in the direction of the sound. Rhoda and the sweet pea exchanged meaningful looks. They had a feeling that whatever this interruption was, it wasn't going to be pleasant.

At the top of the the rise Lilith's brother appeared, followed by another boy about his age. Laughing and talking, they didn't notice where they were until they were actually in the garden. The dandelion stopped breathing.

"Well, look at this," Lilith's brother scoffed. "Keeper of the weeds. So here's where you've been all summer."

Lilith glared at him, her nostrils flared and jaw set determinedly.

"Hey, Miss No-Legs, you think what you're doing is so important. You wanna have something more to do?" The brother moved toward the nearest plant, which happened to be Rhoda, as if he were going to wrench her out of the ground. His chum half gestured as if to stop him, when they heard the girl speak.

"Get out of my garden."

Her brother paused. Lilith spoke again, only this time louder and with more force. She pulled herself up onto her two legs with considerably more vigor and spring than one might have expected.

"Get out of my garden."

The boys were not the only ones who were surprised. Rhoda and the rest of the plants had never heard Lilith speak like this before. Golden Ball zoomed into Lilith's field. Pulsating mightily, the two of them together formed an electric current. Rhoda could not tell where one stopped generating and the other began. The atmosphere, now heavily charged, virtually crackled, and plants and humans alike could feel a peculiar tingling in the air. Any concern about danger lifted from Rhoda's mind. Seeing how strong Lilith was, Rhoda only had room to feel proud of her. All those weeks of hard work had taken shape in the girl's flowing, firm, muscular arms and yes, both of her legs. Lilith had grown about an inch and she was standing straighter! Her hazel eyes, outraged, glinted in her tanned face. She looked positively beautiful, Rhoda thought.

"You so much as touch one flower, even a twig on that bush, and you'll get what you deserve." Her head turned ever so slightly in the direction of the golden particle, who was radiating energy out like a spiral, and it was obvious to Rhoda that Lilith could see it.

The brother, smirking, took a deliberately exaggerated step toward the rhododendron.

"Don't your dare come closer!" Lilith's face was dark with fury. The boy, astounded, stood as if transfixed. "This is not your garden," she said. "It belongs to the plants. They belong to the earth. All of them." She swung her arms widely in an arc indicating the breadth of the garden, with so much intent and grace that it could have been a blessing. "You—" she stamped the unbraced foot, hissing like an angry cat— "do not belong here. I order you to leave!"

The golden ball of energy swirled and sparked. Lilith turned to it once again for just an instant, that glance of recognition lighting up her eyes as if they had bonfires in them. Then she gazed back upon the two who stood facing her dumbfounded, and her eyes were proud.

"All the forces in this garden, be they of this world or of spirit, I call upon you now." Her eyes remained glued to the intruders. "Leave!"

Lilith's brother somehow found himself able to move again. He shifted uneasily from one foot to the other. "You're crazy."

"Leave."

"You witch. You're really a witch! You're out of your mind!"

"GET OUT OF MY GARDEN!" By now the girl's voice had risen to a screech.

"C'mon, let's go." The other boy turned to leave, but still the brother hesitated. Lilith put her good foot in front of her, the calf muscle quivering. And then she started to run toward them. She ran stiffly, but it was unmistakably running. From her lips came an otherworldly cry that seemed to echo in all corners of the garden at once, searing the air with the sheer exhilarating power of her being.

The boys dashed up the dirt path, Lilith panting in pursuit. She couldn't run as quickly as they, but it didn't matter. They sped off as if there really were a witch at their heels.

•

It is now the end of August and the garden has a distinctly changed character to it. In the southwest corner, along with Rhoda, is some very velvety new grass and the sweet pea vine. Sweet peas have a way of spreading easily when they find the soil and climate inviting. The vinelike bush of ribbony pink posies has entwined herself around the rhododendron. They have become the closest of friends.

All the plants now talk to each other—of course not all the time, and not always nicely, for like most of us they sometimes snap and argue and are temperamental and short with one another. But no one ever makes fun of anybody else anymore for being different. Those are the rules.

Lilith still visits the garden, though not as frequently. She is spending most of her time working to move and walk without the brace.

"What I'd still like to know is, who or what are you?" Rhoda is asking this of Golden Ball a bit shyly, not because of the question, but because Sweet Pea is rapturously and uninhibitedly throwing her vines around the rhododendron while at the same time listening with rapt attention. All the garden inhabitants, in fact, are listening and watching with rapt attention.

The one whom Rhoda has nicknamed Golden Ball smiles, if you can imagine this phenomenon occurring in a particle of light. "That is easy to know if you are ready to know it." And the tiny luminous beam seems to grow until, like the sun, it fills Rhoda's entire universe and beyond.

"Feel my energy around you, in you, through you and of you." And Rhoda feels deep within her roots that familiar spark, the spark that had enabled her to extract the life-giving minerals from inside the earth and drink the water that helps her grow.

"I am in all things, of all things," Golden Ball says. "Who I am as a soul in this form is not important. Who you feel yourself to be in my presence is what I am here for. Like you, I have consciousness. My way is different from yours. But like you, I am here to grow.

"Part of growing is in helping others, and so it is with me. When I reach out to experience the world, I change and am changed by it. Do you understand?"

Rhoda rustles her leaves. To the unknowing observer the slight botanical motion is caused by a breeze, but you and I know all the trees, bushes, flowers and yes, weeds are really nodding their heads.

"I can see what you mean," Rhoda says, "but I don't know what to call it." The other plants are intently still for the reply, but it is Sweet Pea who speaks.

"How about love?"

The particle of gold light leaps and spins magnificently, which is its way of jumping for joy.

Rituals

by Kathy Kucsan

Kathy Kucsan is thirty-two and a musician by trade. Performing music somehow led to doing comedy, and she has played the door and rapelled from balconies from Toledo to Caracas. She recently moved from Ann Arbor to Boulder, where she falls in love over and over again with the mountains and the gorgeous psychologist she lives with. Kathy's favorite dream is one of a peaceable planet, where there are no such things as exploitation, abuse and oppression. Men will be gentle and know their places. Children will be treasured. Animals will be respected as living beings. And women will be revered.

Rituals

Trary went outside to stand in the cool night air. It was awful in there; she wished she hadn't come. But Beth loved going to the bar, and Trary had thought that going along would probably be better than sitting home alone in front of the television, eating Chips Ahoy.

Rosemary's was the only gay bar in town. It was an ugly little place with fake wood panelling and a picture of Elvis on the wall, cut out of People magazine and framed. A sad potted palm waved brown tipped leaves in time to Anne Murray singing "You Needed Me," while couples of all sorts clung to each other beneath the glitter ball. That's when Trary had had to get out. Beth was clamped onto some leather-clad dyke with a punk haircut and long red fingernails.

The cement of the sidewalk was cool but Trary sat on it anyway. She talked to herself: *Beth loves me, I know she does, she really does, but if she really does why does she have to dance with that woman? Why does she race around and flirt and ignore me? Why did she go home with Christine Cawhorn two weeks ago? She said it was nothing, I was out of town anyway, and she was lonely. Maybe she doesn't love me. Maybe I'm being stupid. We never really talk about these things. She doesn't take me seriously. Maybe she doesn't love me.*

A yellow Firebird filled with teenage boys zoomed down the street and screeched to a halt in front of Trary. She looked at them. They looked at her. Trary had a hunch they were going to shout at her. She got up and dashed back into Rosemary's.

She ran head on into a tall, well-dressed woman who was on her way out.

"Excuse me!" Trary apologized.

"Hello," the tall woman smiled.

Trary looked into a pair of bright blue eyes.

"Looks like you're in a hurry to get in there," the tall woman said. "I think you'd rather stand here and talk to me, though."

"Well," Trary began.

"Or perhaps you'd just like to come home with me."

"Home?"

"Yes, I think we'd both enjoy that, don't you?" The woman caressed Trary's face. A chill rushed throughout Trary's entire body.

"Well, I—sure. I guess. OK." Trary couldn't take her eyes away from the clear, intriguing blue ones.

"My name is June," said the woman, putting her arm around Trary.

"June?" Trary repeated.

"June," the woman confirmed.

"I hate this place alot," said Trary. "I hate it but I come here alot."

"You poor thing," said June. An odd smirk crept onto her face.

Trary looked at her hopefully. *I don't know what I'm doing but I'm doing it anyway,* she thought.

"Shall we?" suggested June.

"OK," Trary agreed, and followed her to a black Nissan Pulsar. The yellow Firebird full of boys was nowhere to be seen.

Trary looked over at her own yellow, rusted, beat up Datsun, nineteen seventy something. Beth had the keys. Trary climbed into the Pulsar with June, who floored it out of the parking lot.

"I live alone," June announced, "so there's nothing to worry about." She drove with one hand on the steering wheel and the other shoved between her legs.

Trary thought, *Sure, there's nothing to worry about except that you might be some kind of psychopath. . . here I am in this speeding car with you and I know nothing about you.*

"What do you do?" Trary tried. June's suit seemed to be expensive linen. She wore a Rolex. Her car was expensive. Most lesbians Trary knew had cars more beat up than her Datsun; dressing up for a night out at the bar meant flannel shirts and Frye boots.

"I work in the financial field." June flipped on the radio.

OK, she doesn't want to talk about her job. "My lover was kissing someone else when we left," Trary tried a new topic.

"Slut," pronounced June. She shoved her hand further into her crotch. She made a right-hand turn with only one hand on the wheel.

"It happens all the time," Trary admitted. "I should probably leave her."

"I believe in faithfulness and respect," June said. "At least faithfulness in front of your lover. How could she kiss someone else with you right there?"

The word is fidelity, Trary thought, wanting to correct June.

"She thinks I don't mind," Trary said. "We try to have an open relationship, but she's the only one who's open."

"Why do you stay with her her?" June demanded. "If you do mind, why don't you TELL her?"

"I love her," Trary stated simply.

"Love does not mean she gets to ride the bulldozer while you lay in the street," said June. She hit the curb making another right turn.

Lie, not lay, thought Trary. *The word is lie.*

June gunned the Pulsar down a residential street. The sign said Morningside Drive. June pulled into the driveway of a huge house with pine trees all around. There was a black BMW parked in the driveway.

"Is this yours?"

"I told you I live alone," June snapped.

Inside the house, there were plants everywhere. A huge grey cat stared at them from a puffy chair. From the cat's attitude, the chair belonged to the cat and only the cat.

June turned on the stereo. A Sousa march blared.

"How about that," said June, "I used to play the sousaphone in high school."

Trary began to wonder if she might be on Candid Camera.

June put a cassette in the deck, switching off "Under the Double Eagle." The atmosphere in the room became immediately less bizarre. Janis Ian sang "Seventeen." Trary expected New Age instrumental; Janis Ian sounded like an antique.

June got two cokes from the kitchen. She stood in the doorway, half smiling. Her expression was serious, worried. This unnerved Trary, and she got up and went toward June.

"Good!" June's face suddenly softened. "I wasn't sure if you wanted to stay."

Well, Trary wasn't sure either. June was strange. But not boring. She was attractive, too, in an odd way. Trary was charmed by her tiny, sculptured mouth, her too-perfect hair (not a strand out of place), and her blue eyes, intense or aloof and occasionally inviting.

Janis Ian was singing in the bedroom also. June's entire house was wired for sound.

"The bathroom is right through that door." June said, pointing to a door covered by a full-length mirror. Trary glimpsed herself standing there, looking a little lost. She liked what she saw. She liked the smug look, and thought that she would certainly be attracted to herself if she was someone else cruising in a crowded bar.

Trary pushed open the door to the bathroom and flicked on the light. Everything was pink and grey. Everything. Tile, carpet, towels, walls. Some things were only pink or only grey, some were both. Even June's toothbrush. Toothbrushes. There were at least a dozen toothbrushes in the pink toothbrush holder. The soap in the grey soap dish was pink. On the opposite wall was a rack of shower caps. As she peed, Trary looked at them. She counted seven showercaps hanging neatly in a row. They were all varying shades and patterns of pink and greyness. They were extraordinary. June must have searched hard for the pink and grey striped one.

"Can I brush my teeth?" Trary called through the now closed door.

"Use the last toothbrush nearest the wall on the left," June called back. "It's brand new. It can be yours from now on."

Trary wondered if she would get a shower cap, too. She couldn't think of a single one of her friends who had one, who had ever used one.

"Who do all those shower caps and toothbrushes belong to?" Trary asked, emerging from the color coordinated bathroom.

"Lovers," June said nonchalantly.

"You have seven lovers?"

"Sometimes more, sometimes less. I try to stick to seven, that's how many days of the week there are." June held her arms half open. She was lying on the bed.

Trary experienced a rush of revulsion combined with a peculiar sexual urge. She went to June. They kissed. June moaned. Trary felt it again; the urge to run mixed with a strange desire to rip June's clothes off.

June moaned again and writhed underneath Trary, who gently

unbuttoned the expensive blouse and unzipped the linen slacks. June's moans got higher in pitch. She responded to Trary's every touch, no matter how fleeting or light. Trary felt June's small, tight breasts, and kissed her neck. She put her hand inside June's slacks—June wasn't wearing any underwear. Trary barely got her fingers wet before June shuddered and came with a loud sigh.

"Mmmm, that was wonderful," June murmured.

"What?" said Trary. She had just started. June's clothes weren't even off, her own were barely askew.

"I said it was just wonderful." June rolled over and turned out the light. She quickly fell asleep.

Trary sat on the edge of the bed, in the dark. She rolled her eyes toward the ceiling. *This is the weirdest thing,* she kept thinking.

The Janis Ian tape finally clicked off in the living room. Trary wandered around the dark house for a few minutes, afraid to touch anything. She felt empty, the house felt empty. She found the front door and left. June never stirred.

•

Trary walked for a mile down the dark and deserted road before she let any thoughts take hold in her mind. Then she couldn't stop them.

What have I done? What have I DONE? she berated herself. *Why did I do this, let myself be picked up— outside the bar, not inside, where pickups usually happen? I was PICKED UP. How could I do this? I didn't even like her, it wasn't even fun.* June's face flashed before Trary's eyes, haunting her. *June's face and her tiny cries. The wall full of shower caps, the quiet house with two black cars parked out front, and John Phillip Sousa on the stereo. Would Beth understand? Maybe I won't tell Beth. I CAN'T tell Beth. Can I?*

The sky was clear, the moon was full. Trary looked up into the night and begged a UFO to swoop down and rescue her. It seemed the best solution.

Several cars passed by, none slowed down. Her apartment was three miles away and Trary tried to enjoy the walk. She pushed away thoughts of June. How could she really have seven lovers if she fell asleep after ten minutes of lovemaking? Trary looked to the sky for shooting stars and UFO's.

A car slowed next to Trary. Her heart pounded at her shirt; she hunched her shoulders, made herself look very solid, and walked purposefully.

"Can we give you a lift?" a smiling face asked. The car, an old Dodge from the sixties, was full of women. Six pairs of eyes looked out at Trary.

"Do you need a ride? You're kind of far from town," the kind face next to the driver said. Hers was the only set of eyes that wore glasses—stop sign glasses like Trary had worn in the ninth grade.

"Where will I sit?" Trary asked.

"In the back. We can make room."

The three bodies in the back squashed together. Trary climbed in. The car smelled like incense.

As the Dodge pulled back onto the road, one woman said, "We're on our way to a ritual."

Trary didn't say anything. She didn't know anything about rituals, except what she had learned in anthropology class.

"Would you like to join us?" stop sign glasses asked.

"Uh, what would I have to do?" Trary squeaked.

"You can just, like you know, watch. You don't have to DO anything. But, like, I can tell you have some great energy except, like, I can't tell where you'e coming from."

I came from nearly fucking a woman who has seven shower caps hanging in her grey and pink bathroom and has Sousa marches instead of George Winston playing on her stereo. THAT is where I'm coming from. Trary wanted to say this outloud, just to hear how ridiculous it sounded.

"You can just sort of be there," the woman next to Trary said. "It's really very calming." She was very gentle and soft spoken. Her hair was in a french braid.

"I can just be there?"

"You can dance if you want."

"And there will be some chanting," said the driver.

All of the women wore loose, caftan type outfits. Trary realized suddenly that they were passing around a pipe. The old Dodge turned down a dirt road Trary vaguely recognized. They stopped at a clearing where several other women had a fire blazing. Other women materialized from the shadows and joined them. They all wore caftans too. And there were dogs everywhere; most of them wore red bandanas.

"What are you celebrating?" Trary asked no one in particular.

"It's new moon and so it's the time of new beginnings," the car driver answered. "But mostly we're just celebrating the Goddess. We're just thanking her."

The women got out of the Dodge. Trary noticed that they all had little strings around their necks with little bags hanging from the strings.

Guitars and flutes and drums began to play. The women gathered into a circle and whispered a chant. They were chanting names, Trary realized, names of goddesses she had read or heard from somewhere. They chanted at first very quietly, and then louder and louder. Then they sang and the drums played louder. Trary found the rhythm coursing through her body, the urge to move to it became overwhelming.

The chant reached a crescendo, then slowed and quieted. The drums did not stop. A woman directly across from Trary began to speak.

"And if we could all just think of something we would like to draw to us, something that might enrich our lives, something that we can love and cherish, something that will help us do good in the world—think of this something now and bring it to yourself."

Trary thought immediately of Beth. She closed her eyes and saw her, her soft, sometimes scared eyes, her tousled hair. A smile, a frown. All the things about her that Trary loved to look at and touch. *If only I could be enough for you, maybe you would stay near me,* Trary said to the Beth in her mind.

The women were passing around a steaming cup of liquid. Each woman took a sip and passed it to the next. Some closed their eyes, others murmured something before they drank. When it came to Trary, she sipped a warm sweetness. Thirty faces smiled at her.

The dancing began in earnest and Trary let herself be pulled into the gentle swaying. The music got louder and softer, sometimes there were voices. The drums never stopped.

Before the music ended altogether, Trary found herself in a small circle of women. They had their arms clasped around her, embracing her as they danced around her. The circle got tighter and tighter, and

Trary felt each one of them, she felt them dancing and breathing and protecting her. The music ended abruptly, at some indiscernible signal, and the women laughed and hugged one another.

Three of the women Trary had come with headed back to the tan Dodge.

"Shall we drop you off?" one asked.

Trary didn't feel like leaving the warmth of the fire and the women, but went anyway. The ride home was silent, and it was only after she had gotten out of the car and started walking toward her apartment that Trary realized that she hadn't given the driver directions.

Beth was still up. The TV was on with the sound turned off.

"Hi," said Trary.

Beth looked at her, her eyes angry and red. "Where have you been?" she demanded.

"I went home with someone." Trary was at least honest.

Beth made a little groan.

"But I didn't stay," Trary went on. "I left after about an hour and started walking home when I got picked up by a UFO."

Beth stared at her. "You are so full of shit."

"It looked like an old Dodge and was full of women. We danced and danced and sipped magic potion. Wherever they took me was a wonderful place."

Beth blinked. Then she burst into tears.

Trary went to her, afraid to touch her. "Are you OK?"

"No." Beth tentatively put a hand on Trary's arm.

"Beth?"

"I just realized something," whispered Beth.

"What's that?" But Trary knew exactly what Beth meant. It was what they shared; what they meant to each other hung now in the air between them, plain as day. Trary searched Beth's eyes and saw her thinking the same thoughts. Feeling the same feelings.

Beth put her head in Trary's lap. "Maybe we should start this again and do it right this time, OK? Starting now?"

Trary held Beth, cradled her in her arms, kissed her forehead. "Yes, let's do it right, starting now," Trary echoed.

Frost

by Jesse Cougar

Jesse Cougar is the creator of A Poet's Tarot. *She initially wrote* Frost *over a decade ago but it recently underwent thorough revisioning for publication. The remainder of her stories and a novel-in-progress await the skillful and implacable hand of her editor.*

Jesse looks forward and works towards the time when the world will regain balance and thrive again in a state of perfect wildness and complex diversity. She hopes the Earth will be illuminated by the infinite capacity for wonder, knowledge, artistic creativity and love of beauty with which the human (womon) animal is gifted.

Frost

The October light was low like a candle stub, and late. The day had been overcast until now, and as bright as the orange clouds were glowing, they hung low in the mountain land and didn't light the view, or the house, or Kit, watching them. *Too late, sun. Good try, but a little late.* She felt bitter and her hands were cold, very cold, and she just didn't care anymore. She thought of Luna, out walking. *She's probably not cold. And if I wasn't just sitting here fading in the fading light... It's only October. I used to handle the weather better, even in my city days. But then it's warmer inside the city; there it all feels like one big 'inside'. Out here things are different. Here you come to know your strengths by constant use, and your limits by always bumping up against them.*

Well, she felt past those limits now.

"Let's get a house in the country," she'd said to Luna when her money had finally come through. It hadn't seemed then like some ill-conceived fantasy. Then it had felt like coming home: home to Luna.

She remembered once, when their relationship was first verging into passion, Luna had said, "Falling in love is dangerous doings; really we should only do it with good friends." And good friends they'd remained even when they'd plunged into being lovers, and even now, when their lovemaking seemed to be a thing of the past.

Having Luna in her life had always given Kit a way of converting her old disappointments into wisdom and her yearnings into fresh aspirations. Kit felt that she'd known Luna forever, though it had been only for six years, and as lovers just for four. And as long as she'd known her, Luna had been talking about getting out of the city. Then, when Kit had finally asked her, Luna had simply grinned widely and said, "I'm game."

Just like her, Kit mused. Luna seemed alot younger than Kit in her simplistic way of looking at things, but somehow older in the

219

wisdom of her feelings. It was oddly reassuring to Kit that they were the same age.

But they were so different. Luna was light haired, tall and long limbed; Kit was dark haired, rounder and more compact than Luna could ever imagine being. She thought Kit was like a sleek and sensuous feline. Luna was easy-going while Kit's energy seemed to be set at a constant high-level purr. Sometimes their polarity scared Luna. No, not exactly fear. It made her feel distant; she walked long cold hours in the new fall woods.

Cresting a nearby ridge, Luna thought back to when Kit had first posed the idea of moving to the country. Luna had rolled the idea over again and again, savoring it; she had long desired to live her life cradled between mountain breasts. Surely she had loved Kit long enough; they both trusted each other and could depend on their partnership to sustain them through the big changes and hard work entailed in moving to the wilds. And they had both hoped the change of setting would do their relationship good.

Somewhere along the way their loving had fallen into a pattern, a deep but unerotic intimacy. It had happened to alot of other couples they'd known, but Luna hadn't thought it would ever happen to them. She remembered, in the beginning, just a certain way that Kit would raise her eyebrows and widen her pretty eyes, as if to say "Yes?" It was a surefire cue for Luna; she would take Kit and make love to her. It had worked every time, even when they'd been all around, time after time already in one day. And they'd used to spend forever losing themselves in each other's eyes. Now, whenever their eyes met, they'd smile sweetly at each other and so the charge would be defused, if not doused entirely. Luna even tried not returning Kit's smile, but it did no good; then Kit just thought that Luna was depressed or feeling moody. Luna couldn't even remember when they'd last made love; she only hoped Kit wouldn't go and turn to someone new if or when she decided to be sexual again.

As Luna walked, her eyes drank in the natural beauty thirstily, while her mind worked busily over these troubling thoughts. The soothing, even grey sky lay flat overhead through the branches of the bare white birches and the huge black oaks. There were thick mounds of dark clouds at the rim of the sky that came down to touch the hills, now purple in the distance. A lavender mist hung in them.

There was a brilliant streak of orange, ending the day, when Luna eventually turned her direction back towards their new house: home. *Oh Kit, what's happening with us?*

Kit had been so lighthearted and hopeful when they'd first arrived. The house had looked so big and warm and sunny, but they'd quickly found it took a good size wood fire to keep it really warm on the increasingly cold days. Before two months had even passed in their Pennsy mountain haven, their truck had broken down. Then the big old chainsaw that had come with the house had begun acting up, eventually refusing to start. Until they could afford to have it overhauled they were now stuck cutting the four foot lengths of firewood down to stove size by hand, with a bowsaw. It was strenuous work and was one job Kit liked to do less than Luna did.

"This new life is starting to seem not so different from the old one," Kit had said in weariness just that morning. But it *was* different; not any easier or smoother, but here the problems were less abstract, less interpersonal. Here they were more on a survival level, more real.

Except there was still the stalemate of sexuality. Many days Luna had headed home from one of her walks with new resolve, feeling craggy, weathered and wild: ready to meet that lover with whom her romantic thoughts had been occupied. But once home she'd found not the womon of her fantasies, but instead, just good old predictable Kit. Even that name seemed out of place. They had renamed each other in celebration of their new life, but it still seemed to be eluding them.

Inside, the house always felt overheated from the raging woodstove that Kit kept well stoked. And Kit's smiling presence, too, would press onto Luna, and what she knew was meant as warmth and easiness was suffocating. Soon the darkening woods and mountain crags would be gone from Luna's eyes and she could feel herself slide too easily into domestication. Domestic. That was Kit to her now. Damn. She wished she could madden that lovely, complacent, ever-smiling face.

But another new broken resolve would just be useless. As she crossed the open field her thoughts followed her perplexed gaze up to the unlit house. She quickly hopped the small creek over the clear dark water that was covered in fallen yellow leaves, and took the last rise. It wasn't so much the house as the chimney, in its quietude, that worried her. She strode through the yard and into the kitchen, where no hot blast greeted her. By the cold stove sat Kit who watched her enter the room, which was now cool and blue with evening. Luna stopped some feet away.

"Kit?" It sounded foolish, but there was something in Kit's stillness that shouted warning to Luna.

Kit's eyes looked bottomless. "I used up the wood we cut and it felt too late to deal with cutting more. It was getting late, and cold. I'm sorry." Her speech was flat, terribly flat and cold.

Luna felt raw and wide open. She moved slowly, keeping the steady contact of their eyes, fearful and wild like a wild animal. She watched her hands reach to Kit's; they were icy like her own. Her lips began a search that was less kisses than awkward caresses of her open mouth over the cold face—caresses to close Kit's eyes before their sadness drowned her—and to feel her skin, now grown rough with the coming winter. Luna's long form bowed and she went down on one knee, soft now, to blanket her lover.

Kit felt a stirring. She had sunk into a standstill only to find herself being subtly guided in a direction her buoyancy had kept her from before. She felt movement through her, like shivering reflections on a still pond. She laid her head back on the roundness of the chair and in her mind watched a leaf dance down and come to set lightly on the surface tension. She gently started at the ripples as caresses wandered to her bared neck. She felt a cold nose and a warm tongue that left trails of cool wetness as licking flickered up her jaw then settled in between her ear and the crook of her shoulder where Luna's face was buried now, warming.

"Let me warm you. Please," came the whisper as she felt nearly levitated by Luna's quiet motion up. They moved slowly, almost as if injured, and injured was what Luna felt, deep and aching and—longing, yes. "Your hands were too warm, mine couldn't rest there; they sought their own temperature outside, outside you. Maybe you had to reach this chill stillness for me, lover; now we'll grow warm together."

Kit lay on her back in bed with the sleeping bags fluffed up around her. Luna was on top, and her blue plaid woolcoat hung down around them. Her belt and the folds of her thick jeans pressed roughly onto Kit's belly, sending a pang down to her crotch which Luna met with a long thigh brought up between her legs. A long slow ride began, pressing hip to hip, pelvis to soft belly, ribs to ribs. Then arching up and straddling Kit's hips, Luna began to unbutton their thin flannel shirts, never losing pace with the inner time that moved her. Rocking slightly with great tautness of energy, her whole body tensed with the slight friction of her cunt, pushing and rubbing. Kit's pubis was beginning to arch to meet Luna's humping.

Luna's lower lips were flattened against her pants crotch. Feeling them slippery against each other, she dove for the full passion-darkened lips of Kit's luscious mouth, but then changed her course and headed for her newly bared breasts. Taking them each in hand she brought them together; small as they were, she could suckle them both at once. She sucked as both nipples grew stiff and the small gems rose round and red. She plucked them with her tongue and bit them lightly and sometimes rougher and coarsely. She couldn't be gentle and she wouldn't try. Kit's breath became audible: a sudden breathy intake at each nip. A low guttural sound escaped from the depths of Luna's fantasies, through her breast-encircling lips, and it excited her to hear herself.

She bit hard and Kit, grinning, pushed her head away and said, "Get off, mother." With a snort Luna sat back on her haunches, looking haughty and fine. She began to unsnap and unzip first her pants, then Kit's and then two zipper-edged v's appeared, point to point, white bellies and furry pubic hairs, like fur tipped arrows pointing together to that spot where warmth glowed between them. Kit's eyes preceded her head in rolling back, and in her mind she watched a warm sun growing from her cunt: a spreading warmth dawning on her.

Then Luna was reaching in with her tongue, curling ringlets of hair around and around. She probed downward. As her tongue touched clitoris, already reaching to meet that touch, Kit's buttocks rose and Luna pulled her pants down. Kit began to laugh and laugh and tears rolled down her smile lines, tears of laughter and arousal. "Luna, you are too cool."

Through Luna's own joyous sounds words came rushing up; she didn't know where or when they began but they were rushy and gritty and wild like wind and as her tongue whipped around lips, clit, and cunt, words whistled through her head—outstretched like the rest of her to meet this lover. While never missing to meet one tempoed contraction of her lover's clitoris, she talked:

"You're a wild cat, but you'll never get away from me again. I know how to keep you purring; show me your cat dance. You're so soft and sensuous, should I shelter you and shower you with all my love and affection and then be ready to let you go slinking off in the night hot to pounce on some new action should you come into season? Heat! *I'll* stroke you heat. Yesss."

Somewhere words got lost in the rising wind, hissing outside. Inside, Luna dove *inside*, her nose and chin were both ready to enter. Her chin slipped in and she suckled as Kit's strong contractions dripped droplets of misty mucous—musty, sweet, and lightly salty. Her nose rubbing clitoris, her mouth full of warm womon, Luna followed Kit's lead and drifted into peaceful sleep, with Kit's soft thigh as her pillow.

Kit awoke once to undress and cover them, then again to morning. The sun broke brilliantly, lighting the early first snow: a light one, but drifted, blown in on the night's storm winds.

"Hah!" Luna said. "And us with no wood cut."

"I could keep you warm," offered Kit, placing her hands on Luna's slim hips.

But Luna rolled her eyes, her butch resistance bucking. "I have to cut wood!"

"Get off it, mother. Can't you take the cold? Just look at the windows: rainbows from the frost!"

Martha and Estella

by Hannah Wild

Hannah Wild has been a Lesbian-Feminist for all of her fifty-one years on earth. Currently, she and her lover of thirteen years live in Northern California with three literary dogs and two spiritual cats. Hannah has been a writer since she was eight years old. She is still looking forward to the publication of her novel-in-progress, of which Martha and Estella *is a part. She is an avid reader and rock collector. For relaxation, she studies piano and walks on the beach.*

Hannah loves travelling and exploring new places in both inner and outer space. She dreams of owning land and living in a time and place surrounded by Lesbians who are free, creative, and self-sufficient.

This biography was written by Carol Wild.

Martha and Estella

Together with Julia, Elvira, and Susannah, Martha and Estella journeyed to Winter Harbor, Maine in the early part of June, 1936. That summer symbolised for them the beginning of their future lives. Embedded in the experience would be the unfolding of their love and the overlapping of each woman's life with all the others.

Just a few years earlier, Julia Dovetail had sailed into Martha's admittedly drab life to become her benefactress, soon her intellectual companion, thereafter her confidant, surrogate mother, and forever her dear friend. Julia, at the age of forty-five, had decided that she wanted to share her enormous wealth with women less fortunate but no less deserving than she. She had established a scholarship fund, and twenty years later, in 1934, Martha Redbone became a recipient.

Martha had been raised as a solitary daughter with several brothers on her parents' homesteaded farm. The isolation of her growing years on the poor, rock hard farm in the flatlands of western Kansas had rendered a quiet, withdrawn girl who had one asset, her intellect. Julia Dovetail had recognised the rare quality of this gray, muted young woman, and—in addition to establishing the fund for her to live and study at Northwestern—had drawn Martha into her heart and grown closer to this child than she had to anyone since Elvira.

In 1935, their first summer together, Julia and Martha had travelled to Europe. In addition to the cultural awakening she'd experienced, Martha had met many of Julia's oldest friends, women with whom Julia had grown in her formative years and with whom she had forged enduring relationships that had deepened despite separation by time, geography, and other involvements.

The apex of that trip had been their sojourn in England. They'd stayed in the home of Elvira Hartley, Julia's dearest friend and, Martha had realised, her former lover. Although circumstances had prevented Julia and Elvira from continuing their love relationship,

226

they had remained close friends. Elvira had been living for several years prior to the summer of 1935 with her lover Susannah Short in London which was, for Martha, the most dynamic city she had ever experienced.

It was in Elvira's home in London that Martha had met and fallen in love with Estella, Elvira's young niece. It was there that they'd shyly begun their sexual relationship with each other and established an everlasting commitment.

The coming together of all five women in Maine the summer of 1936 was an extension of the intertwining bonds that had formed in London. Julia had had the intervening year to accept, finally, Elvira's relationship with Susannah; the two young women, Martha and Estella, had written letters throughout the winter and spring in which they'd opened themselves, and had grown to know the deepest parts of each other. The three older women were ecstatic witnesses to the young women's new love, and all five were perfectly content to be with each other in the summer's moment of suspended time.

•

The days quickly fell into a mutually agreeable pattern. Martha and Estella would be off very early in the morning leaving the others to sleep late, and lazily let the morning play itself out. The two young women would stroll the beach and climb among the rocks and boulders that were strewn along parts of the shoreline as if by the hand of some enormous sea creature, who had decided to establish a permanent garden. Martha and Estella roamed through the hushed woods where they lingered to lean against a tree, their arms entwined. Gone was their tentative shyness of the previous summer. They now uncovered a passionate desire, one for the other.

They often made love in the deep recesses of the woods, cradled by the soft forest floor as they rocked to each other's rhythm surrounded by the thick foliage beneath whose blanket they caressed each other. Their sighs of passion and exultant cries of joy blended into the other forest sounds, and rose up through the surrounding sentinel trees to linger in the upper branches and merge with the birds' songs. Their desire for each other daily increased. It seemed that the more they explored each other's bodies, the more they wished to . Their passion was prolonged, and increasingly more intense.

"I feel," said Estella one morning as she lay pressed against the earthen floor with Martha's naked body covering hers and Martha's fingers still stroking her moist vagina's lips, "I feel," she said between tiny involuntary gasps, "as if I shall go on vibrating unceasingly. Martha, when you touch me this way I feel as if there is an ocean within me whose tides are ever increasing, and each time I am flung gasping on the shore, each time thinking this is the ultimate, each time, I am lifted once more, drawn back and up into the air to come rushing toward you again. I repeatedly grow fuller and fuller until I feel I am complete, then you take me even higher yet, and I can't imagine anything more. Then, you take me higher still. Oh Martha, I can never have enough of you!" And with that, Estella's focus was gone, her words became trilling sounds, her breath became gasps as she rose up once more within Martha's embrace.

Sometime later, Martha knelt between Estella's open legs, smiling into her eyes as she stroked her thighs with moist fingers. Estella was passive for a while, then took Martha's fingers and entwined them in hers. Martha held herself very still, and waited to be guided by her lover. Estella turned herself round and slid her head between Martha's knees, reaching up and drawing Martha's head down onto her belly. As she began to stroke Martha's thighs with one hand, she took Martha's hand and slipped two of her lover's fingers into her vagina. For several moments, Estella guided Martha's fingers in and out of her vagina, along her labia, quickly on and off her clitoris thus establishing a repetitious pattern while she continually stroked Martha in the same way with her free hand. Then she released Martha's hand, sliding her own along Martha's cheek and neck and shoulders, reaching between their bodies to cup Martha's breast and stroke the nipple, slipping along Martha's side to come across the small of her back and thus to her buttocks which she then began to stroke with both hands. Martha burrowed her face into Estella's pubic hair and maintained the repetitive stroking Estella had initiated, the only difference being that her pace increased with each round of vagina—labia—clitoris. As Estella continued to stroke Martha's buttocks, she also drew them down toward her so that she could reach up into Martha's vagina with her tongue. She slid the tip of her tongue very slowly along Martha's outer labia lips, paused to explore the opening of her vagina, darted quickly to her clitoris where she discovered that rapid vibration of her tongue just barely in contact with Martha's clitoris caused Martha's buttocks to heave up and down so that she held them tighter as her tongue flickered on and off Martha's taut clitoris. She then began to lick all around the outer lips of Martha's labia, and suck on them with her lips, and gently graze them with her teeth. Although it was not the first time they had made love in this way, Martha was so overwhelmed, she nearly became completely passive, but Estella would not have that and reached down to remind Martha's hands of their part in this great adventure. Estella became increasingly excited so that when they climaxed—first Martha and Estella almost immediately after—she began to laugh with joy and she rolled from under Martha to clasp her exhausted lover in her arms saying over and over, "Oh my dear love, oh Martha, it is so magnificent! What we can do for each other!" For an hour or more, Martha lay quietly in their nest, deep within the woods, smiling gently from a great distance, not able to move, lingering in her completely drained, totally satisfied body. Estella alternately clasped her lover and leaned over her chattering in high excitement about their wonderful discovery, or fell back on the ground laughing with pleasure. Finally, Martha began to feel her body come awake again. Estella sat beside her cross-legged, and leaned over her with one hand resting on the damp, rich earth.

"Martha, you simply must come awake, my love. How ever will I explain to the others your boneless state," she teased, tweaking Martha's ribs, then immediately ducking her head to kiss the spot she'd pinched and to lick the "wound," exclaiming, "Did I hurt you! There! That's all better, dear."

"You've taken my will, Estella. I shall never move again. See, I can hardly lift my hand, let alone my entire body." And to prove her point, Martha languidly raised a limp wrist and let her fingers dangle just grazing Estella's knee.

"What you need is some brisk exercise, my girl," chided Estella. "You're much too sedentary, lolling about like this all day."

As Estella teased, Martha's fingers continued to dance lightly on her knee. She smiled from less of a distance into Estella's laughing eyes, and then, in an instant, there was no distance between them at all and Martha's fingers moved along Estellas's thigh and into her vagina once more. Estella placed her hands behind her and leaned back on them as her head dropped back and she looked up to the farthest reaches of the surrounding trees. Martha was fully alert now, and continued to caress lightly as she turned herself around and placed her head between Estella's now outstretched legs, and she used her tongue to arouse Estella as Estella had shown her an hour before it could be done. This time, when the passion had temporarily receded, they sat together on the ground holding and curving into each other. They took each other up into their eyes, and spoke the silent language that would endure for them forever.

•

Afternoons, the five women usually spent together. They worked in the garden, or played a game of whist, or sat under a group of cool elms while some of them sewed or knitted, others browsed through a newspaper or journal, and others lay back in a hammock, lazily swaying to the gentle conversation. Some afternoons they would all take a short hike along the shoreline where they collected odd shells and twisted pieces of driftwood. Julia and Elvira were leery of climbing among the rocks, but sometimes Susannah joined the two younger women and they would climb far out on the huge boulders above the crashing sea. Then sometimes, after lunch and a rest, the five women would go for a drive.

Most evenings, they sat before the fire after dinner. Occasionally, one would read aloud to the others, or two would have a game of chess while others talked or read. But, they always spent the evenings in each others' company, preferring the warmth they took from each other as a group, tacitly agreeing without ever needing to say so that the comradeship they shared fulfilled each of them. They did not wish to lose a drop of these few months they could be all together. Conditions in Europe were increasingly ominous, and they knew that when Elvira, Susannah, and Estella returned to London in the fall, it might be a very long time before they would have the solace of each other's company again, so they wasted not a moment that summer. Much as the two younger women desired each other, they too wanted to be with the others in the evenings, taking great comfort in each of the older women, treasuring their wisdom and strength.

If a quilt could have been made of all the intense interchanges that summer between them in pairs and among these five women, it would have reflected the depth of their trust and love, the breadth of their combined intellects, and the height of their esteem for each other and their value to the future. It would have been a rounded quilt, reflecting the completeness of them individually and in relationship with each of the others. Julia and Elvira, with Susannah as her helpmate, had devoted their lives to the individual enhancement of young women such as Martha and Estella, and in these two because of their brilliant devotion to their goals, they saw the greatest fulfillment of their investment. Martha and Estella had begun and obviously would continue to reach out into the world around them in order to positively affect each person whom they encountered. And they had begun with each other.

Unfortunately, though they had taken to each other deeply and fully, they had not yet discovered how to do their chosen work *and* to be with each other, and this was to be an enduring sorrow for them. But, they had come to recognise where their expertise lay— Martha as a teacher (hopefully of young women since she was beginning to become, under Julia and Elvira's tutelage, a feminist), and Estella as a scientist. It would be many years, however, before they determined how to do their work and also to be continuously with each other.

•

It rained without interruption for several days during the early part of July. The others seemed content to snuggle near the fire, chatting and reading. They had begun the works of Jane Austin, and they took turns reading aloud. All of them took a keen interest in the achievements of the Suffragettes. Julia and Elvira had marched with Mrs. Pankhurst and well remembered the derision they'd encountered from men who had thought them "foolish" to want to disrupt the status quo. They remembered, also, how they had been brought up separate from the men of their generation despite the liberal set of their parents' minds, and that inequity still could arouse sharp anger and bitterness in them. Martha and Estella daily had to struggle with the closed minds of men at their colleges, and knew that their presence there was tenuous, at best. Indeed, Cambridge still did not admit women's colleges into the University, and Estella constantly encountered incredulous stares as she hurried through the town in her gown. They both endured the paternal derision of their male class-mates who continued to view themselves the natural superiors of these quite exceptional young women. The rules may have begun to change, but attitudes remained firmly entrenched.

One particular rainy afternoon, Susannah was elected to read. Martha and Estella, chaffing under the confinement of several days, ventured forth into the gentle rain while the others snuggled in by the fire. Swathed in slickers and wearing high rubber boots, the two young women climbed farther and higher among the rocks than they had previously. The rain was steady and beat into their exposed faces; the wind whipped round them with more fury the higher they went, and the sea roared against the lower rocks sending plumes of spray majestically into the air. The girls felt like two rare sea birds, indeed they nearly appeared to be flying as they fearlessly leapt from rock to rock, ever mounting higher among the scattered monuments. Near the crest of the seashore mountain, they came upon a series of caves not apparent from below, and took shelter in one of them.

Breathlessly, they stood just inside the entrance of their tem-porary home, their hoods thrown back, arms round each other, damp faces glistening and turned toward the sea where they could see far out over the gray thrashing waves. Then, all at once, their arms were within each other's rain slickers, hands reaching beneath damp jer-seys, and their mouths met in gasping, passionate joy, sucking at each other's tongues and lips. Eagerly they caressed beneath their soggy clothes. Buttons on slickers were unfastened, zippers on pants came down, and pants were pushed to ankles as they reached for each other's bare, damp skin. Martha leaned against the cold wall of the cave and clasped Estella against her, moving her hands up and down Estella's back and buttocks, like a swimmer stroking through the sea. Estella drew Martha's thin jersey up under her chin, and dipped her head to suck at her lover's nipples while her hands lav-ished strokes along her belly and down between her legs and into her vagina, sliding through the tangled hair like a fish gliding among seaweed and through its chosen pond to luxuriate in its private back water. Martha came quickly and cried her pleasure into the deep re-cesses of the cave, and her clear joy came resounding back across their heads repeating the sound of her ecstasy in waves of staccato oh-oh-oh that urged Estella to once more bring another cascading wash of pleasure into and through Martha, her fingers fluttering ceaselessly on the tip of Martha's clitoris as Martha had countless orgasms.

Then they were still, Estella leaning against Martha against the cave's wall, cradling Martha's buttocks in her cupped hands. For several moments, the two women lingered as if at the bottom of a lolling wave as it gently rode far out at the horizon's edge. Slowly, they came back to the present, heard the rain beating on the rocks, turned to look out at the surging sea, and listened to the cries of the gulls and pipers.

"I want to taste you," said Martha, and she began to strip away all of Estella's opened clothing: first the soaked slicker, then her jersey. She knelt on the ground and slipped Estella's pants and shoes off, then looked up into Estella's smiling eyes.

"I can never have enough of touching and looking and tonguing you, you know. I always want more," and saying that, she began to lick Estella's body, from her ankles up along her inner thighs where she pressed Estella's legs apart, then across her belly and into her belly button causing Estella to moan. Then she drew Estella to lie down among her scattered clothing on the earthen cave's floor and continued licking across her abdomen, and round her breasts, lingering there for a long while, sucking and biting at her nipples; all this time her hands caressed Estella's thighs and belly and dipped into her pubic hair and came round to her thighs again and onto her belly and on, again, into her pubic hair. Martha's tongue stroked along Estella's neck and all around her face lapping like a cat might, bathing her love, then darting into her mouth, stretching to reach into the recesses of her mouth, flickering along her teeth and gums, licking her lips with the tip of her tongue, and darting quickly in and out of Estella's gasping mouth, never ceasing the entire time her caressing of Estella's belly and thighs and pubic hair. Then Martha's tongue retraced its path moving downward toward Estella's middle, lingering again for a long while on her breasts, sucking and nibbling her nipples as she grasped Estella's breasts in her two hands and gently squeezed them. Then, she turned Estella onto her belly and began to stroke her back with long fingers as her tongue stroked along Estella's buttocks and between them and down and down and up and down between Estella's buttocks so that Estella began to gasp

233

and cry out like a gull in flight and she drew up her knees so that Martha could more easily reach into and under her with her tongue, and Martha now held her buttocks, now caressed her belly, and her relentless tongue continued its journey into and out of Estella until Estella arched and cried out and collapsed prone along the ground panting and gasping for air. Martha lay herself all along her lover's body and covered her in warm, slow caresses, crooning into her ear and gently rocking her, marveling at the repeated waves of passion she felt washing through Estella's lithe body.

They could never have enough of each other.

The Newcomer

by Elizabeth Bonzo-Savage

Elizabeth Bonzo-Savage first defined herself as a writer in the seventies. Before that, her identity was a mixture of public school teacher, university instructor, business owner, parent, back-to-the-land dyke, and parent. Recently, she has added secretary and seeker of enlightenment to her persona. She is a radical lesbian/feminist who lives in Richmond, Virginia with her lover of seventeen years. She published two children's novels, Hey, Van Gogh and The Goldenrod Kids, in the fall of 1988, and is now working on a lesbian novel.

She feels life is a meditation and attempts to avoid negative people and negative energy. She visualizes always a world in which the human family lives peacefully on a bountiful planet with women in their rightful position as leaders and every person striving for full actualization.

The Newcomer

I remember the spring day Margie Baker rattled into Sayersville in her rusty green Volkswagen. In a town with a population of 2,000, you notice things like the arrival of a newcomer. She moved into one of Reverend Jimmy Thompson's furnished apartments. The apartment, in a converted store building, fronted the sidewalk on US 23 where Smith's Exxon, Adkin's Grocery, the U.S. Post Office, and Hetty's Restaurant made up Main Street in Sayersville.

The other streets, which ran parallel to Main, were not visible to cars traveling through town on the highway. But I knew every inch of them: narrow streets lined with neat frame houses which sat back on meager lots shaded by huge, old, sugar maples. I knew, too, the wider lawns of the brick churches scattered among them and the families who left the neat frame houses to fill those churches twice on Sunday and every Wednesday night for prayer meeting.

I worked as a cashier in Adkin's Grocery: not a great job, but it got me out of the house and away from Mom. There wasn't much available in Sayersville for a girl after high school if she didn't get married—a condition I had long ago determined to avoid. At any rate, I pretty much kept up with what went on in town because nearly everyone shopped at Adkin's; the county's only other supermarket was twenty miles away. Margie first came into the store holding onto a six-year-old girl you could tell was hers because they looked alike. They were both little-boned, with black hair and big hazel eyes. Except the kid's mouth was tiny and puckery and Margie had a broad mouth full of sparkling teeth and a loud voice that came as a surprise when she spoke.

I decided this newcomer must be at least thirty years old, when I saw her up close at the check-out counter. She grinned real big, showing all her teeth, when she caught me looking at her. Then she straightened up so her knit shirt pulled tight across her round, ample

236

breasts. Quick as anything, I leaned over to hunt for the price on the milk carton so my hair flopped down and hid my face. But I knew it was too late. There was no way she could have missed anything that flaming red.

When I looked up again Margie was still grinning at me. Then she caught Ron Radcliff, the carry-out, staring at her breasts. She folded her arms across her chest and stared back. I knew my face was red, but his would have made the lights on the volunteer fire truck seem like a flashlight. He concentrated so hard on sacking her groceries he called them off as he put them in the sack: pork and beans, milk, peanut butter, Frosted Flakes, crackers, Pall Malls.

A couple of women who lived on the same street as Mom and me were in line behind Margie. Their eyes bugged out so far I figured they'd both suffer eyestrain well into next week. I had to say, "Next," three times before they emptied their buggies onto the counter. They didn't bother to watch me, either, to make sure I rang up their prices right. And Ron didn't have to listen to their usual comments about the younger generation dawdling at their work. They were so anxious to follow Margie out the door, they forgot to give me Mom's message that she wanted me to bring home cherry-nut ice cream instead of fudge swirl.

I spent the rest of the afternoon in a daze and totally lost my breath when Margie came back a few minutes before my quitting time. She smiled real big at me, but headed right for the meat department where Ron was cleaning up. I heard her tell him she'd bought some wieners, the ones on sale for ninety-eight cents, and when she got home, they weren't in the sack.

He yelled across the store. "Hey, Connie. Do you remember checking out any wieners? I sacked the stuff for this lady, but I can't remember any."

"Nope," I yelled back.

Margie and Ron came up to the counter. She handed me the register tape, pointing with a short, red-nailed finger to a ninety-eight cent total. I thought I remembered checking out something else for ninety-eight cents. Milk, maybe? Or bread? Crackers?

Ron worried it around. "I can't figure out what happened," he said.

"We were busy when she was here," I suggested. "Maybe you

put them in the wrong sack." He didn't make that kind of mistake, but the way he was staring at her nipples pushing out that flimsy shirt she had on, I knew he would agree to anything.

"I'll get a package for you," I told Margie. I came out from behind the counter and streaked past the meat department into the office. "Mr. Adkin," I said, not believing what I was doing, "I need to get off a few minutes early tonight. Mom needs me at home."

"Sure," he answered. He didn't even look up from his ledger. "Tell Ron to take the register until Emily gets here . You can come in early tomorrow to make up your time."

I grinned all the way back through the store because now I could leave with Margie. She grinned, too, when I walked out with her. Going down the street I had to cut my stride way down so I wouldn't run away from her. She had little short legs and was wearing spike-heeled sandals. Her apartment was only two blocks from the store and I couldn't think of anything besides the weather to talk about before we got there. It didn't matter, though, because she still asked me in for a coke.

I guess she hadn't had a chance to clean things up since she'd moved in. The place smelled like a flooded basement. The floors were gritty and the green paint on the walls was streaked. Nails and light green squares showed where the former tenants had hung pictures. The couch was worn and greasy. I felt sorry for Margie. You would really expect more from Reverend Thompson. Mom kept our garage looking better than this.

Books were the only thing I could see that had been unpacked. The stack on the scarred coffee table were titles I didn't recognize. Most of them were about women.

"You read these?" I asked when she came back with the coke.

"Parts of them. You want to borrow some?"

"Maybe." I picked one up and it fell open the way a book does that's been opened a lot to one place. I closed it quick when I saw the word clitoris. Margie grinned some more.

"How old are you, Connie?" she asked.

"Nineteen."

"Have you lived in Sayersville all your life?"

"Yeah. I thought about joining the navy or getting a job up north once I graduated. Maybe in Dayton or Columbus."

"Why didn't you?"

"Everyone said the navy wasn't any life for a girl. And big cities are too dangerous. Besides, there was just Mom and me. I didn't want to leave her alone." Suddenly I couldn't understand why I thought Mom needed me. She was healthy: a big strong woman. Big arms, big legs, big behind, big boobs. "And then I got this job at Adkin's Grocery." I felt more ridiculous, but I kept on. "I'm saving my money. Maybe I'll go to school or something." I didn't sound convincing, even to me.

Margie sat on the arm of the couch and stared at me. That bothered me some. I'd never had a female look at me that way before. Not that I hadn't wanted them to. I was glad my long legs weren't skinny and that I had firm, pointy breasts. My naturally curly hair wasn't too bad, either, except that it was a kind of mousy brown.

I bent over my coke to hide my face and found my eyes gazing at her legs. She had on the shortest shorts I'd ever seen and those spike-heeled sandals were too much. My ears were hot enough to catch my hair on fire. I had to get out of there. I killed my coke and got up.

"I have to go. Mom gets mad if I'm late for supper. She says if she goes to all the trouble to fix it, the least I can do is show up before it gets cold." Margie laughed, loud and free. I didn't know any women who laughed that way, but I liked it—a lot.

I left and crossed the street to Hetty's Restaurant. I ordered a coke and took it to a booth near the window so I could see Margie's apartment. I made myself remember all the girls I'd ever had a crush on and how they had always ignored me or used me to help them patch things up with their boyfriends. I put myself through the hell of every one of those fiascoes, trying to squelch the excitement stirring in my guts. But I still kept looking across the street. After four cokes, I gave up and went home.

I watched for Margie every day at the store and hung around Hetty's until I was afraid people would think I was queer or something. But I didn't see her again until Sunday morning when I went to church with Mom. I was sitting in my spot with the choir and Ron was playing the organ. Everything went along just like always until Margie came in with her kid. When Ron saw her, his foot slipped on the volume pedal so the music made a fanfare for her. She dragged her kid clear up to the front row and sat close to the choir loft. I had a lot of trouble remembering the words I was supposed to be singing.

She had on a tight, low-cut dress that looked like it belonged in a bar instead of church and those same spike-heeled shoes. The way her hair was curled made her eyes look even bigger. Ron gave her a "you're really special" smile. The rest of the men pretended not to notice her. The women kept their faces blank. I would have given a lot to be sitting beside God and looking into their heads that morning.

After church I got away from Mom and hurried outside so I could watch Margie some more. She was standing there in the fresh spring air being friendly. Some of the women's faces began to get that compassionate look they kept for sinners and poor people. Margie was talking real soft like she was afraid her voice would scare them off.

"Your sermon was *so* inspiring," she said to Reverend Thompson. "And everyone here is *so* friendly. It's very different from living in the city."

"We're glad to have you," Thompson said. "I hope you'll consider our church your home."

"Well, I had thought I would visit all the churches before I decided which one to attend," Margie said hesitantly. "But you've all been *so* kind."

Reverend Thompson beamed and looked at her kid. "We have a wonderful youth department, too," he said. "I know your daughter would be happy here."

Margie looked at the faces pushing up to her and bowed her head a little. "It would mean a lot to Kathy to have a place to belong—you know, like family. It's hard for children when their parents are divorced." I could see her eyes get misty. The women took a backward step. Except for Reverend Thompson's wife. She reached for Margie's hand and patted it.

"Don't you worry about Kathy. She'll be just fine as soon as she makes some new friends," she assured Margie. I knew it wouldn't be long before the Women's Home Mission Circle made Margie their project.

Margie smiled at the ring of faces and looked over their heads at me. Her tears went away quick. I smiled back and headed in her di-

direction, but Ron moved faster. He planted himself between me and her.

"Want a ride home?" he asked her. "I'm going that way." The liar. He lived clear on the other end of town.

She nodded and they got into his car: Ron and Margie in the front seat and her kid in the back. I turned away, then, so I wouldn't have to see his blond, shaggy head next to hers.

When they drove off, I practically shoved Mom into my Honda so I could follow them. Ron stopped at Margie's apartment and I pulled over in front of Hetty's.

"Why are you stopping here?" Mom complained. Ron and Margie were getting out of the car.

"I want to get you some pistachio ice cream," I said. "They didn't have any at the store yesterday."

"Well, hurry up. I don't want to sit out here all day." When I came out of the restaurant, Ron's car was gone. Mom was frowning at Margie's apartment. "I hope Ron doesn't get mixed up with that woman," she sniffed. "He's such a nice boy."

"So do I," I said.

I had to hang around the house for Sunday dinner to keep Mom company, but the minute the dishes were done, I got in my Honda and headed back to Hetty's. I drove around the block so I would have to park on Margie's side of the street. Before I got out of the car she was standing in her door. She grinned at me like the cat who knows the canary is as good as caught. I hardly waited for her invitation before I was into her apartment.

She took me back to the kitchen and plunked a coke and a bag of corn chips on the tiny, formica-topped table. Then she opened a beer for herself. We talked some about Mom and me. She was good with small talk, I began to feel easy around her.

"Have you been divorced long?" I asked.

"Since Kathy was three." She opened a pack of Pall Malls and lit one. I liked the way she twisted her mouth around so she wouldn't blow smoke on me when she exhaled.

"How come you got divorced?"

"Charlie found someone he liked better. I guess he got tired of the wife and baby scene." She crossed one of her legs over the other so it came close to mine. I decided Charlie was a real chump.

241

"That must have been hard," I said, hoping she didn't notice how breathy my voice was.

"Not really. I was pretty tired of Charlie, too. *And* his credit cards and the bill collectors. Charlie was a big spender." She took a long draw on her Pall Mall. "It wasn't so bad. I learned I could take care of myself. And then I found a whole bunch of girlfriends." She laughed so I didn't see any need to feel bad for her over Charlie.

"Why did you come to Sayersville?"

She kind of hesitated and then shrugged. "You do what you have to do," she said. "Charlie disappeared and so did the support money. I'm trying to locate him or get money from his family for Kathy. A kid shouldn't have to suffer because the parents fuck up."

I couldn't think of anything to say after that. Margie was quiet a long time. She put out her cigarette stub and lit another. She stared at me through the smoke that drifted between us. "He was a good dancer," she said. "A lousy father, but a good dancer." Her foot started moving like she was keeping time to music. "You dance?" she asked.

"Not very well." I didn't feel like explaining that I hated dancing with guys and that I didn't know any women who danced together.

"Poor baby," she said. "I'll have to teach you." She tapped her toe on my leg and I nearly choked on my coke. Then she seemed to forget all about the dancing. She looked around the apartment and curled up her nose like a kid getting ready to stick out its tongue.

"Have you ever seen such a trashy place?" she asked. "The good reverend should be paying me to live here instead of me paying him." She looked around the room again and then out into the alley. She pointed to the second story window of the apartment building across from hers.

"See that fuzzy redhead peering out the window?" she queried. "She comes down every day to have coffee and spends the whole afternoon telling me about her gentlemen friends. She even asked if I was interested in getting into the business." She raised her eyebrows after that tidbit. She sighed a little. "I guess she's like me—doing what she has to do. Anyway, if I have to be her therapist, she's going to pay for it." I got the feeling she had just had a brainstorm. "My time ought to be worth at least twenty bucks." Margie laughed at the thought and leaned on the table so her breasts rubbed against

242

my arm. I didn't hear what else she said. All I could think of was how I wanted to know if the rest of her felt as good as her breasts.

When I realized she had stopped talking, I was so flustered I couldn't remember what our conversation had been about. I blurted out the first thing that came to my mind.

"Are you coming to church tonight?"

"Do you want me to?" Her husky voice raised the hair on my arms and shot my temperature up ten degrees.

"Yeah."

"Then I will." The way she said that made it sound like she was promising a lot more than one night at church. But her next words got me right in the gut. "Ron asked me, too."

"I guess he's picking you up," I said, wishing I didn't sound so much like a peevish kid.

"This time he is."

I got up to leave. I felt sick, as if all the times I'd had to face seeing a girl I liked go off with some guy had suddenly settled on me in one big hurt.

"See you around," I said, heading for the door.

"How about tomorrow after work," she suggested. Her eyes were as innocent as a child who has just learned to say fuck.

"Maybe," I mumbled and beat it out of there.

I skipped church that night so I wouldn't have to see her with Ron. Mom was a little upset, but I told her something I ate hadn't agreed with me. So she left me alone and went on to church with her friends. I spent the whole evening thinking how I was never going back to Margie's again. She was just like every other woman—out to get a man. I didn't need that kind of punishment. I convinced myself I could stay away from her, right up to the minute I walked onto her front porch the next day and banged on her door.

When she let me in she was wearing those shorts again, but she was barefooted which made her seem tinier than ever. When she walked away from me I could see her buttocks peeking out from the shorts and my legs got so rubbery I had to plunk into the first chair I saw. I was still quivering when she asked if I wanted to pass up my coke for a beer.

"Sure," I said, blocking out the sudden picture I had of Mom. There was nothing innocent about the way Margie looked at me when she handed me that beer. And there wasn't much innocent about me when I finally left that evening, either.

In the weeks that followed I hung around Margie like a kid who's just discovered the candy store. I couldn't stay away. And she didn't try to stop me. She even found places to send Kathy so we could be alone. I went by her place every evening after work. And the minute Mom got settled in her chair after supper and turned on the TV, I headed for Margie's again. Mom got real bitchy about me being gone so much, but for the first time in my life, I ignored her.

Sometimes Margie and I played cards or watched television. Sometimes we took Kathy to Hetty's for ice cream. Sometimes we would turn down the lights and dance. I was holding her real close one night and we were sort of moving to the music, but not much, when she tilted back her head and looked up at me.

"Do you ever think of leaving here, Connie?" she asked.

"Not anymore."

She smacked me on the behind. "There's a whole world out there you don't know anything about. You need some experiences."

"I can get all the experiences I need right here." I was feeling pretty worldly at the moment.

She smacked me again. "That's not the kind I mean. You're being wasted here. What do you plan to do with your life? Get married and have a bunch of kids?"

"What are you—crazy?" I saw she was serious so I considered how it would be to leave. I got excited about it until I remembered Mom. I was all she had since Dad died. "I can't leave Mom," I said, suddenly feeling like I was somehow not being fair to Mom *or* to myself. "Besides, I have you."

She was quiet for a minute, like she was studying on something. "I'm a free spirit, Connie. I never stay long in one place. Who's going to love you when I'm gone? The girls you went to school with?"

"Sure. Just like they did before you came." She laughed then, that free and easy laugh. We stopped talking after that.

For a few days I worried that she was planning to leave, but things went on as usual so I settled back to enjoy it. But then Ron started hanging around. It got so he was at Margie's almost as much as I was.

"Why do you let him come around all the time?" I asked Margie once.

She shrugged and got a far-away look in her eyes. "You know what I always say, Connie. You do what you have to do. Besides," she added, "the engine in my bug blew up and he's going to fix it. A car means freedom, you know. He's even going to get the parts wholesale for me."

"How generous," I said in my most sarcastic tone. She just smiled and pulled my face down until our lips touched.

For the next three weeks Ron worked on her car in the alley behind the apartment while Kathy and I sat on the back stoop and watched. Margie hung around the car and asked questions. The only thing I found to be glad about was that she had replaced her shorts with jeans.

Ron kept working later and later and I kept staying later and later. I was determined not to give him a chance at Margie because any idiot could see what he was thinking. I would stay until midnight and then I'd go home to Mom sitting in front of the television finishing off the last of her ice cream and accusing me with her eyes.

Finally she couldn't hold her tongue any longer. "You're seeing too much of that woman," she told me when I came in.

"What woman?"

"You know what woman. That Margie woman. The one who's divorced and chases after men."

"Who said that?"

"Everybody's saying it."

"Well, they're wrong."

"What do you call the way she's going after Ron? His mother told me he's with her all the time. And him just a boy, no older than you."

"I've heard it's not the age, but the experience that counts."

"See there." Her voice shook indignantly. "You never talked to me that way before. I don't want you around her ever again. I raised you to be a good girl. I'm not going to have it spoiled now."

I stared at her. She shoved another mound of ice cream between her lips. I thought about Margie, carefully cutting into a bowl of ice cream, popping the bites clean and quick into her mouth. I thought about how Margie and I were together: how we laughed and how we loved. I thought about Ron, doing everything he could to get her body. I thought of her telling me I needed more experiences; that I was being wasted here. I thought about how everyone treated Margie—as if she was contaminated in some way. Just because she didn't follow their rules. I remembered how she was always saying, you do what you have to do. I felt my guts turn over. Could I do what I had to do? If it hadn't been so late, I would have gone right then to talk with her. But I couldn't face another row with Mom. So I waited until morning.

I left early the next day so I could stop by Margie's on my way to work. I knew she usually slept late, but I knocked loud enough to wake her and everyone else on the block. I didn't care who heard me. I had to see her. When she didn't come to the door, I went around to the alley. Her VW was gone.

I swallowed hard and knocked on the back door. It swung open. I stepped into the empty apartment. There was an envelope on the kitchen table. It was addressed to me.

"Sorry to leave like this, sweet thing," she'd written, "but we do what we have to do. Charlie's family told me loud and clear to get lost. Kathy doesn't need that, so I'm off to Columbus. I have friends there. If you can ever tear yourself away from here, you're welcome to come stay with me. I'm not promising any permanent commitment, but there are lots of opportunities there—jobs, school, etc. And I would love to have you warm my bed until you got settled. Also, you'll find many kindred spirits, if you know what I mean. P.S. Kathy says love and kisses."

I stepped out onto the stoop and pulled the door shut. I looked at the empty spot where her VW should be. She was gone. I couldn't blame her. There was nothing in Sayersville for her. If only I had acted earlier. I should have come to her last night. She would have taken me with her.

I read the letter again. It was full of life and promise. I felt the beginnings of a grin tug at the corners of my mouth. I put the letter in my pocket and looked up to see the redhead hurrying across the alley.

"You looking for Margie?" she asked.

"Not now."

"That's good because she skipped out last night. The reverend's going to shit in his sock. She owed him three months back rent, he told me. I got screwed out of twenty bucks, too. She told me she needed it for the kid. Looks more like she needed it to get out of town." She took a cigarette from the pocket of her blue flowered smock, put it to her lips, then stopped and tilted her head to one side. "I'll bet that boy got screwed over her car, too."

I laughed. "Not the way he had in mind."

She poked her finger against my chest. "She screw you, too?"

"You could say that." I laughed again and touched the letter in my pocket. I was still laughing at the end of the week when I threw my bags into my Honda and headed for Columbus. I guessed I would be the newcomer there.

Romance

Hot Flashes

by Joan Bridget

Joan Bridget moved to Canada from Ireland in 1975. She has lived in Ottawa, Toronto, Vancouver and Kingston since then and is now, again, living in Toronto. She has published poetry in A Room of One's Own *and* Upstream.

Hot Flashes

She has bright blue eyes. She says her eyes are hazel and indeed when I look at them—deep into them—they are hazel. But sometimes they are blue—not just ordinary, beautiful blue, but a flashing sapphire blue. Her eyes light everywhere inside me—deep and shallow places.

Oh, I've wanted to touch her, to whisper in her ear—anything, just the soft slip of sounds off my tongue—and to hear her whisper back. She is tall and dark and wears black—I would prefer splashes of colour, sensuous and extravagant against her skin, but that is not who she is. She is an artist and this year, then, she must wear black. Maybe black is just cheaper and easier—all black things in one's closet must save a lot of thought and planning about what to wear; just pick one or two things and there you are—dressed and coordinated.

It has been a long time since I've wanted anyone—wanted them against my skin, in my breath, in my bed. But I do want her.

There are one or two problems. She is young; I am not. And I don't know if she wants me. But her eyes flirt—softly, shyly; she blushes and gets bolder. I am shy and confused. I have been alone too long.

For weeks I have tortured myself with her—delicately, beautifully. I plan where I will run into her, but I do not plan what I will say and so I'm often left dumb and awkward when we meet.

At the women's bar she is carrying a tray of drinks and I almost just reach out to hug her. It is a shock, to feel this hug reach out of me. I stop just in time, and we look each other in the eyes for a few moments. Her eyes are blue again. But maybe blue is the colour of woman lust: the colour of the flash of feeling that passes uncensored and wild from woman to woman.

I kept my head and the moment passed. I went into the hallway to catch my breath, my back against the wall.

Five years I have been living alone, no casual lovers, no serious lovers. Life is predictable and controlled. I work, I eat, I visit friends, they visit me, I write, walk the cats—a regular, productive, happy life. These flashes of blue I do not need. But I do want, now that I know them. And I am afraid. Have I forgotten how to do this dance? The steps are awkward. Is there no grace because I haven't practiced in such a long time?

This is just middle-aged madness; it will pass if I ignore it. She seeps into my dreams by night and day. Such a lovely smile. My body has long seemed a trusted, reliable friend, but now I take off all my clothes and examine myself in the mirror. My body is soft, scarred, heavy in the hips—and hairy. I am anxious about exposing myself—naked in need and in fact—to anyone, especially someone young and, in my mind, perfect.

On my body there are two big ugly scars and they are both precious to me. So much they represent—death and life, yes, but also triumph over struggle and pain. I do not scar prettily: no thin, neat, contained lines; rather they spread, break open and pucker—as if they are telling of the huge emotional sprawl inside me. I have struggled so long for containment; I see it as part of happiness, or at least, contentment. And here I am, for months firmly balanced (where I have fought so long to be), and then I have dreams of this woman growing up—free, wild, compelling.

Balance, I think, is only a moment in time, a place to take brief bearings before the next step off into space—to fly or to fall.

There are other things, too. I have watched others flitting about their affairs, lovers coming and going faster than a fiddler's elbow. It has frightened me to see such huge expenditures of emotion on such transitory relationships. This part of myself I have confined, held captive. It has not been a difficult captivity, not often have I longed to escape. But now, now—oh, I would love one wild moment of letting go, emotionally and physically, to dive and float in some new dimension, to be only in the moment—loose, whole, expanded.

For weeks now I have been meeting her: safe flirting and conversation. I try to find out a little about her life—to know her through little things. But in some ways I don't want to know her that way—I want to know her physically, although this will not tell me much more about her than I know. Slowly it's dawned on me that I am no longer content to see her, to live in fantasy. But the deliberate act of asking her for more has been too much for me. I've waited for the perfect moment, knowing it will likely never arrive.

I do not know if the moment is perfect or not. I know only that it's come, and we've arranged to meet.

Carefully I select what to wear: the soft slide of fabric on my skin, what colours and textures, what looks good, what is good to touch—how I want her to see me, and how I want to see myself. Never have I dressed so consciously, not ever. I want to yield and be yielded to, to create these aspects of me that exist side by side, all at once. As the clothes slide on and off of me I touch myself: my shoulder, breast, the curve of my hip. My hands skim over my pubic hair, not daring to touch deeper, closer—not now. I must be ready on time.

When I see her I don't care what I look like, for once again I am lost in her eyes, her smile. For a moment I have nothing to say, my breath is—somewhere else. Then I feel awkward, clumsy; I trip phrases out, then remember not to say anything but what I mean: thoughts that are mine and not just conventional phrases; "You are beautiful."

We talk for hours about all kinds of things. About nothing. Our eyes say delicious things, converse all on their own, a counterpoint to time and place. She says, "Come to my studio, it is not far from here." Oh yes, I say, yes.

I do not clearly remember her studio from that time, only that the light from the street makes rectangles on the floor, red and blue flashing. And I remember the sounds, too—the steady swoosh of cars on wet pavement, voices loud and unexpectedly clear, and deep inside all this: our breath.

Because she is young I have thought she would be shy. I clearly have forgotten the arrogance of youth, its boundless self-confidence. It is I who am shy. This taking off of clothes used to be a delicious pleasure, something that was done quickly, in the moment of passion—garments tossed aside in a heap to fall where they might—or to be undone slowly, deliberately, to arouse. Now it means to uncover myself, layer by layer, to put off the persona which I have carefully selected to wear. I remember some essential things I should have thought to mention before, things that can be hidden no longer.

My hand hesitates as I begin to disassemble my clothes. She comes close to me, holds me in her arms, rocks me gently. I kiss her neck, lost for a moment in her scent and the feel of her skin. I put my lips to her ear. "I have only one breast," I whisper.
Softly she breathes in my hair. "Yes I know." Something finally releases in me, slides away.

And she is not what I've fantasized. She is real, tall and slender, like no woman I've ever been with before. Her skin is dark, her breasts hardly fill my hand, my mouth, and oh, she is sensuous. I run my hands over her back, she touches my thigh—her touch firm and knowing—and I am lost. I do not know where she and I begin or end. Our moments of awkwardness pass and blend into an urgency to explore each other. "No," she moves my hand a little, "touch me here". I feel my body ease into freedom and ecstasy with her. This dance I have not forgotten. I know how to lead and how to follow, how to listen to the sure rhythm of our bodies... how to be alive.

RAINBOW